# Children and Biography

# New Directions in Life Narrative

*New Directions in Life Narrative* explores the concept of life narrative across the mediums of written work, oral narratives, photography, documentary film, visual art, performance and social media. The series nurtures theoretical, methodological and interpretive innovation in life writing research, supporting projects that apply new combinations of philosophy, critical theory and methodology to the study of life narrative, providing new ways of reading diverse and always evolving forms. It advances interdisciplinary approaches to life narrative, combining the insights of life writing scholarship with those of cognate fields such as art history, history, anthropology, comparative literary studies, law, sociolinguistics, media studies, medicine, philosophy, psychology and sociology. The series strives towards an international scope that mirrors its community, offering a forum for the study of works in translations not previously studied as well as publishing studies of non-Anglophone works.

**Series Editors**
Kate Douglas, Flinders University, Australia
Anna Poletti, Utrecht University, Netherlands
John Zuern, University of Hawaii, USA

**Editorial Advisory Board**
Dr Ebony Coletu (Penn State University, USA); Dr Ana Belén Martínez García (University of Navarra, Spain); Associate Professor Claire Lynch (Brunel University, UK); Professor Pramod K. Nayar (The University of Hyderabad, India); Dr Nick Tembo (The University of Malawi); Professor Jianling Liu (Shanghai Jiao Tong University, China); Professor Gerardo Necoechea (Instituto Nacional de Antropología e Historia, Mexico); Dr Laurie McNeill (University of British Columbia, Canada)

**Forthcoming Titles**
*The Death Memoir in Contemporary Culture*, Claire Nally
*Inhumanities*, Gillian Whitlock
*Reading Mediated Life Narratives*, Amy Carlson
*Human Rights in Graphic Life Narrative*, Olga Michael

# Children and Biography

*Reading and Writing Life Stories*

Kate Douglas

BLOOMSBURY ACADEMIC
LONDON • NEW YORK • OXFORD • NEW DELHI • SYDNEY

BLOOMSBURY ACADEMIC
Bloomsbury Publishing Plc
50 Bedford Square, London, WC1B 3DP, UK
1385 Broadway, New York, NY 10018, USA
29 Earlsfort Terrace, Dublin 2, Ireland

BLOOMSBURY, BLOOMSBURY ACADEMIC and the Diana logo are trademarks of Bloomsbury Publishing Plc

First published in Great Britain 2023
Paperback edition published 2024

Copyright © Kate Douglas, 2023

Kate Douglas has asserted her right under the Copyright, Designs and Patents Act, 1988, to be identified as Author of this work.

For legal purposes the Acknowledgements on pp. vii–viii constitute an extension of this copyright page.

Series design by Rebecca Heselton
Cover image: *My Mummy* by Darcy Douglas-Spencer

All rights reserved. No part of this publication may be reproduced or transmitted in any form or by any means, electronic or mechanical, including photocopying, recording, or any information storage or retrieval system, without prior permission in writing from the publishers.

Bloomsbury Publishing Plc does not have any control over, or responsibility for, any third-party websites referred to or in this book. All internet addresses given in this book were correct at the time of going to press. The author and publisher regret any inconvenience caused if addresses have changed or sites have ceased to exist, but can accept no responsibility for any such changes.

A catalogue record for this book is available from the British Library.

Library of Congress Cataloging-in-Publication Data

Names: Douglas, Kate, 1974– author.
Title: Children and biography : reading and writing life stories / Kate Douglas.
Other titles: Reading and writing life stories
Description: London ; New York : Bloomsbury Academic, 2023. | Series: New directions in life narrative | Includes bibliographical references and index.
Identifiers: LCCN 2022010258 | ISBN 9781350236363 (hb) | ISBN 9781350236400 (pb) | ISBN 9781350236370 (epdf) | ISBN 9781350236387 (ebook) | ISBN 9781350236394
Subjects: LCSH: Biography as a literary form–History and criticism. | Children–Books and reading. | Children–Biography–History and criticism. | Children–Biography–Authorship. | Autobiography–Child authors.
Classification: LCC CT21 .D69 2022 | DDC 809/.93592–dc23/eng/20220615
LC record available at https://lccn.loc.gov/2022010258

ISBN: HB: 978-1-3502-3636-3
PB: 978-1-3502-3640-0
ePDF: 978-1-3502-3637-0
eBook: 978-1-3502-3638-7

Series: New Directions in Life Narrative

Typeset by Newgen KnowledgeWorks Pvt. Ltd., Chennai, India

To find out more about our authors and books visit www.bloomsbury.com and sign up for our newsletters.

# Contents

| | |
|---|---|
| List of figures | vi |
| Acknowledgements | vii |
| | |
| Introduction: The *Value Tales* | 1 |
| 1  Biographies for children: A literary and cultural history | 19 |
| 2  Biography for children in the twenty-first century | 39 |
| 3  Reading the heroic life: *Kids Who Did* | 65 |
| 4  'Tales of Trusty Hounds': Posthuman biography for children | 83 |
| 5  Children's picture books as collaborative biography | 101 |
| 6  'Biography of a Detention Centre': Children's drawings as auto/biographical testimony | 123 |
| 7  'Five Reasons My Mum Is the Best': Children and biographical practice | 141 |
| 8  My lockdown diary: Childhood biography during Covid-19 | 169 |
| Conclusion: What next for children's biography? | 191 |
| | |
| References | 199 |
| Index | 215 |

# Figures

| | | |
|---|---|---:|
| 2.1 | 'Superhero Greta' from *Little People, Big Dreams: Greta Thunberg* | 46 |
| 2.2 | Rosa Parks 'Why Should I Move?' from *Great Women Who Made History* | 51 |
| 2.3 | 'Young Ada Lovelace' from *Women in Science: Ada Lovelace* | 56 |
| 5.1 | From *My Beautiful Birds* | 117 |
| 7.1 | 'Best Mum' | 152 |
| 7.2 | 'Mothers' Day' | 154 |
| 7.3 | 'Mom's Superpowers' | 155 |
| 7.4 | 'Mother of the Year' | 157 |
| 7.5 | 'To My Amazing Mothers' | 158 |
| 7.6 | 'Best Mum Ever' | 160 |
| 7.7 | 'Why My Mum Is the Best' | 161 |
| 8.1 | 'Who Are You Home With?' | 181 |
| 8.2 | 'Appreciation Day (a)' | 182 |
| 8.3 | 'Appreciation Day (b)' | 183 |
| 8.4 | 'Write a Note to You in the Future (a)' | 185 |
| 8.5 | 'Write a Note to You in the Future (b)' | 187 |

# Acknowledgements

My deepest thanks to my editor Lucy Brown at Bloomsbury for her engagement and enthusiasm throughout this project. I began this book at the strangest of times and I appreciated your positive communication and the clarity and diligence of your approach throughout.

To Gillian Whitlock who has always encouraged me to approach life narrative research with courage and confidence. Through you, I have learned to always approach new subject areas and methods with positivity and self-belief.

Thank you to Karen Douglas (always) for your chats, encouragement, and always believing in me and the value of my work. Thanks to Danni, Ella, Josh and Darcy for your support of me and for the project as it developed. Thanks for the noise, but mostly for the quiet.

Thank you to my dearest work colleagues and friends Lisa Bennett and Kylie Cardell. I am indebted to your unwavering encouragement and positivity through this project and through all of our personal and professional adventures. I am very lucky to have you in my corner, always.

Thank you to Pamela Graham and Edith Hill who worked persistently and creatively as research assistants on this project. I am incredibly grateful to have had your support at various stages of this project. Thank you also to my friends and colleagues, Marina Deller, Craig Howes, Phillip Kavanagh, Emma Maguire, Kris Natalier, Anna Poletti and John Zuern for productive conversations about this research and for sharing your ideas on this project during its various stages.

During periods of lockdown, this research was supported expertly by my 'rebel dogs' and 'rebel cats': Jasper, Junior, Socks, Dottie and Dasha. They are best study buddies a girl could ever want.

Draft chapters of this book were presented at the International Auto/Biography conferences in Madrid (2019) and Adelaide (2021), the American Comparative Literatures Association conference (2020) and the Australian

Literary Studies Convention (2021). I benefited greatly from feedback gained from these presentations.

Most importantly, I would like to acknowledge and thank the children who participated in the reading groups for this project and to those who contributed their biographical texts. The children's engaged and enthusiastic responses and work launched these chapters and my understanding of children's engagement with biography. The children's collaboration in this project was central to its completion. I thank them for their time, creativity and unending enthusiasm for non-fiction. I would also like to extend my heartfelt thanks to the mothers who contributed their children's texts and shared their own understandings of children's biography with me. I feel very fortunate to have had the opportunity to learn so much from those I met during this project.

This research was completed with the support of the Flinders University Social and Behavioural Sciences Research Ethics Committee (Project numbers 2147, 4239 and 8649).

Finally, this book is dedicated to my favourite child reader, Darcy Douglas-Spencer, who inspires me every day to work and to not work. You have instilled in me a love of children's literature, and the capacity to read these books much more carefully, through your eyes.

# Introduction: The *Value Tales*

I went to primary (elementary) school in a large country town in New South Wales, Australia. This was the 1980s; my school library was small, in retrospect, but at the time, for me, it was filled with untapped treasures. Like many children my age, I borrowed several books per week and devoured them all. I happily read from a variety of genres, but one particular set of books has stuck firmly in my mind. The *Value Tales*, by Spencer Johnson and Ann Donegan Johnson, and illustrated by Stephen Pileggi, was a set of forty-three American biographies for children, produced in the mid-1970s. I cannot remember how many of the forty-three books my school library stocked, but I can recall eagerly waiting for another book to come on display so that I could cheerfully obsess over the faraway, foreign subjects represented.

It turns out, I am not alone in my love of the *Value Tales*. There are hundreds of reviewers on book reviews website Goodreads offering fond, nostalgic reflections on the positive impact these books had on them. Here are some indicative comments:

> I read these as a child, and they had a profound effect on my values and view of right & wrong.

> Originally published in 1977, this book was my introduction to feminism. I will always have a special place in my heart for this book and for Nellie Bly because this was the first time I remember thinking that I wasn't limited to 'girl' stuff.

> Fantastic, highly recommendable series … On the whole, I love these types of books; they made history, science, and important life lessons come alive for myself and so many young readers. On that front, they continue to accomplish much good.

> The first series of books I ever loved to read by myself, and still remember fondly to this day, despite not seeing them in at least 20 years at this point. As a kid, they opened up whole new worlds to me.[1]

The comments align with the series title. The *Value Tales*, overtly and unapologetically, aim to provide moral guidance and explicit values for children to follow, and this is what the readers report gaining from their reading.

The *Value Tales* were large picture books of roughly sixty pages long. They presented the stories of well-known historical figures. The focus of each book was a particular positive character trait of the person represented: 'the value of caring', 'the value of commitment' and so on. Each of the historical figures had an imaginary cartoon friend who helped them in their journey. Though the stories offer limited knowledge of the histories represented and are often referred to as 'fictionalised biography', perhaps because of the inclusion of the imaginary friends, the books offer insights into the life represented, and this information is tailored for a child readership. Importantly, this book collection offers a window into what biography for children looked like in Western contexts during the 1970s and 1980s.

What drew me to these books were their large bright covers and the unfamiliarity of the subjects: I was in Australia and these books were about international characters whom I knew little or nothing about. As I have argued elsewhere, this is often how autobiographies and biographies are constructed – to offer something new, for instance, the life of an unknown subject within a familiar theme, genre or form (Douglas, 2010). And this is what happens in the *Value Tales*. The subjects gain their appeal as the form becomes increasingly recognizable with each book read. These are neatly packaged biographies for easy consumption.

Though predictably for their time, many of the subjects were conventional heroes: very well-known, commonly revered historical figures such as explorers and adventurers (Christopher Columbus, Captain James Cook, Jacques Cousteau), science and medical pioneers (Marie Curie, Thomas Edison, Alexander Graham Bell, Florence Nightingale, Louis Pasteur), creative artists (Beethoven, Lucille Ball, Charles Dickens), sporting stars (Arthur Ashe, Jackie Robinson, Wilma Rudolph) and activists (Jane Addams, Nellie Bly, Cesar Chavez, Terry Fox, Helen Keller, Eleanor Roosevelt and Harriet Tubman). But the books, perhaps remarkably for their time, make sound efforts towards diversity in representation with the inclusion of Cochise (an Apache leader during the Apache Wars) and Sacagawea (a young Lemhi Shoshone woman who travelled with explorers Lewis and Clark through the United States and supported their understanding of Indigenous cultures), as well as numerous historical figures who were not white. The *Value Tales* also include representations of disability. And the series also extends well beyond the United States in its representation of subjects.

There was a lot to value about the *Value Tales*. The series aimed to appeal to the stakeholders of children's literature which includes children, but of course, it is not children who are most commonly those purchasing and displaying these books. Stakeholders include teachers, librarians and parents. The *Value Tales* offers their subjects as role models for children. This is not so surprising; children have always been given stories that are inspiring, and these books (implicitly or explicitly) ask children to connect these biographical stories to their own sense of the world and its histories. As I discuss in Chapter 1, biographies, in one form or another have always been a popular genre for child readers. Children have been reading biographies for as long as children have been reading. The reasons for these books' existence and circulation have been remarkably consistent across decades, even centuries. Biographies have aligned closely with ideas and values around child development and education of the time, whether moral or intellectual. One of the critiques we might immediately make about biographies for children, then, is that they tend to conform to predictable templates for understanding and representing human endeavour and achievement. The books and their subjects assert and define what makes a valuable life through what they include and what they omit. However, where this might have been problematic, for instance, in the pre-twentieth and twenty-first-centuries, the publication of deeply conservative, homogenous, biographical texts for children, the genre has more lately become a genre of possibility when it comes to more radical representations of marginal subjects and histories. These representations show children a more diverse world.

Biographies written and illustrated for children have become a burgeoning literary genre in the twenty-first century, with more books being published than ever. However, as an important subgenre of auto/biography and of children's literature, these texts have not been considered in a full-length study. The significance of this study is its positioning of these biographical texts within a wide variety of theoretical disciplines including life narrative, childhood studies, children's education, human rights, children's literature, creative writing and readership studies. My central research questions include what trends in forms and themes have emerged in twenty-first-century biography for children. How do children interpret biography, and what do these texts reveal about children's relationship to truth? What is biography's role in developing empathy, educating liberal citizens and instilling a sense of personal empowerment for child readers? How do children themselves write biographically?

## Biography

'Biographers pretend they know people', wrote Virginia Woolf in 1927. This provocative definition immediately invites us to think about the distance, whether spatial, temporal even ideological, between the biographical author and the subject. It asks us to consider the reason that a biography is being written, and who stands to gain what from its production and circulation. Defining biography in a rudimentary sense, scholars Nigel Hamilton (2010) and Hermione Lee (2009: 5) posit that biography is someone's life story being told by someone other than the subject. Biography is thought to be distinct from autobiography, then, by the apparent separation between the author and the subject and events of the subject's life. But as implied by Woolf's quote earlier, the extent of this distance or separation will vary from text to text.

Ruth Hoberman (2001: 109) explains that biography is often considered as a 'subcategory of historical writing'. Sometimes referred to as personal histories, biographies locate the subject in time and space, so that the story of one person can reveal something of the socio-cultural or political flavour of life in the time or place in which the subject lived. Biographies are led by, and also limited to, the facts of the subject's life, such as birth, death and documented events from their life – what can be known and proven about a life. Even the more innovative contemporary examples I discuss through this project tend to adhere to these genre conventions. These aspects of biography's style continue to be an important part of what makes the genre recognizable. Biographies try to evoke a subject's 'inner life ... to make its subject "come alive"' (Hoberman

2001: 109). This acknowledges the craft of biography. Biography requires a reader who finds a story accessible. The relaying of the facts and dates of a life or stale, seemingly objective descriptions are unlikely to achieve this accessibility. Throughout this study I consider the myriad stylistic and thematic ways that biographies are crafted as important, accessible stories to engage their readers, whether young or adult.

Biography as the diverse form we see now has its origins in the fifteenth century. But what we might include as biographical text dates back much further, as Hoberman (2001: 110) argues, 'funeral orations, post-funeral songs of mourning and praise ... inscriptions on monuments' are all examples of biography. Biography is not limited to the written word, but is inclusive of material and visual forms; it is an ever-evolving form. Early biography, for instance, in Greek and Roman times, was largely didactic and offered 'models for imitation' (Hoberman, 2001: 110) During the Middle Ages 'hagiography', that is, biographical writings of the lives of saints, dominated European biography, and Hoberman notes similar themes in Indian, Japanese, Chinese and Islamic biographies during this period, which also focussed on gods, prophets, religious leaders, warriors and other heroes (Hoberman, 2001: 110). In the eighteenth century, literary biography peaked in England and was characterized by significant lives and the broader search for meaning in lives. Nineteenth-century biographies were 'long and respectful' and meticulously researched (Hoberman, 2001: 110).

The most significant historical shift in biography was in the twentieth century with the idea of 'new biography' and the publication of Lytton Strachey's *Eminent Victorians* (1918). Strachey argued that a biographer's mandate was not to simply celebrate the subject and their achievements, but rather 'the biography must shape his/her material and expose his/her subject's less complimentary features in the interest of constructing a coherent, artful, and convincing portrait' (Hoberman, 2001: 110). And in the twenty-first century we have come to understand biography in this way. Though biography, for the most part, continues to invite the reader to consider what they are reading as a representation of a true subject and life, as Jenny Coleman (2010: 19) contends, we also understand that the biographer, like the novelist, makes choices about inclusion and omission, shapes the narrative and constructs characters.

Strachey's ideas emancipated authors of biography, inviting craft, creativity and speculation into the biographer's toolkit. As biography has evolved, there has been a deeper response to the notion of new biography and what biography might do and achieve in the world. In her book *Metabiography*, Caitríona Ní Dhúill (2020: 2) notes that biography as a genre and a practice calls for 'a dizzying array of incompatible viewpoints', giving weight to the potential inclusivity of the form and a move away from notions of its inherent conservatism and limitations. For Ní Dhúill (2020),

> biography itself, as a genre, cultural practice, and approach to the past, has been taken to task, rightly, for its own complicity with a patriarchal culture with cults of individualism and heroism, myths of sole achievement, and fictions of (self-) authorship and agency that underwrite and are underwritten by the singular name. (15)

One of the central concerns of biography today is that the form has traditionally overlooked marginal subjects. But, as Hoberman (2001: 112) argues, biography's continued popularity presents an opportunity for the form, for instance, to challenge 'a culture's assumptions about what the successful life looks like, and who is worth remembering'.

If we are to open up biography as a genre with unlimited potential, we must first face up to the problems of its past, specifically, its deeply entrenched conservatism and unbalanced attention to particular types of male subjects. Ní Dhúill (2020) explains,

> The 'masculinism' of biography works at three levels. Most obvious is the historical tendency of the genre to focus on male lives. This has begun to give ground in recent decades to a welcome proliferation of female lives; queer and trans lives, which have remained on the margins, are now beginning to come into their own. But taken over the genre's full historical reach, the quantitative problem of ratio remains. The masculinism is most simply and starkly illustrated by the male to female ratio in standard biographical dictionaries. In the *British Dictionary of National Biography*, begun in 1885 ... five percent of the biographical subjects included were women. In the 2004 *Oxford Dictionary of National Biography* ... the proportion of women is ten percent. (188)

In 2021, as I am writing this book, biography remains a popular literary genre. Twenty-first-century critics of biography, like Ní Dhúill (2020), have sought to unsettle the genre by asking questions about its past and its evolution into present forms. This involves not only a criticism of what biography has been, but also a sense of optimism regarding recent shifts in biographical practice, for instance, an increased representation of minority subjects and a trend towards stylistic experimentation, and its capacity to provoke new conversations about ethics, form, style and so on. Ní Dhúill (2020: 189) argues that life writing and memoir, as examples of non-fiction genres, have exceeded biography in terms of representation,

> While the proliferation of life writing and memoir in recent years has generated increasing interest in the narration of previously 'unknown' lives, that is, lives made known to the reader only through the biographical text itself, mainstream biography remains indissociable from concepts or prior cultural prominence or achievement.

But such a conception of biography locates it too strongly in the past rather than asserting the myriad new forms that define twenty-first-century biography, which Pamela Graham (2016) argues might include biopics, Wikipedia, online obituaries, creative non-fiction biographies (such as Rebecca Skloot's *The Immortal Life of Henrietta Lacks* and Helen Garner's *Joe Cinque's Consolation*), graphic biography, and social media memorial texts. Graham (2016) argues that we might consider such forms new modes of 'new biography' that extend Strachey's original thinking about biography's capacity to be radical and changing. Such twenty-first-century new biographies 'make visible, revise and remake biographical politics, ethics and epistemologies' (14). More recently, leading biography scholar W. Craig Howes has used the term 'biobits' to explore the 'traces and fragments' that might exist outside of and within 'bio'-'graphe' – the life and the writing. It is not in our best interests to place limits on a genre that we want to see become more inclusive (n.p.). Howes (2020) has productively used the 'biobit' to describe how short-form biography, and visual and graphic texts, have become significant sites of genre change, for instance, television documentary, songs and other forms of flash biography. Howes argues that short form biography has been around for a long time, but, now, its proliferation prompts the question, how important is narrative to this form of life narrative?

Biographies for children have become a fascinating microcosm of the genre of biography more generally. As I will discuss in Chapter 1, the shifts and expanses suggested above that have affected biography, generally through its history, have not surprisingly characterized biographies for children: a move away from conservatism in representation and forms, towards wider consideration of subjects. Though biographies for children have been around for a very long time, in the late twentieth and twenty-first centuries, we can see a significant shift in the politics and ideological bases of these books.

## Children and biography: Reading and writing life stories

There has been some insightful scholarship on biographies for children from different locations and periods in literary history, which I discuss in Chapter 1. However, this book is the first extended study of biography, broadly defined, produced for and written by children. As argued above, biography is an inclusive broad church that includes the representations of diverse subjects including well-known historical figures, biographies of objects and sites, as well as (increasingly) the life stories of marginal subjects including children themselves, 'rebels', and the posthuman – such as animals. Biographies for children can be picture books, books for early readers, chapter books or information-based non-fiction – such as science or history texts. The wide publication and circulation of biographies for children tells us something about what stakeholders (writers, publishers, educators, parents) perceive to be important for children to read now.

As a global community, we are now deeply interested in how children engage with the world they live in. Public debates about children's books and reading practices have intensified with the rise of technologies and children's engagements with them. Now, debates about children's reading most often relate to panics about reading being on the decline, and also extend to discussions of content, for instance, the age-appropriateness of certain books.

In a fast-changing, often uncertain world, children's relationship to knowledge, 'truth' and role models has become an urgent issue. Biographies for children overtly engage with fundamental questions about knowledge, facts and how we acquire them. In an age of mass information and news sources, children face considerable challenges to negotiate facts and competing representations of the world; since biographies commonly offer children a 'way in' to historical knowledge, literary scholarship offers a means for considering the cultural work that these texts might engage in. How do these literatures speak to the big issues of our time? For instance, biographies for children open up discussions of wide-ranging, timely, micro- and macro-social issues such as bullying, vulnerability, leadership and heroism (Anderson and Cavallaro, 2000; Jones and Watkins, 2002).

Biographies for children have become increasingly popular texts in the twenty-first century (see genre and market research by Albers, 2016; Alexander and Jarman, 2018; Bender, 2013; Clark, 2016; Onwuemezi, 2018; Rosen, 2015). This aligns with the continued, general popularity of children's literature. As Kathy G. Short (2018: 95) notes, 'while other readership have stagnated, the sales of children's books have continued to rise'. Short (2018: 287) notes a strong trend towards 'books that matter' and 'books that reflect the diversity of our society and the world'. The rising popularity of non-fiction books for children follows the 'memoir boom' of the late 1990s and 2000s, during which autobiographies and memoirs became one of the most popular genres for adult readers (Couser, 2011; Douglas, 2010; Rak, 2013). Children's literature historian, Leonard Marcus has argued, 'The picture book biography is among the most dynamic genres ... a reflection perhaps of an urgently felt need for role models and heroes in a complex world' ('NYU Georgiou Library', 2015: n.p.). They provide a popular and early introduction to 'true' life stories of scientists, activists, innovators and other public, heroic figures. Biographies written and illustrated for children explore some of the most pressing issues affecting children now, such as the representation of knowledge, environmental change, health crises, education, and personal and cultural development. From *Goodnight Stories for Rebel Girls* through to the numerous adaptations of Malala Yousafzai's life story, these books are assumed to offer diverse, inspirational examples for children to follow.

But there is a lot we do not know about these books. For instance, their significance to life narrative scholarship more generally or to scholarship on children's literature. In this book I aim to produce new knowledge on how these texts are produced and read, and the cultural work they do, and to foreground children's voices in discussions of how children read life narrative and are engaged in its production.

I present a brief history of the form in Chapter 1 before focussing on the twenty-first-century trends that have characterized this genre and practice. My focus is texts published in English in Australia, North America and Europe, whilst respecting the form's cultural and linguistic diversities. As much as a global study is warranted and would yield fascinating results, text access, my own linguistic limits and the time-consuming practicalities of research have imposed some boundaries on this project. I hope that the project's limits might allow for focus and depth that provide meaningful insights into the texts and practices I explore.

I approach this project as a life-narrative scholar. I work within the broad field of life narrative or auto/biography studies. I find these umbrella terms useful, as others in my field such as Sidonie Smith and Julia Watson (2010) have in their central works *Reading Autobiography: A Guide for Interpreting Life Narratives* and *Getting a Life: Everyday Uses of Autobiography* (1996) have done. These concepts can be used to define the myriad ways in which life stories are constructed and circulated every day. Life narrative encompasses diverse 'truth' genres such as autobiography, biography, memoir, letters, diaries, documentary, social media and so on. What makes life narrative texts different from fictional ones is that life narratives are constructed and presented as offering *a truth* (which is, of course, different to *the truth* or any objective notion of truth). All life narration involves creative crafting, choices about inclusion and omission. And this is what scholars working in this disciplinary area find unendingly fascinating, and this is what we explore in our scholarship.

One of the central journals in my field is *a/b: Auto/Biography Studies*. In using the term 'auto/biography' in the title, the journal affirms the breadth of the genre in terms of what sorts of texts and scholarship 'a/b' encompasses. Further, it asserts the genre work that might be accomplished at the intersection of autobiography and biography. In *Children and Biography: Reading and Writing Life Stories*, I am interested in the inevitable slippage between autobiography and biography. Interrogating the '/' or 'slash' involves considering the ways in which autobiographical representations might permeate biography and biographical or relational representations might pervade autobiography. What are the implications of these slippages in biography for children, particularly when it comes to thinking about the inevitability of children experiencing their lives relationally?

Much of my previous research, notably *Contesting Childhood* (2010), has focussed on autobiographies written *about* childhood by adults. Adults have been, historically, more likely to tell stories about children than children. And when adults tell stories about children and childhood, certain narratives tend to be dominant at particular points in history. Children's literature scholars M. O. Grenby and Andrea Immel (2009: 19) argue that, 'ideas about children's books are inextricably bound up with cultural constructs of childhood'. Literatures about children and childhood or for children and childhood tend to reveal a lot about the social and cultural position of children at the time of the text's production. They show the investments that are made in childhood, as well as fears and desires about what childhood is and should be.

This study operates in this space, but aims to provocatively extend our sense of children as stakeholders in non-fictional literatures written for them and about their lives. In this research I work at the intersection of childhood studies, children's literature, and life-narrative studies and ask what can we learn about children's world views from the ways they interpret non-fiction? What does the production of biography for children now tell us about children's perceived relationship to the truth and cultural representations of real lives and heroes? And what happens when children make biographical texts? What does this production reveal about what children think biography is and can do in the world?

Fiona McCulloch (2011: 3) posits that, 'childhood is a vague term and notoriously fluid regarding when it ends, dependent upon the historical period in which it is being addressed. It is also a concept that differs geographically and culturally'. And Hugh Cunningham (2014: 1) reminds us that 'we need to distinguish between children as human beings and childhood as a shifting set of ideas'. Literatures for children reflect the ideologies of childhood prevalent at the time in which they are produced, and this is a central theme for this study. I follow scholarly definitions of children's literature as books written for children of different ages, including those containing visual and verbal narratives (Coats, 2018; Jaques, 2015; McCulloch, 2011). I take Grenby's (2007: 277) point that children's literature can be difficult to categorize: is children's literature any books that children read or books designed particularly for children? And how can we account for literature as diverse as for three-year-olds and eighteen-year-olds? The parameters of this study are literatures produced for and by child readers aged between five and twelve (primary-school-aged children). I choose these limits in recognition that these are the target ages for children's literature. At the upper level of this age group, young readers tend to graduate to young adult (YA) literatures or even adult literatures. And though primary-school-aged children can and might read literatures not intended for or marketed for them, it is these literatures that offer containment and focus for the present study.

## Approach

This project uses interdisciplinary methods by combining textual and contextual analyses with a readership study of child readers, and analyses of life-narrative texts produced by children. To date, there are no studies of child readers in life-narrative scholarship. I aim to open up vital conversations on this topic; for instance, what is changing behind this idea of 'heroes' for kids? How do these books and their reception show us that? What are the consequences of these changes for how we model life paths for children? What representations do children reject?

My analysis builds on the close reading strategies developed in my previous life narrative studies: *Contesting Childhood* (2010) and with Anna Poletti, *Life Narratives and Youth Cultures* (2016); identifying patterns and themes; analysing literary and visual techniques. I ask: What techniques are used to bring 'true' stories to children's attentions? How do these biographies draw real-life evidence to construct a life narrative for a child reader? How do they construct knowledge and facts within the text? Drawing on readership studies with children (Backman, 2020; Iordanaki, 2020), I will consider my reading of biographical texts for children in light of children's interpretations made in focus groups. Focus groups have proven to be a quick way of gathering readership data with children. They allow children to gain confidence in building on ideas expressed by other children and have ensured that child-directed discussions emerge. The focus groups will appear in Chapters 3 and 4 of this study. Analyses of children's own life narratives, drawing and writing, is central to Chapters 6, 7 and 8 of this project. Drawing on children's interpretation of their work, alongside my own analyses and anchoring within the theories of this project, will hopefully offer some potent insights into children's contributions to and relationship with biography.

\* \* \*

Chapter 1 focusses on biographies produced for child readers and offers a literary-historical overview. I argue that biography has been the leading form of life narratives produced for children, historically. A particular focus in this chapter is the ideological, moral, religious and educational value these texts have been constructed and/or perceived to have by stakeholders engaged in their circulation (particularly in the United States and the UK at different historical moments).

Chapter 2 moves the discussion into the twenty-first century, noting the emergence of key biography-for-children series such as *Little People, Big Dreams* which includes biographical picture books of young people such as Anne Frank and sketches of the younger years of other famous figures such as Frida Kahlo, Marie Curie and Stephen Hawking. Similarly, *Women in Science* features subjects such as Jane Goodall, Ada Lovelace, Rachel Carson and Temple Grandin, and Kate Pankhurst's *Fantastically Great Women Who Made History* (2016) and *Fantastically Great Women Who Changed the World* (2016), which contains a mix of biographical sketches about women, including young women, who had an impact upon history. Perhaps the most famous biographical series so far in the twenty-first century is Elena Favilli's and Francesca Cavallo's *Goodnight Stories for Rebel Girls* (2017–21). Chapter 2 asks, why these people, and these stories, now? In this chapter I engage in close textual analysis of the biographical representations made in these books. In constructing biographical sketches of 'great' women, what's included and what's left out and why? What assumptions are made, for instance, about age-appropriate content (in terms of subjects)?

Literary studies tend to focus on textual analysis, with less attention given to reading practices (Bode and Dixon, 2009). In life writing studies, there is little known about how readers comprehend and interpret non-fictional texts, and empirical data simply is not yet available. In combining textual analysis and readership studies, this project will address this gap.

In two of the chapters that follow, through focus group questions and discussion with children, the project will generate important, original data on children's readership allowing us to discover how children read these books and how they process the information, facts and truths these texts construct.

Chapter 3 observes that where many biographies for children published in the past focussed on adult stories, or what now-famous adults were like as children, many of the twenty-first-century biographical narratives focus on the life narratives of children, asserting the value of children's lives. Most recently, Kirsty Murray's *Kids Who Did: Real Kids Who Ruled, Rebelled, Survived and Thrived* (2019) showcases 'forty true stories' celebrating children who have,

> protested, prayed, rebelled, saved lives, earned a fortune, lost everything, become world-famous, or fought to survive war and oppression. Fearless kids, feral kids, Olympic champions, human-rights crusaders, climate-change warriors, princes and prisoners, workers and whiz-kids.

Collectively, these texts purport to show child readers how children can be powerful and change the world, despite any public discourse to the contrary. However, there are assumptions and ideologies in these texts that we might scrutinize (particularly around heroics and what makes a valuable life). But how do child readers respond to these biographies? By engaging in observational, close-reading activities (of *Kids Who Did*) with child readers (aged from eight to ten, in four focus groups of six), this chapter will explore what these biographies might tell us about how young readers are responding to these representations. I imagined (or hypothesized) that children would like to read notable stories about other children. And this is why I selected *Kids Who Did* for the readership chapter of this book.

Chapter 4 takes the focus away from the human in exploring biographical representations of animals. Kimberly Hamilton's *Rebel Dogs: Heroic Tales of Trusty Hounds* (2019) effectively rides the coattails of the aforementioned *Rebel Girls* (etc.) book series. The book covers are very similar, they share the same structure, and work to engage a similarly aged readership. Of course, this is not the first biographical text about dogs for child readers. Amazon lists eighty-eight results in a search for the 'biographies for readers aged 9–12', including the search term 'dog'. Expanding the search to 'animals' includes over a thousand results, with biographical subjects including US presidential pets; animals that served in war and conflict; animals as muses for famous conservationists, activists and artists; and animals engaged in therapeutic pursuits. This chapter draws on theoretical work on animal biography and posthumanism and life narrative to read a selection of heroic animal biographies and consider how they are framed to do cultural work (whether individualizing or celebrating particular animal lives, or as literary activism, for instance). How do these texts seek to construct a relationship between texts (and their ideas) and the child reader?

Chapter 5 considers issues-based picture books and explores their biographical methods. In 2017, Alexandra Alter wrote a piece for *The Guardian* titled 'Why Children's Authors are Taking on the Refugee Crisis'. Alter notes an exponential growth in children's books about asylum-seeking in the past two years. Though some of these books are fiction, notably, many are non-fiction and draw on texts and methods from life writing: for instance, picture books based on true stories, actual testimony or interviews with asylum-seekers and refugees, and archival research. For example, Suzanne Del Rizzo's *My Beautiful Birds* (2017) is based on a true story of a Syrian boy living in Jordan in the Zaatari refugee camp who had tamed wild birds, and Francesca Sanna's *The Journey* (2016) is based on the story of two girls that Sanna met in a refugee camp in Italy, and other interviews she conducted with refugees, to create a 'collage' of personal stories.

This chapter explores *My Beautiful Birds* and *The Journey* as examples of children's books that offer biographical narratives as source of historical, social and cultural knowledge on the experience of child asylum-seekers. These books aim to make the lives of child refugees visible to child readers. Within the contexts of displaced and disappearing migrant children, these picture books seek to tell stories and share testimony that might otherwise disappear. How do these texts draw on life narrative methods (such as oral testimony and interviewing) and documents of life to construct life narrative texts for children, and to authorize these texts, more generally? I argue that these biographical picture books – their authors and illustrators – become witnesses to, and conduits for, the circulation of asylum-seeker testimony. In their construction, they reveal something of the perceived value of sharing trauma narratives with child readers.

Chapter 6 links with Chapter 5 to consider how child and adult life narratives exist in biographical dialogue to explore the experience and representation of cultural displacement and asylum seeking. Children's testimony of their refugee and asylum-seeker status is vital in the wider circulation and reception of knowledge of the asylum-seeker or refugee experience in the Australian context and beyond. This chapter considers a small archive of children's drawings which form part of The Australian Human Rights Commission (2014) Forgotten Children report. These are thirteen drawings by detained asylum-seekers aged between four and seventeen. My aim in this chapter is to frame these drawings as auto/biographical texts that significantly become powerful biographies of place and space as well as an imagined Australia and Australians.

Children are not only readers of biographies, but also produce them, readily and often, in their everyday lives. Chapter 7 draws on Sidonie Smith's and Julia Watson's (1996) notion of 'everyday uses of autobiography' and interdisciplinary theories of childhood and youth, for instance, on children's drawings and children as creative, social actors to read some biographical texts (indeed, ante-autobiographical texts, to borrow Claire Lynch's 2013 concept) produced by children. It reports the findings of a small study into biographical texts children have made at school of their parents or other family members. Children are routinely required to draw and/or write about their family members – for instance, as a 'getting-to-know-you' activity at the start of the school, or on days like Mothers'/Fathers' Day. In this study, ten parents of nine-year-old children were asked to share biographical texts produced by their child; these texts are reproduced in photographic form and analysed in this chapter. What do these texts tell us about children and how they construct relationships via biographical practice and representation?

Children's life writing has often been marginalized or is missing from official histories and accounts of childhood. Chapter 8 offers an example of children's life writing: lockdown diaries produced during the Covid-19 pandemic by South Australian primary-school children. During this time, most school children were away from their extended family and friends, schools, sports and so on, for an extended period of time. 'My Lockdown Diary' was produced by New Zealand artist Stephen McCarthy and released as a free, downloadable tool for children to make a record of their experiences during lockdown. In reading 'My Lockdown Diaries' we have an opportunity to document children's experiences at a significant point in history. I read these diaries against the grain of diary, exploring the biographical representations that they make. This chapter affirms a more general argument of this book study, that children more readily produce auto/biographical relational lives.

The conclusion explores the implications of what I have observed across this survey of biographical texts produced for children, and also what happens when children produce their own life narrative texts of consequence. This chapter will look at directions for future research, particular ways that researchers might place children's voices and writing at the centre of future inquiries in ways that facilitate genuine agency for child authors. The conclusion also considers ways we might engage with diversity in life narrative for and by children, for instance, in translation or in oral and visual formats.

\* \* \*

I commenced this project in 2020 and concluded it in 2021. These years will be marked in the memory of the generations that lived through them. It was also a time when reading gained broad attention as a vital cultural pursuit, with lists emerging around the sorts of reading people might turn to during a pandemic.

I started a children's non-fiction book club for Chapter 3 of this project, and this was initially the only chapter I had thought children (as readers or as writers) would appear in. But as the project developed, so did the children's presence in the project. They ended up playing a role in Chapter 4 also, but more generally in my thinking as I revised all the chapters and developed my understanding of the production, circulation and reception of biographies for children. If my ideas have become more sophisticated as this project has developed (which I dearly hope they have) I owe this to what the child readers taught me during and following our time together. What started as a literary studies project has become much more child-centred and collaborative than I could have ever hoped it might be, and I am deeply grateful for this opportunity.

## Note

1. Review 1: Lauren Ann Tull (15 January 2019). Available online: https://www.goodreads.com/book/show/20406368-valuetale-set.
   Review 2: Zoe's Human (25 November 2013). Available online: https://www.goodreads.com/book/show/27268126-the-value-of-fairness.
   Review 3: Jondania (15 April 2018) and Review 4: Chad (28 May 2009). Available online: https://www.goodreads.com/book/show/196827.The_Value_of_Believing_in_Yourself.

# 1

# Biographies for children: A literary and cultural history

The wonderful Kids' Book Club, as mentioned in the introduction, will feature in two chapters of this study. During one of my sessions with the children, I asked the members, ten nine-year-olds, 'do you know what biography is?' Six of them said 'no'. The other three responded:

Is it when you write a true story?

I think these are stories about old men, like your grandfather.

Is it a story about a famous person?

These answers are not far off. But they also tell us that, for the most part, the target audience for children's biography does not know much about what biography is and who or what it is for. This is surprising considering, as I hope to show in this Chapter 1, biography has been a robust subgenre of children's literature for over three hundred years. But it is also a diverse and ever-changing genre in its presentation, and the genre labels attached to it have varied over time. Perhaps children read and enjoy it because of the ways it arrives to them – via teachers, librarians, parents, bookstores etcetera.

*Children and Biography: Reading and Writing Life Stories* is a study that predominantly examines twenty-first-century biographies for children. However, recent developments in the genre can be productively contextualized within literary history. As Carrie Hintz and Eric L. Tribunella (2019: 309) argue, when we think about non-fiction for children, 'we often conceive it as purely didactic – or a teaching – genre'. This has certainly been a focus of biography for children through literary history; the genre has included texts ranging from religious instruction through to science education, all appearing through the accessible lens of biography. Biographical texts have long played a role in children's literature: as role modelling texts, conversion narratives and as cautionary tales. A particular focus in this chapter is the ideological, moral, religious and educational value these texts have been constructed or perceived to have by stakeholders engaged in their circulation, for instance, in the United States and the UK at different moments in literary history.

This chapter also explores the rise in biographies seeking to represent diverse lives, particularly in the United States in the late twentieth century. These texts show a shifting sense of what biography might achieve, particularly in moving away from its conservative roots. The case studies that appear at the end of this chapter signal the significant changes that have characterized biography for children in the twenty-first century who had their foundation in the late twentieth century.

The development and circulation of biographies for children aligns closely with the evolving socio-cultural position of the child at the time of publication. As Karen Coats (2018: 11) argues, the history of children's literature cannot be considered separately from the history of childhood. Biographies for children also reveal and respond to cultural perceptions of children's literacy and biography's relationship to constructions of literate citizenship. Biography during this period has been characterized by its shifting role, from being exclusively purposed as moral instruction and the conveyance of factual knowledge, towards books 'designed to enliven the reading experience and spark imaginative response' (Hintz and Tribunella, 2019: 310). In the late twentieth century, biographies for children had become an expansive and diverse genre characterized by diversity in representation, radical revisionist histories and inspirational education texts aimed at opening up children's worldview.

## Pre-eighteenth and eighteenth-century Britain and Europe

Fiona McCulloch, in thinking about how to define children's literature, suggests that before there was children's literature, children were reading books that were not intended for them. There is 'evidence of children reading fables as far back as ancient Greece, Rome, Egypt and Sumer', McCulloch (2011: 29) explains. In medieval Britain, children were reading 'fables, courtesy books, journals, ballads, saints' lives, romances and chapbooks, which were short cheap books sold by peddlers' (McCulloch, 2011: 29). And oral traditions were also an important way in which children received stories 'for instance, ruling class children would hear fables told by servants' (McCulloch, 2011: 29).

This changed, McCulloch (2011: 30) argues, with the advent of the printing press in the fifteenth century, which brought books into wider circulation. Though there were still few books written for children, in the sixteenth century, children who could read were encouraged to focus on religious texts. These were moralizing tales, and a common theme was death due to the high infant mortality rates (McCulloch, 2011: 31). In France and England, fairy tales were read by children, but they tended to reproduce gender roles and satisfy patriarchal ideals (McCulloch, 2011: 34).

In their study of genres of children's literature, Hintz and Tribunella (2019) consider the history of non-fiction for children and point to 'conduct books' of the sixteenth century as an early example of biographical writing for children. In these books, certain lives were held up for children's admiration and as guides to appropriate behaviour. Books such as Baldassare Castiglione's *The Book of the Courtier* (1528) offered 'knowledge of the classics, fluency in the fine arts, and elegant manners' as examples to follow. There are clear class stakes here in terms of who might be expected to read conduct books. Some were aimed at men and women, but many were aimed at a mixed readership or for children especially. Up until the eighteenth century, these were the main forms of non-fiction writing intended for a child readership.[1] Hintz and Tribunella (2019) also point to Puritan biographies for children from the seventeenth century, for example, James Janeway's *A Token for Children* (1671) which offered true stories of 'repentant children to inspire them to embrace the Puritan faith' (316). Similar to conduct books, such books show how, prior to the nineteenth century, most biographies for children focused on religious instruction. Recurrent themes were duty to God and parents, respect for teachers and upholding the social and political status quo (Hintz and Tribunella, 2019).

Though Hintz and Tribunella (2019) locate early non-fiction for children in the sixteenth century, most scholars agree that biographies for children found their moment in the eighteenth century, when Puritan ideas were replaced by Enlightenment thinking. The rise of children's literature more generally aligned with changing perspectives on children's education. These were influenced by John Locke's writings about children's education and development. In 'An Essay Concerning Human Understanding' (1689) and 'Some Thoughts Concerning Education' (1693), Locke argued that children's development was most significantly affected by their socialization. For Locke, children's minds were *tabula rasa*, their learning came predominantly from their environment. Children are driven by curiosity. Therefore, education had a vital role to play in children's futures. Children's literature should therefore focus less on language and morality and more on its capacity for more general education and inspiration.

Children's literature scholar Matthew Grenby (2007: 277) explains how children's publishing in the UK developed in a noticeable way from the mid-eighteenth century, and by the 1790s it was a 'flourishing branch of print culture'. Children's books became commercial products – books that parents may like and want to buy and read to their children. Grenby (2009) explains,

> for the first time, publishers ... began to devote substantial resources to a product that was marketed at children and their guardians ... children's books were different in appearance, and in cost ... Separate advertisements were placed in newspapers. Reviews began to appear in periodicals. By the end of the eighteenth century, an author could start to think of himself, or more typically herself, as a writer for children only. (6)

Grenby (2009: 7) contextualizes this shift in light of a number of different factors. Firstly, the fact that there were 'more children around'. Grenby (2009: 7) writes, 'the English population rose by about 20 percent between 1720 and 1770. What these demographic and cultural shifts meant was a society increasingly full of, and concerned with, children, and willing to invest in them both emotionally and financially.' Education was also an important factor; there was an increased recognition that children required education, particularly religious education, to enter the adult world (Grenby, 2009: 7). Grenby (2009: 8) also points to developments in the book trade as enabling the production of children's books: new printing methods, particularly for illustrations, and new binding techniques brought the cost of books down.

The rise of the middle class meant more people were able to buy books. And the physical attractiveness of books made them desirable commercial products and were also status symbols during a time when social mobility was becoming more desirable and possible. Also, around this time, literature was becoming more professionalized. With less emphasis on patronage, the open market paved the way for mass-market books of which children's books were becoming a part. This was also a time of significant change in relation to the status of the novel, as Grenby (2009) discusses:

> At the start of the eighteenth century, the novel had been widely seen as a moral form suitable for the whole family. Increasingly though, novelists were declining to act as guardians of the moral welfare of the nation and its youth, and the didactic element was replaced by greater emphasis on form, style and narrative, amatory and erotic elements, or psychological complexity. These shifts encouraged a new literature for children. In effect, children's literature filled the void which the novel's rise to maturity, and move away from moral didacticism, had left behind. (8)

So, where the novel might have left didacticism behind, children's literature was to have it as a central focus. McCulloch (2011) explains that,

> children's books, then, became an immensely powerful ideological tool in the surveillance and guidance of children and their parents in teaching children to be compliant, obedient and subservient. On the other hand, such tales offered children heroes and heroines that they could identify with and a literature which was separate from adult novels and directed specifically at their entertainment. (38)

Samuel Pickering Jr (1977), researching in the US context, has similar findings. Children's literature also became a distinct category of its own in the United States in the second part of the eighteenth century. Stories produced explicitly *for* children began to emerge from the mid-eighteenth century onwards, initially in the form of fanciful tales and fictional stories. Publisher John Newbery was a key figure in early-children's publishing, publishing *A Little Pretty Pocket Book* in 1744. This book, McCulloch (2011: 36) explains, represented something of a turning point in that it is often thought of as the first modern children's book, marketed specifically for children. The book also attempts to 'entertain as well as instruct' (McCulloch, 2011: 36), which made it significant for its time, imagining a reader who needed, but importantly also deserved, more than simple moral instruction.

However, as the eighteenth century progressed, moral panic about the effects of the novel on 'young minds', especially young women, gained momentum, there was a turn backwards in favour of 'instructive' rather than 'imaginative' texts (Pickering, 1977: 9). Within this context, and because of its perceived proximity to the truth, biography had a role to play! Writers and educators became more mindful of the possibilities afforded by non-fiction to teach religion, history and social awareness to children. In 1793, John Macgowan, Scottish Baptist minister and author, wrote *The Life of Joseph, the Son of Israel: In Eight Books, Chiefly Designed for the Use of Youth*. This anthology represents an early example of biographical writing for children that centred on moral education. *The Interesting and Affecting History of Prince Lee Boo: A Native of the Pelew Islands, Brought to England by Capt. Wilson* was published in 1789 and is another early example of non-fiction writing aimed at young readers. The manuscript of which is held in the US Library of Congress engages young readers with 'true' exotic tales from faraway places. Augustin Louis Josse's *Juvenile Biography; or, Lives of Celebrated Children; To Which Are Added Moral Reflexions, Translated by Mrs. Cummyng*, was published in 1801. Josse was a French Catholic priest, so this biography offered explicit moral education for children in the forms of admirable children whose lives are held up as exemplary. Two similar British examples are *Juvenile Biography; Being Some Account of the Childhood of Persons Who Were Eminent in Maturer Years for Piety, Genius, and Learning*, published in 1824 and Ebenezer Miller's *Scripture History, With the Lives of the Most Celebrated Apostles. Designed for the Improvement of Youth*, published in 1815. The elongated titles of these books provided a transparent sense of their tone and their objective. These books were not circulated for children's entertainment; they were exclusively morality tales.

As Pickering (1977) explains, in the late eighteenth century, in place of the novel and the fairy tale, late-eighteenth-century writers for children looked to a new genre that might be conducive to the sorts of heavy-handed morality tales that were the focus of the day. This new form was the 'fictional biography'. Their subjects were animals and inanimate objects, for example *The Life and Perambulations of a Mouse* (1783) by Dorothy Kilner, and *The Adventures of a*

*Silver Penny* (1790) by Richard Johnson. These books offered moral teachings to children such as humility and selflessness. The prevailing message was that good things happen to those who are good, so, these books also acted as cautionary tales of what might happen to children who do not follow the teachings within. These books are revealing for what they demonstrate about the cultural position of children and also children's reading at this time. Those championing these texts did not see children as active agents in reading, nor deserving of entertainment, diversity or intellectual stimulation. Children's right to read books that were meaningful to them was dependent on other (adult) stakeholders' belief in what reading was morally good for them.

## Nineteenth- and twentieth-centuries biography for children: The United States and the UK

As Roni Natov (2018: 103) suggests, again in the nineteenth century there was a growing sense that children's literature could and should be entertaining for children and not simply didactic. Biographies had a role to play here because they were commonly thought to offer both entertainment and education to children, and a lot more besides. Biography's relationship with historical subjects and events meant that it was well positioned to present rollicking adventure tales to children, whilst also offering role models for their information and solid values to admire and follow.

Perhaps not surprisingly (given the prevalence of libraries and archives in the United States) on nineteenth-century biographies for children, we know more about the US context than any other. R. Gordon Kelly's (1973) study 'American Biographies for Children, 1870–1900' reveals that there are some common subjects of children's biography from the late nineteenth century. The most prominent subjects include the US presidents (for instance, Lincoln and Washington), explorers (for instance, Columbus, Vasco da Gama, Magellan, Drake) and colonial-era pioneers (Stuyvesant, Hudson, Crockett). Biographies offering 'heroes for boys' and 'heroes for girls' (including Queen Elizabeth I, Queen Victoria, Pocahontas, Harriett Beecher Stowe, Florence Nightingale and Louisa May Alcott) were also popular according to Kelly. These nooks were constructed and circulated by authors and publishers to be read primarily by those under the age of eighteen (Kelly, 1973). Institutionally promoted reading lists were one way that biographies for children found their readership during the late nineteenth century. In 1890, John F. Sargent compiled the list 'Reading for the Young' under the auspices of the American Library Association. Sargent's list complemented 'Books for the Young' by Caroline Hewins, a much shorter list which had appeared eight years before and on which Sargent drew in compiling his own selections. A third list, the 'Catalogue of Books', compiled by the Carnegie Library of Pittsburgh in 1907, supplements Sargent and assigns each title to the appropriate grade in school' (Kelly, 1973: 125). Thus, biographies were being recommended to children by institutional stakeholders and this was because of their apparent representations of heroes. These subjects were presented to children as models to follow.

Leonard Marcus (1980) also notes that there are particular figures who recur in biographies for children in the United States:

> The writing and illustration of biographies for children is most often an attempt at praise. Folk heroes like Johnny Appleseed and Joan of Arc, and inventors and statesmen like Benjamin Franklin recur in the lists … Infamous people do not receive attention, usually, except as moral foils. The psychology of evil – psychology as such – is not the underlying concern of most biographies for children. Rather, the central character's life in children's biographies is often offered as an exemplum, as a model for the child. Young George Washington, little readers have been told again and again, chopped down a cherry tree but never, never told a lie. (15)

On the emergence of biographies for children in the nineteenth century in the United States, Ivy Linton Stabell (2013) offers some important context, suggesting how children's biographies were instruments of American identity and nationalism. Stabell (2013: 91) explains, 'Biographies – which not only identify key Americans to admire, but also outline how to admire them – were frequently written for the "rising generation" in order to instill values that would in turn ensure the state's survival'. So, George Washington and Benjamin Franklin were persistent subjects of children's biographies. *The Life of Washington* (1800) by Mason Locke Weems offered transparent, practical, civic-minded values for children to follow, for instance, obedience and self-sacrifice. Stabell (2013: 94) contends that 'these works taught children how to be citizens in a capitalist market economy'. This was much more complex than simply instilling particular political values within children. The possibility of young Americans 'channeling' and 'becoming a Washington', 'is crucial to understanding the function of the patriot's biographies … especially those written with children in mind', Stabell (2013: 91) argues. So, children's biographies at this time revealed the 'symbolic weight' of children as 'representative of a community's future' (Stabell, 2013: 94). Stabell (2013: 94) refers to biographies for children as a 'vital genre' for exploring 'a community's ambitions and fears'. This is in line with more general cultural anxieties about children and childhood as symbolic of the collective future.

Suzanne Rahn's (1991) inquiry into children's historical fiction and non-fiction gives some insight into publishing trends for children over this same period in the United States. Though her study does not focus on biography until her overview reaches the 1970s, she explores biography as a subgenre of historical non-fiction. Rahn points to a boom in biography for children in the 1960s and 1970s. She states that in the United States in the 1970s,

> historical nonfiction was thriving – enjoying exponential growth in quality, creativity, popularity, and prestige. Paradoxically, some of the same trends that had worked against historical fiction were working for nonfiction. The 'story biographies' of past decades, for one thing, had been chiefly 'inspirational' – which meant inaccurate, over-reverent, and dull. The quirks and eccentricities of great men like the Founding Fathers, let alone their faults, were conscientiously ironed flat. Now the reaction against traditional authority created a new readiness to see such men with less reverence – as human beings rather than animated monuments. (19)

Rahn (1991) highlights the author Jean Fritz who wrote 'brief biographies of the Founding Fathers' from 1973. What was significant about Fritz's approach was the use of humour. In her representations, Fritz did not shy away from the eccentricities of her subjects; she wrote about 'Sam Adams's unwillingness to ride a horse' and 'John Hancock's craving to be liked by everyone' seeing these as 'traits with which children could sympathise' (19–20). Rather than relying on fictional dialogue to suture the narrative, Fritz located 'odd yet authentic' details that she thought might appeal to child readers, such as 'Sam training his dog Queue to bark at Redcoats, John's passion for gold lace' (19–20). Rahn (1991) argues,

> Fritz insisted that children deserved, and wanted, the same faithfulness to fact expected in biography for adults; she even provided scholarly endnotes for her books. To top it off, her early biographies were written for a fairly young age group – third or fourth graders – an age for which the most blatant fictionalizing had always been deemed necessary. Fritz's approach, once discovered, proved irresistible. She has had numerous imitators, and biography for children may never be the same again. (19–20)

And Rahn is correct. Such an approach, towards the fun and quirky, which give direct attention to the reading desires of children has been foundational for the success of series like *Horrible Histories* published from the early 2000s, which I discuss briefly in Chapter 2, and the *Rebel* book series, which I explore in Chapters 2 and 4. Children's literature scholar Perry Nodelman (2015: 36) argues that the education versus entertainment discussion regarding what children's literature is 'for' is central to debates about how children's literature has evolved. In Chapter 2 I discuss how twenty-first-century biographies for children have shown how the form 'has its cake and eats it too' when it comes to effectively blending entertainment and education within these books.

Judith V. Lechner (1997: 230), writing during the 1990s, observes how biography for children has changed since the 1950s and 1960s where perfect, unbelievable male role models were the norm. Biographies came to be more multifaceted, with an emphasis on learning through mistakes. In the late twentieth century, children were being encouraged, even explicitly invited, to think critically about biography. Lechner (1997: 239) argues, 'If children are to become critical readers of biographies, it is important that they become aware of the fact that not all "factual" books are accurate and there are ways to try to uncover the "truth"'. There are other potential payoffs in inviting children to engage critically in biography, for instance, it develops their critical capacities more generally. And these are important, transferrable life skills. In Chapter 2, I discuss how many twenty-first-century biographies for children have lists for 'further reading' which explicitly encourage children to investigate further, to read between the lines and to be critical. As Lechner (1997: 240) persuasively argues, 'One of the most valuable lessons children can learn from reading biographies is that "getting the facts straight" is a continuous and exciting process'.

Linda Girard (1989) points to the wide publication of biographies for children in the latter part of the twentieth century as evidence of its success. According to an American Library Association survey from 1985, eleven biographies for children book series were being published across eight publishers (Children's Press, Dillon, Hamish Hamilton, Harcourt, Lerner, Random, Troll and Franklin Watts; Girard, 1989). Other publishers publishing single titles at this time included Atheneum, Dutton, Harper and Row, Houghton Mifflin (Clarion), Lippincott, Little Brown, Lothrop, Macmillan, Morrow, Putnam and Albert Whitman. Rahn (1991) also explains how the mid-to-late-twentieth century was an important time for children's biography as it became increasingly recognized and rewarded for its 'literariness':

> A special category for nonfiction was created in the Boston Globe-Horn Book Awards for children's literature, and by 1980 nonfiction was showing up with much greater frequency among the Newbery Honor Books, reaching a kind of climax in 1988, when the Newbery Award itself went to Russell Freedman's *Lincoln: A Photobiography*. Historical nonfiction picture books won Caldecott Awards in 1980 (Ox-Cart Man) and 1984 (The Glorious Flight). In 1986 Jean Fritz was given the Laura Ingalls Wilder Award for her contribution for children's literature. (21)

Gale Eaton's (2006) study, *Well-Dressed Role Models: The Portrayal of Women in Biographies for Children*, surveys the representation of historical women in biographies for children. She looks at biographies of Queen Elizabeth I, published in the UK and the United States from 1852 to 2002, then takes a 'snapshot' approach and looks at what was published in 1941, 1971 and 1996. The lists of biographies (included as appendices at the back of the book) also reveal recurring biographical subjects. They include writers, activists, and presidents' wives. Names that consistently appear across the lists are Pocahontas, Florence Nightingale, Emily Dickinson, Beatrix Potter, Phyllis Wheatley, Martha Jefferson, Jane Adams, Emma Goldman, Marie Curie, Mary Shelley, Queen Victoria and Eleanor Roosevelt. The 1996 list includes Maya Angelou, Anne Frank, Aretha Franklin and Gloria Estefan.

As biography and children's literature have evolved as genres, they have done so in line with changes in the cultural position of children and a deeper sense of what non-fiction literatures such as biography are for and might achieve in the world. In this overview of pre-twenty-first-century biographies for children, we can see an evolving genre in terms of diversity and revisionist histories, for example. However, this evolution has been arguably slow, and biography remains tainted by evidence of its continued conservatism. For example, Susan Gardner (1991), in her study of biographies for children about Christopher Columbus, notes how these biographies have not changed in the years she surveys 1932–91. Gardner (1991: 275) surveys thirty-six children's books and finds little in the way of revisionist history, or in acknowledging the shameful colonial past of the United States. So, in the twentieth century, there remained work to be done in terms of opening the genre of children's biography to produce, circulate and have children consider alternative subjects and histories that would broaden their understanding of biography's capacity to represent a world that all children might recognize.

## Representation of minority subjects: Mid-twentieth-century African American biographies for children

Biographers for children saw this genre as one that could agitate for social change. What better way to change futures than to write directly to children? This final section of this chapter considers some examples of how mid-to-late-twentieth-century biographies for children in the United States offered representations of minority subjects and in doing so, invited children to consider alternative histories. As Sara VanderHaagen (2018: 18) argues, 'biographies are an influential, though understudied, aspect of Western educational culture and American public memory'. They are assumed to have a didactic function in terms of role modelling identity formation for children (VanderHaagen, 2018: 34). These books invite child readers to critically engage with historical figures and consider their own role as 'agents of the future' (VanderHaagen, 2018: 1). Rahn (1991: 21) similarly argues that in the United States, in the twentieth century, biography for children was taking responsibility for 'filling in the gaps and correcting the distortions of traditional history textbooks and curricula'. The difference here was textbooks versus tradebooks. Where textbooks, endorsed by educational institutions (which were, in turn, influenced by government institutions) tended to be more conservative in their representations of American subjects and histories, tradebooks published by mainstream publishers and guided by different cultural gatekeepers, became important sites for alternative histories to be told and new subjects to be presented to child readers.

For example, Julia Mickenberg explains, 'school curricula and school textbooks generally supported the racial status quo during the years leading up to the civil rights movement's full flowering in the 1960s' (2002: 65). But as Elizabeth Marshall notes, in the early-to-mid-twentieth century, there were various non-fiction genres engaged in the larger project of bringing diverse histories and subjects to child readers, 'children's literature, periodicals, and other media for youth have long provided an outlet for adults to communicate anti-racist, pro-labor, feminist, and other social justice pedagogies through life writing' (2019: 169). Elizabeth Ross Haynes's *Unsung Heroes* (1921) contained 'seventeen sketches of African American men and women' and Hallie Quinn Brown's 'Homespun Heroines and Other Women of Distinction', 'a collection of more than fifty sketches about African American women' (VanderHaagen, 2018: 38). Marshall (2019), refers to W. E. B. Du Bois, Augustus Dill and Jessie Fauset's creation of *The Brownies' Book for African American Youth* (1920–1), which contained short biographies of famous African Americans including Harriet Tubman, Benjamin Banneker, Crispus Attucks and Phillis Wheatley. As it developed, authors and critics saw a need for the periodical to integrate education alongside entertainment so that it could 'become a vehicle for political change' (VanderHaagen, 2018: 38).

VanderHaagen (2018) refers to a letter published in a 1920 children's periodical by the National Association for the Advancement of Colored People. The letter's author, a young reader named Audrey Wright explains, 'It is surprising to know … how many high school girls know nothing or very little about our own Negro heroines such as Harriet Tubman, Frances Harper and Sojourner Truth … I believe if you could give us a short sketch of their lives every month' (35). VanderHaagen (2018) explains how young women 'had a void that could be filled with a regular diet of brief biographies', and so, from here, biography consistently became a means by which African American authors could engage in 'public remembrance for children and young people' (35). And this idea, of 'the Black child reader as a political actor persisted throughout the Harlem Renaissance and into the 1930s' (VanderHaagen, 2018: 38).

VanderHaagen (2018) argues that this is a point of distinction between contemporary biographies for children and early, radical biographies for children such as these African American biographies for children:

> Whereas contemporary biographies for children of all backgrounds tend to obscure their moral designs, biographical sketches and texts written by, about, and for African Americans during the 1920s convey historical information with the explicit goal of supplying young readers with politically and racially significant African American role models. In these texts, the conservative genre of biography becomes a rhetorical resource for pursuing progressive purposes such as historical recovery and racial uplift. (36)

While I will take up VanderHaagen's first point critically in Chapter 2, her final point here is a crucial one on how these radical biographies have been effective in turning the genre's traditions on itself. Biography, long known for its didactic methods, became and continues to be a mode primed for educational purposes.

So, these biographical representations invited American children to consider a broader view of history and, in particular, gave African American children and children from other minority cultures recognizable subjects to engage with. Rahn (1991) explains how

> Milton Meltzer gave young people a whole new look at history with his biographies of men and women like Thoreau, Thaddeus Stevens, Lydia Maria Child, and Dorothea Lange; with *In Their Own Words* (1964–67), a three-volume compilation of the unheard voices of Black Americans; with the sagas of Jewish Americans, Chinese Americans, Japanese Americans; with accounts of world slavery, American peace movements, Reconstruction, the Depression, and poverty in America. Paul and Dorothy Goble retold Custer's Last Stand from the Indian's point of view in *Red Hawk's Account of Custer's Last Battle* (1969); Paul Goble's *Death of the Iron Horse* (1987) chronicles another, more obscure battle which the Indians also won. (21)

These stories had either never been told before, or never told to children in this way (Rahn, 1991: 21). And the method of telling is crucially important here. For instance, offering new, marginal perspectives on well-known historical events invites children to consider and further investigate larger questions about truth and history. Julia Mickenberg (2002) argues that biographies of African American civil rights leaders, penned in the 1940s and 1950s are a good example of this change and indeed the broader, radical potential of biographies for children. Mickenberg (2002) writes:

> These biographies showed children a model of civic duty that hinged upon the need for brave, non-conforming individuals to struggle against injustice and to rally members of the community to join in that struggle. Within these historical tales are an implicit or explicit commentary on the power of history and stories and on education in general. This embedded commentary encouraged children to connect what they were reading to the world in which they currently lived. (71)

Thus, the representations made in the biographies are not simply important for their representation of a particular life and history, but for the tools for historical investigation that they invite children to acquire when they read biography.

Hintz and Tribunella (2019) concur that twentieth-century biographies for children were engaged in a project to represent complex histories and minority groups. But such an endeavour illuminates some of the particular challenges faced by the genre:

> Biographies such as Shirly Graham's *There Was Once a Slave: The Heroic Story of Frederick Douglass* (1947) and Dorothy Sterling's *Freedom Train: The Story of Harriet Tubman* (1954) taught child readers to resist authority when it was morally wrong. At the same time, these books present an idealistic vision of the United States as encouraging and nurturing ideals of protest for the purpose of enacting political change. (317)

As I argue in Chapter 2, this balance remains a challenging one for children's biography. As gatekeepers of children's literature such as writers, publishers and teachers aim to bring these books to children, they are conscious of the contexts within which these texts emerge and the other gatekeepers such as governments, public school systems, parents and the media that they must satisfy. Thus 'radical' offerings might look like baby steps but nevertheless represent significant steps away from the narrow conservatism that had previously characterized the majority of biographies published for children.

In her study, Mickenberg (2002: 65) focuses on 1945–65, the 'early years of the Cold War' to explain how politically left-wing writers and activists brought their expertise to children's literature to offer biographies that 'implicitly challenged post-war racial hierarchies, communicated radical ideas about citizenship and made a direct connection between past struggles against slavery and present struggles for civil rights'. Authors such as Shirley Graham, Ann Petry, Dorothy Sterling and Emma Gelders Sterne, 'the former two were African American, the latter two Jewish', (Mickenberg, 2002: 71) wrote biographies about African Americans, particularly women, and 'other figures from the past who struggled for emancipation and civil rights' (Mickenberg, 2002: 71). An important example of this writing was 'Juvenile Black Biography' which aimed to rewrite US history as part of the civil rights movement (Mickenberg, 2002: 65). These books were explicitly child-centred and pro-child, while aiming to teach independent thinking and the courage to speak out against injustice (Mickenberg, 2002: 78). Mickenberg (2002) explains:

> Children reading these books thus learned that independent thinking and rebellion against injustice were traits and behaviours worth emulating; they learned this at a time in American history, the 1950s, when children and youth were being vilified and branded 'juvenile delinquents' for challenging adult authority, blamed for being angry at the hypocritical society into which they had been born. (86)

In such examples, biography emerges as a genuine site for consciousness raising, of providing information and perspectives on issues that might be unfamiliar to their readers. As Mickenberg (2002: 86) summarizes, 'although these biographies implicitly urge children to be brave, independent thinkers, children are also made to understand that *adults* have the responsibility, along with the power, to make the world better for the young people who will inherit it' (emphasis in the original).

VanderHaagen (2018) makes similar observations in her studies of twentieth-century African American biographies for children. She looks at changes in publishing in the United States in the 1960s and 1970s, arguing that children's publishing became more diverse during this period with significantly more publications by and about African Americans. This was the result of 'institutional and commercial barriers [that] had been challenged by the civil rights movement ... [and] the emergence of Black Power discourse and the Black Arts Movement intensified the demand for children's books that accurately reflected the 'Black experience.' (VanderHaagen, 2018: 39). VanderHaagen (2018: 39) explains that though authors were writing for Black children, these works were increasingly being promoted by white teachers and librarians and thus the readership for these biographies grew significantly.

VanderHaagen's (2018) study focuses on an analysis of twenty-eight biographies of Sojourner Truth, the early-nineteenth-century women's rights activist and abolitionist. VanderHaagen (2018: 19) notes that from the mid-1960s to 2010 more than forty biographies were published about the life of Sojourner Truth. She explains that 'the number of biographies about Truth and other African American women dramatically increased' and that coincided with the way that 'the civil rights and women's rights movements of the 1960s galvanized African American feminists, who began to explicitly theorize their experiences and traditions during the 1970s and 1980s' (VanderHaagen, 2018: 19). And this had ongoing effects. VanderHaagen (2018) writes that

> many African American writers and historians enthusiastically ... [produced] a veritable 'flood' of biographies and historical texts about African Americans ... the first Coretta Scott King Award – a book prize honoring books for children about African American history and experience – was given in 1970 to Lillie Patterson for a children's biography of Martin Luther King Jr. In 1976, fifty years after Carter G. Woodson proposed Negro History Week, Black History Month became a recognized period of remembrance in the United States, particularly in public schools. (21–2)

Biography, like other literary genres, responds to literary trends. Similar books came to be published following the success of books in the same genre. Biography also mirrors cultural change, but in the examples cited earlier, it is also an important driver in it.

## Conclusion

In her 1972 discussion of the genre, Marilyn Jurich asked, 'What's left out of biography for children?' and isolated a series of observations. Though a very US-centric assessment, the issues Jurich points to include: an oversimplification of what makes people successful or heroic, the omission of 'necessary violence' (which I think alludes to the whitewashing of history), the infallible hero (pointing to the racism and sexism that goes unexamined in certain representations of history) and the lack of women represented in biographies for children (Jurich, 1972: 2). For Jurich (1972: 6), biographies for children lack critical engagement with core historical issues and questions. Her suggestions for 'new directions' include 'more lives of ordinary people', increased representations of flawed persons, more representations of children's lives, and a book on writing biography *for* children (Jurich, 1972: 6).

In this chapter's discussion of pre-twenty-first-century biography for children, we can see Jurich's (1972) assessments and mandates coming to fruition. Biography has had a consistent, close alignment with children's moral and historical education. This has resulted in its representations being too often limited by the prevailing conservative contexts within which it has been produced. And this has been particularly apparent when it comes to the social positioning children as vehicles for the perpetuation of dominant values.

However, we can see significant shifts and ideological progression in terms of subjects represented within children's biography from the mid-twentieth century onwards. There has been a strong and growing sense of biography's potential as a radical genre which might open up children's interpretations of history and present opportunities for the consideration of previously marginalized subjects. As biographies for children have come to offer increasingly diverse representations, this has, in turn, opened up productive conversations about what sorts of representations are possible for a child readership. Such conversations (indeed, debates) occur at the intersection of popular media and interdisciplinary scholarly inquiry, for instance, children's literature, childhood studies, education and psychology. What subjects are 'okay' to share with children? What representations do children require protection from? Twentieth-century biography for children increasingly became a literature of inspiration, but at the same time, 'biographies for children were also expected to be more frank about the lives of their subjects than they had been in the past' (Hintz and Tribunella, 2019: 317). Revealing the inspirational aspects of subjects' lives as well as their hardships and failures (and everything in between) allows children various points of access to biography and the lives of others. This, I argue in Chapter 2, is what characterizes biography for children in the twenty-first century.

## Note

1  Hintz and Tribunella (2019) explain that conduct books continued to be popular in the nineteenth and twentieth centuries in both England and the United States, with a focus on self-improvement.

# 2

# Biography for children in the twenty-first century

Online bookseller Amazon has a rich selection of biographies for children published before and in the twenty-first century in its 'Children's Biographies' section. But even with a cursory glance, it becomes clear that the twenty-first century, and more particularly, the past decade, has been a boom period for the publication of biography for children. Many of these texts recount the lives of artists, sportspeople, political activists and pioneering scientists. One of the most popular book series of the past two years is the *Little People, Big Dreams* series (created by Maria Isabel Sánchez Vegara). The series includes biographical picture books of young people such as Anne Frank and sketches the younger years of other famous figures such as Frida Kahlo, Marie Curie and Stephen Hawking. The goal of these books is to show the childhood as formative to the accomplished adult figures these children became. No matter your humble or challenging beginnings, you might just leave an indelible mark on history! In taking this approach, such books borrow the traditional tools and themes of biography to write new, contemporary hero tales for children.

But as these books might benefit from donning the conservative and ever-popular cloak of biography, recent biographies for children can be read as having diverse ideological and pedagogical agendas. Biographies for children, in their paratextual presentation, often emphasize their relationship to national curricula and STEM or STEAM education. Their authors are commonly historians or allied scholars. But at the core of these books, broadly speaking, is a child-centred focus on the ways that non-fiction literatures and more potently, biography, can empower children. For example, picture book series *Women in Science* (with various authors and illustrators) features subjects such as Jane Goodall, Ada Lovelace, Rachel Carson and Temple Grandin, and

Kate Pankhurst's *Fantastically Great Women Who Made History* (2018) and *Fantastically Great Women Who Changed the World* (2016) contain a mix of biographical sketches about women, including young women, who had an impact upon history. Both collections seek to bring subjects to children's attention; in most instances, children are unlikely to have heard of these pioneering women, and so the series seeks to insert these women more centrally in history.

Perhaps the darling of the biography-for-children phenomenon has been *The Goodnight Stories for Rebel Girls* (2017–) series. It has become a publishing phenomenon and has also spawned a plethora of imitation series. Aimed at slightly older readers than the aforementioned picture book series, *The Rebel* series, framed as 'goodnight' or 'bedtime stories', challenge the notion of an easy, settling story for children to fall asleep to. The title 'goodnight' rather than 'bedtime' stories possibly works better for an older readership. With their exploration of powerful, often marginalized women from history, it is more likely that the books will spark engagement and inspire child readers to ask questions as they read them before bed.

The abovementioned examples speak to the current popularity of the 'great women' mode of biography for children. This interest in women's lives and the publication of girl's and women's life stories is not unexpected. It aligns with feminist goals and wider cultural pursuits; women's lives have too often been sidelined, even erased from history. Feminist life writers and life writing scholars have been engaged in this wider project of bringing women's stories into the public sphere, robustly for the past three decades (Fuchs, 2004; Huff, 2005; Jolly, 2008; Smith and Watson, 2010). More recently, life writing scholars have engaged with the narratives of girls (Douglas and Poletti, 2016; Maguire, 2018; García, 2018, 2019, 2020). The aim here is to recognize girls as prolific producers of life narratives across various locations, cultural spaces and in diverse forms. Scholars aim to elevate such texts for wider readerly consideration and critical engagement.

Life writing for and by children can also be considered part of these broader agendas, to insert marginal stories into history. This chapter considers what makes the subjects represented in these biographies as 'great', 'heroic' and 'rebellious' at this cultural moment, considering what we already know about the history of biography as a form (as explored in Chapter 1). These recent children's books are transparent in their goal of offering particular types of knowledge transfer to young children, on people and subjects considered to be of value to child readers. I cannot discuss each book in this incredibly rich publishing domain, so I will focus on the three series cited above which I see as indicative of what is being published and read at this time. Each series is highly successful and ground breaking in its own right; all of the books articulate a shared goal: to represent women who transgressed cultural expectations of their time, and, in doing so, became remarkable.

But further, in bringing these stories into the context of biographies for children, there are more specific ideologies and values at work. For example, to what extent might we see the agendas of individual or liberal feminism at work in these feminist biographies for children? To what extent are women's accomplishments benchmarked against traditionally masculinist markers of success? Focusing on women's achievements in such realms can devalue domestic roles and relationships. Celebrating individual achievements may come at the expense of recognizing women's or girls' collective action.

Literature has limits, and there are many contemporary examples within biography to attest to the genre remaining true to conventions and parameters. But there is also a strong impulse within these new biographies to use the master's tools to dismantle the master's house. Such approaches recognize the enduring power of biography, and the capacity for biographers to take the genre in new directions.

Elizabeth Marshall (2019: 169) contends that, 'life writing for young readers reveals cultural fault lines, especially when these narratives challenge familiar "truths" about … history, identity, and childhood'. Here, Marshall (2019) attends to the potential of life writing for children to be radical and to approach current issues in potent ways. Similarly, Linda Walvoord Girard suggests biography's 'urgency' by arguing, 'well-done biography has a sense of urgency, of burning significance. More than usefulness or timeliness, more than lifelike portrayal or eye-catching art, more than soap opera drama or flat examples of goodness, urgency is a revision at the core of narrative' (Girard, 1990: 1). Biographies for children have found their moment because they aim to address marginality and diversity. Their goal is to take responsibility for showing children, who represent the future, an alternate past (and present) to what they might have learned in other historical texts. Of course, in doing so, they also function to reinforce new heroic models for children, particularly in relation to particular modes of feminism. In looking at these book series, I engage in close textual analysis of the biographical representations (written and visual) made in these books. In constructing biographical sketches of great women, what's included and what's left out? What assumptions are made, for instance, about age-appropriate content (in terms of subjects)?

## *Little People, Big Dreams*

I first encountered these books in 2018 at an airport bookshop when looking for a present for my then seven-year-old daughter. I saw the 'Anne Frank' book and thought this would be an important read for her. Adapting and transforming well-known adult life stories for children is not a new trend, as I have argued elsewhere (Douglas, 2019). Anh Do's *The Little Refugee* (2011) rewrites his migration story *The Happiest Refugee* (2010) for a child readership. Malala Yousafzai's *I Am Malala: The Girl Who Stood Up for Education and was Shot by the Taliban* was published in 2013 and adapted the following year (into a very different text) for young readers. In 2017, Malala published another memoir – a picture book for readers aged four to eight years – *Malala's Magic Pencil*, by Malala Yousafzai, illustrated by Kerascoët. There are many other examples. Authors potentially have much to gain from such adaptions, most obviously, an increased readership, book sales and the literary kudos associated with crossing literary genres.

Though *Little People, Big Dreams* does not offer direct adaptations of previously published materials, almost all of its subjects have previously been the focus of biographical representation. The series is incredibly diverse it its approach, for instance, famous figures from histories and previously marginal subjects that also appear in the other book series I discuss in this chapter (Anne Frank, Rosa Parks, Ada Lovelace, Frida Kahlo, Marie Curie, Emmeline Pankhurst, Jane Austen, Harriet Tubman, Josephine Baker, Jane Goodall). It is not surprising that subjects recur across series. There are a range of reasons for this, for instance, more information about the subject's life is in circulation and there is reader interest. Contemporary contexts, for instance, political events such as the Black Lives Matter movement reinvigorate histories in which

Black people brought about powerful cultural change. A growing cultural engagement with climate change, or women's role in science, for instance, ignites a readership for pioneering science and environment subjects. And such books are bound to sell if they offer recognizable subjects and thus pique the interests of adults who are also parents!

The *Little People, Big Dreams* book series functions as an introduction to biography for children, aged roughly four–eight years old. Spanish author Sánchez Vegara worked in advertising for over twenty years, but her dream was to create this book series. She self-published the first book in the series as a birthday gift for her twin nieces. She explains,

> I had discovered a ton of great children's books for my oldest nephew Ernest; full of brave, enthusiastic boys ready to conquer the world. But these sorts of books didn't seem to exist for little girls, and so I thought to myself, wouldn't it be great to change that? I wanted to show Alba and Claudia some real female characters who had had the determination to believe in their dreams and make these dreams a reality. (Q&A with Maria Isabel Sánchez Vegara, 2018)

Sánchez Vegara correctly predicted the appetite for such books (and the other that would follow). Now the titles have been published in over twenty languages with 3.9 million copies sold. There are over seventy illustrators involved in the project. Of the myriad titles in the series, the collection now includes an interactive journal, colouring book, matching game, learning cards, and 'board books' for baby and toddler readers which are often adaptations of previous titles. The books also now appear in thematic box sets such as 'Women in Science' and 'Women in Art'.

Early childhood education scholar Hani Morgan (2009: 219) reminds us that literature has a role to play in teaching diversity and multiple perspectives to children. In the twenty-first century, this has resulted in a rise in culturally authentic picture books (Morgan, 2009: 226). So, it is not surprising that, at the time of writing, amongst those books 'coming soon' in the *Little People, Big Dreams* series are books on Michelle Obama, Ruth Bader Ginsberg and Kamala Harris. The books are focused on a diversity of subjects including activists, artists, athletes, BIPOC, Black voices, eco heroes, LGBTQ, scientists, musicians, trailblazers, women and writers.

It is easy to imagine this book in primary school libraries and classrooms. They are likely attractive to the child's eye, and as previously argued, the subjects will be recognizable to adults. Sánchez Vegara, explains, 'I like to think the success of the series really boils down to one main factor: children love to read true stories about other children – like them – achieving great things. It gives them the strength and the courage to believe in themselves and dream BIG' (Q&A with Maria Isabel Sánchez Vegara, 2018).

The notion of 'big dreams' is important and a key issue in how children are thought to think about their own future and the relationship of reading and books to this. There is an obvious neoliberal or meritocratic tone to such life lessons for children. It suggests that if you work hard, stand up for your rights and attend to your individual talents, you will naturally be rewarded because that is the way the world works. This is not to argue that the books in the series each fall into this trap, but that it is useful to read them with this critical eye. As argued in Chapter 1, reading non-fiction has, consistently throughout history, been one of the core ways that children are encouraged to learn about the world and explore their place in it. Further, as Marshall (2019) posits, 'life writing for the child is often also *about* children, and these representations can contest understanding of childhood as a period of innocence' (169; emphasis in the original). Biographies for children that represent the lives of children offer a point of entry for children to think about how childhood is socially constructed, and how children negotiate their own identities around these constructions.

In this section I focus on two of the books from the *Little People, Big Dreams* series: *Megan Rapinoe* (Vegara and Weckman, 2021) and *Greta Thunberg* (Vegara and Weckman, 2020). Of the wealth of choices in this series, I chose these two biographical subjects as examples that are different to those that I discuss elsewhere in this chapter (historical figures). Megan Rapinoe and Greta Thunberg are recognizable figures in the present; they will be known to many of the child readers who encounter the book. I present these examples as further demonstration of the broad foci of biography for children and the cultural work they do around identification. Twenty-first-century biographies for children are not just about revising histories, but about centring on important figures from the present and encouraging children's engagement.

It is important that Greta Thunberg achieved acclaim *as a child,* and this is what will be emphasized in *Little People, Big Dreams: Greta Thunberg*. It is not particularly common for children to receive recognition as social actors during childhood, so the celebration of the young Greta is an important achievement of this book. At a time of increasing global recognition of what children can accomplish when it comes to activism and political change, biography for children cannot only be concerned with children looking to adults for inspiration; they must look to children too. In an illustrative style resembling folk art, *Greta Thunberg* opens with a bright, colourful representation of young Greta, her parents and her dog by her side, planting flowers. Greta is positioned as insightful, in fact, more insightful than 'most grown-ups', 'Greta was a little Swedish girl who learnt from her parents to turn off the lights, not to waste water and never throw out food: three simple lessons for being kind to nature that most grown-ups haven't quite learned yet'. Greta's lineage is explained: apart from having parents who have guided her environmental journey, her great-grand-uncle Svanete was a 'brilliant scientist' who discovered global warming.

Smart adults aside, the book explains that it is adults that have been destroying the planet, 'even though adults have known this for a long time, not much has been done to change it'. As she, her father and her dog walk along the street, Greta sees exhaust fumes emanating from a car, 'Greta wondered what would be left of the planet when she grew up'. So, the book represents the complex scientific phenomenon of global warming in accessible ways for child readers (planting flowers is good; car exhaust fumes are bad; polar bears losing their homes is bad). But the book also assumes that young readers will follow Greta's journey as she is represented as a deep thinker, genuinely worried about the future of the planet. Greta's diagnosis as neurodiverse, having selective mutism and Asperger's syndrome, is also presented and contextualized within her environmental concerns ('she would only speak and pay attention to what was really important to her'). Children are often ostracized or discriminated against for being neurodiverse, so, Greta's positioning here in relation to these conditions is important. They become her superpowers!

In a two-page illustration (Figure 2.1), Greta is shown to be flying above the smokestacks in her town, her signature yellow coat becomes her cape. A 'G' adorns her chest like Superman's or Superwoman's 'S'. Greta will be powerful and bring change. We learn that this change started by Greta and her family 'walking the walk' by making changes in their everyday lives (giving up air

**Figure 2.1** 'Superhero Greta' from *Little People, Big Dreams: Greta Thunberg*. Courtesy of Frances Lincoln, 2020.

travel and refraining from eating meat) are simple lessons that might be followed. Then comes Greta's most famous move: to play truant from school every Friday and protest on the steps of the Swedish parliament. More and more students joined her every week, 'it was time for children to wake up the adults!'. In illustrative panels, the book represents children all over the world holding hand-written signs in their own languages protesting for change, just like Greta. A double-page image offers a close-up of Greta's face and flowing hair. In Greta's hair are a wave of protest signs, all in different languages, allowing the reader to see Greta's influence. Though the cause is still centred on Greta, the energies of one person have inspired many children to act. 'Greta is no longer alone', the final double page explains, as other children are shown wearing capes, just like Greta.

Environmental change and activism are prominent concerns for children today, as I found with the children in my book club (in Chapters 3 and 4), it was a topic that emerged in almost all of our conversations. Another subject that recurs often with children is sporting heroes. Children growing up now have a much greater exposure to women's sports, and to an assortment of sports more generally, for instance, through watching the Olympics and

Paralympics and often having a range of channels and streaming services to choose from. Further, there is a greater understanding now of the importance of sports and other physical activities for children's mental and physical health. Within these new contexts, it is unsurprisingly very common for children to idolize sportspeople, as it has always been.

Fascinatingly, the *Little People, Big Dreams* series has only eight books about sportspeople: Muhammed Ali, Wilma Rudolph, Evonne Goolagong, Billie Jean King, Jesse Owens, Pelé, Ayrton Senna and Megan Rapinoe. This lack of attention may be because sportspeople are over-represented as subjects of biographical inquiry. The sporting subjects in the *Little People, Big Dreams* series are predominantly Black, Indigenous, People of Colour (BIPOC), which asserts the series' commitment to diverse representations and to educate child readers on these subjects. Of the three non-BIPOC subjects, two are lesbians, and it is one of these subjects, Megan Rapinoe, that I discuss here.

'Little Megan' is shown through cute cartoonish illustrations to have an idyllic childhood with her twin sister and brother. When it came to playing soccer, she was way ahead of the other children chasing her down. Just three (double) pages into the book, the reader is introduced to the book's central conflict: Megan, dressed in sports clothing, stands at the classroom door, feeling like an outsider. The reader learns that by the time Megan was in the sixth grade, she no longer felt like she fit in. The girls in her class did not want to play sports with her, they were too busy with boys, and 'Megan wasn't sure she was interested in boys'. So, her sporting abilities, her gender and sexuality are positioned as reasons why Megan stood out from her peers. But Megan is comfortable in who she is. With other, overtly feminine girls looking on and pointing at Megan, the book offers this affirmation as a smiling Megan walks down the school hallway, 'she knew there were lots of ways to be a girl. She just wanted to be herself'. On the double page that follows, Megan is shown to be happy and well supported (by her sister, her parents and her teammates) as she plays soccer, 'she was invincible!'

Megan's sexuality, alluded to in the early parts of the book, is given an assertive rainbow-coloured two-page representation towards the end of the book. Though the book centres on Megan's life and development, as one of the best soccer players in the world, and one who brought recognition to women's sport in ground-breaking ways, this knowledge about her sexuality, cannot be omitted. It is crucial to Rapinoe's public image, 'Before she went to the London Olympics, she told the world she was gay. She wanted to be an example for other gay athletes'. Sexuality, though still a controversial topic in many parts of the world, is generally something that children of different ages are encouraged to know and think about in 2021 (contrary to previous periods in history). The main issue here, as in many biographies for children, is positive role modelling of diverse lives and experiences. And where we would not have expected to see such representations of sexuality in biographies for children, even ten–twenty years ago, what we know now is that having the opportunity to learn about diverse lives and experiences is an important part of children's education, their personal and moral development. As Marshall (2019: 168) argues, 'life writing before and about the child as a potentially critical practice that allows educators to privilege narratives of diversity. Including intersecting linguistic, ethnic, racial, gender, religious and sexual identities in the classroom'. The educative potential, and capacity to act as a tool for social justice, is a clear goal of this book.

* * *

In her discussion of Latinx children's books, author Monica Brown (2019) explains that,

> Latinx children's book give children wings and act as tools for change ... offer models for meaningful and soaring lives ... I wrote picturebook biographies about them because I wanted to share their stories with children. (202)

The subjects of her biographies include leaders of the farm workers' movement in the United States: Dolores Huerta and Cesar Chavez, Chilean poet Pablo Neruda, Mexican artist Frida Khalo and Brazilian footballer Pelé. Her work has been translated into eight languages. Biographers for children see the genre as one of significant potential, particularly when it comes to engaging with children from minority cultures. The *Little People, Big Dreams* books have a clear focus on finding subjects that will inspire the next generation of leaders across different creative and sporting fields, education, the sciences, industries, activism and political domains. But to arrive at this place, where we can now see biography for children overtly celebrating diversity in the present in ways that the *Little People, Big Dreams* series does, we might also look at series such as *Fantastically Great Women* and *Women in Science* which look back in history to present and explore foundational and often marginalized histories in the same celebratory ways that the *Little People, Big Dreams* books attempt to. In doing so, they invite child readers to understand that there have always been women like Greta Thunberg and Megan Rapinoe in the world; we just have not always been able to see them.

## *Fantastically Great Women*

This set of four picture books by Kate Pankhurst published between 2016 and 2020 is aimed at readers aged six and above.[1] The books are beautifully illustrated in fun, comic style that is constructed to be instantly recognizable and appealing to children. The books feature the short biographies of women ranging from adventurers, scientists, sportspeople, artists, authors and fashion designers (a notable aside, the author is a descent of Emmeline Pankhurst who features in the first book). The range of subjects, and the titular assertion that these are 'great women' who 'made history', 'changed the world', 'worked wonders' and 'saved the planet' urges child readers to see that the world has been changed and built by a diversity of women. So, gender *and* race immediately become central to the books' presentation, and this aligns with the representation of women from different racial and cultural backgrounds on each of the book covers.

The books are structured as a trail for child readers to follow. In *Great Women Who Made History* children are asked to 'travel through some fantastically great history with' and the book's subjects are named. The book emphasizes its interactivity; this is not a book with the simple aim of relaying information to children. The introductory pages are filled with recognizable symbols from children's literature such as fairy tale (magic potions, lamps, treasure chests). The pages with the biographical stories on them are a mix of illustrations and rich written text. The pages are very busy and non-linear in their construction, drawing on different textual genres such as puzzles, 'Wanted' and 'Reward' posters, speech bubbles and prose narration. The fonts are changing in style and size. Each story has a different minimal but striking colour scheme to the one before it. The biographical sketches offer the child a reading adventure;

the reader's eyes will be drawn to different parts of the page all at once. So, the child is engaged in an active reading journey, having to locate the linear narrative and follow the story.

The biographies themselves present key knowledge about the subject' life (background, how they came to be remarkable, key events and achievements from their life), and the final part of each biography is framed as a lesson: what these stories show us about what women can do. For instance, Noor Inayat Khan was the first female wireless operator to be sent to Nazi-occupied France during the Second World War, a secret agent, and brave in capture, refusing to give up any secret information. She died a prisoner of war; the biography's lesson is, 'Noor was one of the most remarkable agents of World War Two. Her work showed that in extreme situations ordinary people are capable of extraordinary things.'

With subjects as Frida Kahlo, Sacagawea, Rosa Parks, Qiu Jun, Harriet Tubman, Boudicca, these books read like adventure stories. There is a strong focus on women of colour which is one of the ways that these books seek to overtly represent women's diverse histories, while offering representations that young readers are encouraged to identify with. These books are not simply concerned with looking at the past but signalling future possibilities for child readers. When difficult histories are represented, the books are bound by age-appropriate representations, for instance, avoiding overt representations of sexism and misogyny, violence or trauma. But the stories find a way through, to show and explore injustice and mistreatment. For example, the story of Rosa Parks is presented in a simple way, the narration designed to open up conversations between adult and child reader. The double-page story begins on the bottom, left page and explains through a short narration, told via the bus window of the yellow and green 'Montgomery Bus':

> At the time, strict laws kept white and Black people separate. This was called segregation. One law said that if a bus got busy, Black people had to give up their seats for white people.

This statement may be confronting to a child reader. Depending on their context and personal experiences, they may not have any insight into the traumatic histories affecting African Americans, so, this story offers a point of entry to such complex histories. Such is the potential power of biography for children. As Marshall (2019: 168) notes, 'critically-minded educators have long employed life writing to teach parallel histories and to spark social action within and outside of the classroom'. Children's literature and representations of difficult subject matter can challenge official histories, offering children different stories and points of access (Marshall, 2019: 168).

The narrative of Rose Parks continues, 'Rosa Parks stood up for herself and others by sitting down. Taking the bus home in Montgomery, Alabama, in December 1955, she had no idea that she was about to do something amazing'. Rosa is presented as a smartly dressed woman with over-sized glasses and a little handbag, she is pointing at the bus-stop sign.

**Figure 2.2** Rosa Parks 'Why Should I Move?' from *Great Women Who Made History*. Courtesy Bloomsbury Publishing, 2016.

The narrative is presented in short bursts with accompanying pictures to ensure accessibility for a complex subject (Figure 2.2). When asked to move by the driver, 'Rosa thought to herself, why should I move?', and it is likely that child readers would nod their heads in agreement. There is a smart, effective use of colour in the image to the right of these words. It is Rosa, the Black woman, who is represented in bright clothing and foregrounds the image, 'Rosa did not budge'. The white people are drawn in black and white. This is a powerful subversion of hierarchies, positioning Rosa Parks as powerful and right in her convictions. The reader learns that Rosa Parks was arrested, and the conclusion of the narrative explains how her stance prompted significant cultural change, 'News of Rosa's arrest spread quickly. Soon as other Black people decided to stop using buses until the law was changed. Eventually that law, and many other unfair laws, were changed'.

Children are raised to be obedient, not to challenge authority figures. So, this representation of Parks is important in explaining the difference between misdirected disobedience and standing up for one's rights. When disobedience is represented in biography for children, the representations are always carefully constructed and justified. There are no rebels without causes!

The *Great Women* books also function as a subtle introduction to feminism, a call to action for the child addressees of the books. Most of these women did things that women were not supposed to do; they achieved 'firsts' such as Dr Elizabeth Blackwell who was the first woman to ever be awarded a degree in medicine and Valentina Tereshkova was the first woman in space. The book explains:

> To make history you need to be brave, bold, and believe in yourself – just like the women in this book. They lived in times when women weren't expected to have big ideas, be in charge or to have exciting ambitions – but that didn't stop them. Their extraordinary deeds and words didn't just make history, they helped shape the way we live today. *Read on and prepare to be inspired.*

The final page of *Great Women Who Made History* reads 'how will you make history?' This powerful call to action emphasizes the powerful interactivity inherent in all of these books (which I discuss further on in this chapter).

## Women in Science

Non-fiction science books are an incredibly popular genre for young readers. A quick search of any bookseller website reveals a plethora of titles, most often information book focusing on the body, the solar system, the environment, scientific experiments, inventions and engineering feats. But there is also a robust movement in non-fiction-science books towards biography and the human stories behind the wonderous inventions and so forth. As children tend to learn in integrated, interdisciplinary spaces, biographies of scientists allow educators to teach English, history and science all at once, for example. They also allow for complex ideas about science to be made more accessible to child readers.

These books also attend to the strong push towards engaging young women in science education. Though women have made significant contributions to science across history, these have not always been recognized due to the socio-cultural position of women at various points in history. Further, in the twentieth century, there has been a significant focus on Science, Technology, Engineering and Mathematics (STEM) education for young women. For example, the abovementioned *Little People, Big Dreams* series has a woman in science sub-collection of titles. Biography has a role to play in encouraging young women to see that a career in science is possible.

*Women in Science* is a four-book series published in 2020 and focusing on four women who made significant contributions to science through history (Rachel Carson, Jane Goodall, Temple Grandin, Ada Lovelace). These books are very similar to the *Fantastically Great Women* books, particularly in terms of illustrative style and approach to subject. But their focus on just one life allows for a more in-depth biographical narration to be presented. For instance, Ada Lovelace appears in *Great Women Who Made History*. In this two-page narration we learn that Ada had an incredible mind and was born in an age of great invention when it came to machines. Though the two pages effectively distil the most important aspects of Ada's career, there is a strong focus on her gender and her ability to break through where others did not. For instance, again, in snapshot narrative form, Ada's story is imprinted on the gold machine symbolic of her pioneering invention. In her work with mathematician Charles Babbage, she is shown to have the superior mind,

> studying the thrilling invention, Ada's imagination whirred and spun until ... **PING!** Her extraordinary mind went one step further than Charles's had. Ada realised that the Analytical Engine could do more than just make calculations.

Even when Ada's famous poet father is mentioned, he is not named as Lord Byron. So, the focus in this brief narration is singularly on Ada; other details must not detract from her achievements. Comparatively, the *Women in Science* biography of Ada Lovelace had thirty-two pages in which to tell her story. Like *Great Women*, the *Women in Science* books are structured as an adventure for children to follow. The pages offer a mix of illustration and different formats of text (information comes to the reader in different, often novelty-framed text boxes and speech bubbles) inviting, but not requiring, a linear reading. The reader is often invited to read-between-the lines, finding extra pieces of information and clues hidden in images on the page.

The opening page offers a map pointing to 'Important Places in Ada's Life', locating her in the UK and Europe, and allowing children to see where these places are in relation to their own geographic location. The map also flags significant events that happened for Ada at these locations and includes page references of where these events will be explored in greater detail. This gives the young reader an investigative mandate to explore the book in linear and non-linear ways (moving back and forth, to and from this page).

The page that follows is an introduction, text only, that presents the book's mandate: to write Ada Lovelace into history through children's biography. The book explains:

> Throughout history, there have always been women scientists. But because they often didn't have the right to work in professional jobs, their work – often alongside fathers, husbands or brothers – was generally ignored. Over recent decades, historians have uncovered all the little-known achievements of many women scientists and now they are starting to get the attention they deserve.

Every time you play a computer game or talk with your friend on your smartphone, you can only do so because of the pioneering work by Ada Lovelace. (5)

So, like the *Great Women* biographical sketch, the agenda is to use all available space to foreground Ada, her life and her achievements. For a child reader, though, her achievements cannot be presented in the abstract, they need to be coded in a way that is accessible to the child reader (you could not have computer games without her). This is not reductive, but a clever presentation of information.

The biography is structured in a predictable way, nodding to the conventions of the form in its commencement of the narration at Ada's birth. The strong feminist tone begins from this event; we learn that Ada never knew her famous father Lord Byron. Her mother is represented as standing in front of a blackboard filled with mathematical equations, Ada in her arms and a child's rocking horse toy at her feet. It is clear that Ada's mother will be responsible for her childhood-wellbeing and her education. Meanwhile, Lord Byron is illustrated, comically, reading his own book, hand raised, with his speech bubble exclaiming 'I'm a genius'. The reader is invited to see him as the opposite. But even more potently, the overt critique of Lord Byron in a children's science biography functions as a fun literary 'smackdown' in which popular, genre non-fiction speaks assertively back to the canon (Figure 2.3).

Complete with Ada's cute companion cat Mrs. Puff, *Women in Science: Ada Lovelace* aims to make complex subject matter, mathematics and computer systems, accessible and engaging for young children. Despite her strict upbringing, Ada is represented as a free-thinking creative. She is a young woman who was supported to become a scientist by her mother at a time when very few young women were afforded such opportunities. When her 'flying machine' is represented, Ada is magically represented on a flying horse (11). But the young reader is reminded that Ada is more than a cartoon character; she is a real person as the real-life portrait shows (7). She is compared to Leonardo Da Vinci (who child readers might be more familiar with), and this juxtaposition is important in terms of elevating Ada as a historical scientist of note.

**Figure 2.3** 'Young Ada Lovelace' from *Women in Science: Ada Lovelace*, p. 7. Courtesy of Salariya Press, 2020.

In the pages that follow, Ada's robust collaborations with fellow scientists Mary Somerville and Charles Babbage are emphasized. She is represented as a strong individual, but also a strong team-player, something that child readers will likely connect with. There are no overt hierarchies of gender or class represented when they are at work together. And just like her famous father is marginalized in the text, so too is Ada's husband Lord William King-Noel. As part of one short paragraph on her marriage, the reader is told, 'She had three children with Lord William and continued her studies in science and mathematics' (18). It is clear to the reader that these details of Ada's life are not what the book will foreground. Women's lives are more commonly represented considering their experiences as wives and mothers, and of the supporters of men's careers. Not this book! It proceeds to explore her relationship with another collaborator, Professor Augustus De Morgan who she corresponded with and shared ideas.

In the page that follows, Ada's work is contextualized alongside notable contemporaries Charles Darwin and Michael Faraday. Their work has received more recognition in mainstream history than Ada's, but in this book, it does not. *Women in Science: Ada Lovelace* points to the injustice of Ada being listed as only the translator of works published by Babbage in which her ideas were central. Though the book explains that 'Babbage was very grateful to her for her ideas and contributions. He called her "the enchantress of number"' (24); the preceding image of Babbage makes him appear smug and sniggering, short in stature with spiked hair and giving a side glance with speech bubble saying, 'this will change the world'. It appears he knows he has taken advantage. Ada in comparison appears sophisticated and poised as she works.

We learn that Ada Lovelace died at age thirty-six from cancer. Though she was not adequately acknowledged in her lifetime, the latter pages of the book explain her legacy. She introduced the idea of algorithms which allowed for the development of software that we all rely on today. As a portrait of Ada literally looks over the people in the illustration as they work on their computers, iPads, phones and computer games, a young woman remarks, 'Ada is watching over us' (26). The child reader is invited to consider how her work has had a significant and lasting impact on their everyday lives.

## *Goodnight Stories for Rebel Girls*

Arguably *the* most famous of all biographies for children now, *Goodnight Stories for Rebel Girls* franchise has become a worldwide phenomenon. The first book was published in 2017 and, according to its back-cover blurb, contains '100 stories of heroic women from Elizabeth I to Serena Williams'; the biographies are each one-page long, and each story is simply, but strikingly illustrated with sixty illustrators represented in the first book. Its publication was initially crowd funded, the preface states. But its rampant success shows the broad appetite for a book such as this. The authors, Elena Favilli and Francesca Cavallo, explain the overwhelming sense of trust they felt from their backers as they assembled this book:

> The amount of trust is not something women get to experience very often … Most of the extraordinary women featured in this book never experienced this kind of trust. No matter the importance of their discoveries, the audacity of their adventures, the width of their genius – they were constantly belittled, forgotten, in some cases almost erased from history.
> It is important that girls understand the obstacles that lie in front of them. It is just as important that they know these obstacles are not insurmountable. (xi)

These books are centrally about raising awareness of the wonderful things that these particular women achieved and their impact on history, while also alerting young readers to the fact that if they have not heard of them, this is a problem! In selecting these narratives to share with their readers, the authors seek to find a kind of coverage that will allow for recognizable names and not-so-recognizable names across many fields, geographic locations and ages.

The first *Rebel Girls* book was such a success that several books have followed: *Goodnight Stories for Rebel Girls 2* (2018); *100 Immigrant Women Who Changed the World* (2020);

*Rebel Girls Champions: 25 Tales of Unstoppable Athletes* (2021); *Rebel Girls Lead: 25 Tales of Powerful Women* (2021); five-chapter books focusing on individual subjects represented in the other books (including Ada Lovelace); and *One-Hundred Real-Life Tales of Black Girl Magic* (2021).

The books' successes have been nothing short of incredible. *Rebel Girls* now has an app, a podcast, toys and other merchandize, and will soon expand to live theatre. There have also been many spinoffs, for example, Ben Brooks's series *Stories of Boys Who Dared to Be Different* (2018) and *Stories of Kids Who Dared to be Different* (2018), Kimberlie Hamilton's *Rebel Dogs: Heroic Tales of Trusty Hounds* (2019) and *Rebel Cats: Brave Tales of Feisty Felines* (2018) (I discuss *Rebel Dogs* in Chapter 5), and in the Australian context, *Shout Out to the Girls: A Celebration of Awesome Australian Women* (2018) and most recently Karen Wyld and Jaelyn Biumaiwai's *Heroes, Rebels and Innovators: Inspiring Aboriginal and Torres Strait Islander People from History* (2021), which I discuss in the conclusion to this book.

The popularity of these books speaks to the ongoing and increasing popularity of biography for children. The persistence of the 'rebel' figure aligns these books with particular current and historical political movements that have fought for equality, aimed to draw attention to injustice, and encouraged young people to do so. Movements such as Black Lives Matter, #MeToo and Time's Up, Fridays for Future/School Strike for Climate and March for our Lives, to name some prominent examples, have brought the ideologies and practices of protests into prominent view. When such issues are represented within biography for children, they become recognizable, accessible and invite children to consider who gets to be heard and celebrated in the public sphere now, and why.

There is a lot that has and could be said about the *Rebel* books, for instance, the first book's controversial inclusion of Margaret Thatcher and Aung San Suu Kyi, and its being banned in Turkey for its potential to corrupt young women.[2] The books have also been controversial for being overtly marketed to 'girl' readers, their potential exclusion of boy readers.[3] We might also consider how drawing gendered lines around books and readings might impact on non-binary or trans-children. Is it more positive for children to select their own books outside of gendered reading norms? Children's books have often been inappropriately gendered.

These issues considered, how are authors like Favilli and Cavallo (and the others cited in this chapter) to justify their projects? Quite simply, through being provocative and confident in their convictions. These books do directly address and attempt to engage children who identify as a 'girl'. This is a feminist project concerned with equality and balancing representation and empowering young girls. As discussed in Chapter 1, through history, biographies for children have often been gendered in their ideological approach to gender – in their confirmation of particular gender roles. *Rebel Girls* (and the aforementioned books in this chapter) aim to encourage young women to believe they can take on any career they wish to, for example.

As I reach the conclusion of this chapter, I want to bring something original to the discussion of the *Rebel Girls* books. I consider how these books are overtly interactive. This flags work in future chapters on how children might be overtly inspired by biographies aimed at them. How might child readers interact with biographies, naturally, and how are they encouraged to do so by books like *Rebel Girls*?

In both the first and second *Goodnight Stories* books, after a hundred stories and illustrations, the child reader is invited to create: 'Write Your Story', a lined page requests. The page begins with the prompt, 'Once upon a time,'. The adjacent page asks that the reader to 'Draw You Own Portrait'. This might seem, at first glance, like an afterthought, a tokenistic engagement strategy. But as I discuss in Chapters 6 and 8 of this book, children like writing and drawing as much as they like reading (sometimes more!) and it is instinctive for twenty-first-century children to want to 'hack' and interact with non-fiction books. I am thinking of the success of another children's book franchise, the *Wreck My Journal* books, a series of interactive journals which ask their child readers to 'wreck' the pages, for instance, glue items to the pages, colour outside the lines, wet the pages, paint the pages, poke holes in them, spill something on them. The *Wreck My Journal* books are aimed at a similar age group to *Rebel Girls* (eight +) but have had broad appeal amongst older reader/creators too. The emphasis in these books is on making a mess, on not being neat, which seems to go against the grain of traditional activity books for children, with an emphasis on independence and creativity. Again, such projects seem to be in line with twenty-first-century thinking on childhood development and creativity. And this is a point I circle back to in Chapter 8 of this project which looks at children's Covid-19 'lockdown diaries'.

The two pages at the back of the *Rebel Girls* and *Rebel Girls 2* books seem congruent to what has gone before. They act as a call to action: the reader of this book might have a story similar to those within the books and situating their story in this way is an important political act. The reader is invited to acquire and demonstrate the skills of an auto biographer.

It is perhaps not surprising that a *Rebel Girl* book followed what was singularly focused on readers writing their own auto/biographical text. This book, when completed, would be an auto/biography of its author. Provocatively titled, *I am a Rebel Girl by (insert your name): a Journal to Start Revolutions*, the authors' introduction offers simple messages with the focus on girl power,

> Dearest Rebel,
> 
> Growing up as little girls, we've been taught to color within the lines that other people have drawn for us. We've been taught to say 'yes' even when we wanted to say 'no'. We've been taught to take up as little space as we could.
> 
> It's time to stop passing these lessons on.
> 
> With this journal, we give you a mirror to explore your identity without fear. (xi)

With minimal illustration in the book itself, the aim is to tap into the reader's creativity over the 200+ pages of the book. *I Am a Rebel Girl*'s focus is illustrations and short writing exercises that encourage the reader to represent the self, imaginatively and creatively. Some of the prompts include, 'This is how I see myself', 'This is me upside down', 'My everyday look', 'This is how I sit' and 'This is how I sleep'. Other thematic prompts include reflections and aspirations, for instance, 'Things I think about when the lights go out', 'My secret wishes' and 'People I want to meet'. The book aligns itself with popular therapeutic theories regarding embracing vulnerability and aspects of the self that we do not always feel comfortable with. There is also a strong focus on aspiration and accomplishment, not in the neo-liberal sense of a work ethics equals success, but more in line with simply embracing and documenting your abilities and creative skills in the pursuit of accomplishments. The creative autobiographical tasks in *I Am a Rebel Girl* ask children to think broadly about what aspects of their lives they might share, for instance, a gorgeously drawn double page that resembles a retro record player asks children to write their 'Rebel Girls playlist' by DJ (insert your name). Other prompts include the more predictable 'Dear future me' and 'Books I am going to write' which ask for some aspirational writing from future creatives. The prompt, 'This award goes to … me!' asks the young reader to think about themselves in light of the *Rebel Girls* stories they have read. What is remarkable about you that might make you the subject of an award (or biography) some day?

The prompts in the book go beyond autobiographical representations towards more outward-looking questions, which again loop back to issues and representations from the *Rebel Girls* books. *I Am a Rebel Girl* contains prompts on women's rights and advocacy, including 'I have the right to' which is an illustration of a young woman flying a plane with a paper trailing behind, reminiscent of sky writing or a smoke trail. The trail is where the children write about their rights. Other themes are overtly feminist, asking readers to like things about themselves that society might tell them they should not, 'Love notes to my favourite body parts', 'Fears I have', 'I will not be tamed', 'My march', 'Things my friends are good at', 'Rebel Girls I am proud of'. The latter two prompts ask for celebratory biographical thinking around the young women around them. As the readers will have found from reading *Rebel Girls*, biography provides a means to elevate subjects in positive and empowering ways. Similarly, 'This is My Family', 'Interview with the Bravest Woman I Know' and 'Here's What My Family Think of Me' blur the boundaries between autobiography and biography, asking young readers to think about the relationality of auto/biography – the extent to which life storytelling can never be about just one subject.

So, *I Am a Rebel Girl* asks the reader/participant to think about life and the self in the now and the future, and their life in relation to the lives of others.

In doing so, this interactive rebel book equips its readers with skills to analyse biography and to acquire skills to write it too (observing, interviewing, building evidence, drawing, writing, for instance). There is a strong sense, emerging from these biographical books for children and their associated activity books, that reading inspires action. After reading the books, children might want to act or to do something that is meaningful for and empowering to them.

## Conclusion

I may seem, at times, an uncritical cheerleader for these contemporary biographies for children. These are attractive and enjoyable books and an exciting addition to the corpus of contemporary biography. But it is easy to see the prescriptions and the limits of this form. Certain lives are privileged that adhere to recognizable templates for success or remarkability. And though these writers and publishers are unlikely peddlers of narrow ideologies, they obviously want to sell their books. As previously argued, one of the limits of biographical representation is that individuals tend to be celebrated over collective action. History is full of such examples; a heroic person is celebrated and becomes symbolic of larger cultural and political histories. Individual life stories make history intelligible. Of course, this is problematic. We (adults) and children might want to know what lies beside or behind the narrative we are receiving. What narratives are we missing? This has been the persistent mantra of life-narrative scholars. Though, as I have argued in this chapter, some biographical subjects and their stories exist in repetition, such narratives can be seen to open doors for stories we have not yet heard and this can be seen as the framework for *Little People, Big Dreams*. Perhaps the sales of more famous subjects allow for the publication of emerging narratives?

In the latter part of this chapter, I introduced the potential for biographies for children to open up the genre to children's reception of these texts and their ideas, and children's creation of their own texts. This curiosity about how children interact with biographies is something I consider further in the Chapter 3. Where many biographies for children published in the past focused on adult stories, or what now famous adults were like as children, we can now see a trend in the production of biographical narratives that focus solely on the lives of children. Kirsty Murray's *Kids Who Did: Real Kids Who Ruled, Rebelled, Survived and Thrived* (2019) showcases 'Forty true stories' celebrating children who have

> protested, prayed, rebelled, saved lives, earned a fortune, lost everything, become world-famous, or fought to survive war and oppression. Fearless kids, feral kids, Olympic champions, human-rights crusaders, climate-change warriors, princes and prisoners, workers and whiz-kids.

Collectively, these texts purport to show child readers how children can be powerful and change the world, despite any public discourse to the contrary. How do child readers respond to these biographies? This is the focus of Chapter 3.

## Notes

1. Like the *Rebel Girls* series, there are also two activity books associated with the *Great Women* books: Kate Pankhurst's *Fantastically Great Women Who Made History Activity Book*, which invites young readers to document their own ideas and practices, particularly on how they too might be 'great'. The book's blurb suggests, 'the world is full of amazing women, including you! Create beautiful postcards to send to some of the fantastically great women in your life and use the pages of this book to write down your own hopes and dreams for how you will change the world'.
2. *Goodnight Stories for Rebel Girls* can only be sold to adults in Turkey and its cover must be concealed for fear of it being a corrupting influence on young readers.
3. See Tricia Lowther (2018) 'Why No Stories for Rebel Children? Don't Divide Young Readers by Gender' in which she argues that 'labelling books by gender only reinforces stereotypes'. Why are child readers being segregated into gendered readership groups?

# 3

# Reading the heroic life: *Kids Who Did*

The short narrative, 'Childhood in Chains', recounts the story of Iqbal Masih, a twelve-year-old boy in Pakistan who is one of thousands of 'bonded labourers' in the 1990s around the time when this practice was about to be abolished. The story explains Iqbal's and his friends' journey in holding the government accountable to its promise to abolish child slavery. Before his murder, Iqbal became a spokesperson for the fight, started gaining an education, and inspired and empowered other children to gain freedom. He also developed relationships with children across the globe who would continue to fight for children's rights.

Iqbal's story is one of '40 true stories' in Kirsty Murray's *Kids Who Did: Real Kids Who Ruled, Rebelled, Survived and Thrived* (2019) celebrating children from across the globe who have,

> protested, prayed, rebelled, saved lives, earned a fortune, lost everything, become world-famous, or fought to survive war and oppression. Fearless kids, feral kids, Olympic champions, human-rights crusaders, climate-change warriors, princes and prisoners, workers and whiz-kids.

Collectively, these texts purport to show child readers how children can be powerful and can change the world, despite any public discourse to the contrary. This book differs from some of those biographies for children discussed in this study because the heroes *are* children. Children commonly read about children, and children often read about heroes, so, this would seem to be a winning combination. As Margery Hourihan (1997) argues, quest and hero stories endure over time, and are common to children's literature (Hourihan, 1997: 2). They are also highly influential stories and act as 'agents of cultural transmission' (Hourihan, 1997: 3–4). Particular heroic stories have been told again and again, for instance, that European men are superior to other races and animals, and that woman are born to serve (Hourihan, 1997: 2). Hourihan (1997) argues as follows:

> Only in the last few decades have people begun to question its message, to argue that those with different coloured skins are not inherently inferior, that women are not naturally subordinate, that the relentless conquest of nature may have appalling consequences.
>
> If Western society is to become less violent, less destructive of nature more genuinely equitable, we need to tell different stories, especially to children, but we also need to understand the hero story and its appeal, to deconstruct it and see how it functions. (1–4)

*Kids Who Did* represents an attempt to redress this issue; it seeks to add nuance and indeed subvert the conventional hero narrative. The assertion of child heroes, child heroes of colour and girl heroes helps recognize the familiarity and appeal of the hero narrative for children, and extend and revise it in productive ways. As Caitríona Ní Dhúill (2020: 19) rightly asserts, 'heroism is a construct of the biographical text, not a pre-existing quality of the person it represents'. In *Kids Who Did*, the child readers are invited to consider a diversity of possible lives for children, and a range of reasons why we might consider a child's contribution to the world as heroic. Though diversity is the order of the day when it comes to contemporary biographies for children (this even extends to the posthuman, as I discuss in Chapter 4), I imagined (or hypothesized) that children would like to read notable stories about other children. This is why I selected *Kids Who Did* for the readership chapter of this book.

Scholars across a variety of disciplines including education and psychology are deeply engaged with children's reading behaviours. There are many studies that observe how and when children read. These studies cover diverse and significant ground including the effects of learning and neurodiversity on how children read; reading with technology; children's cultural background and its impact on their reading; general studies of literacy and comprehension; or motivation, frequency or quantity of reading (e.g. Aliagas and Margallo, 2017; Barzillai et al., 2018; Barone, 2011; Merga and Roni, 2018; Van Bergen et al., 2018). Such research provides a constructive foundation for the current project. Further, there are studies that have shown that there are myriad benefits from children reading collectively, participating in shared reading activities, including literacy support, independent meaning-making and the opportunity to engage critically with diverse topics and perspectives (Carter and Montgomery, 2017; Maine et al., 2020; Norwich and Koutsouris, 2020). As Kristen L. Drogos (2021: 117) notes, book clubs have the capacity to raise consciousness critically on the subject of racism in children. In Chapters 1 and 2 of this project, I discussed how biographies for children have long been considered a didactic genre, aiming to educate children on what it is to live a good life, to contribute to history and so forth. And this literary imperative has been complicated and given some radical nuance by the diverse biographies for children in circulation in the twenty-first century. Thus, the theoretical discussion begun in Chapter 2 deserves extension, and I aim to do so in this chapter by considering some of the effects of these texts on child readers themselves.

I formulated the present study imagining the potential benefits for those child readers participating, as well as for scholars seeking to know more about children as readers of non-fiction. To my knowledge, this chapter represents the first study of children as readers of biographical texts and the first inquiry to consider how children read and interpret the latest wave of biographies written and published for them. How do children make meaning from these texts? Children are often overlooked as literary stakeholders (as research by Robin Hoffman, 2010; Rachel Skrlac Lo and Sue Dahlstrom, 2020 has previously shown). But the meanings that children make from reading literary texts and, in this instance, life narratives, can provide significant insight into how they interpret their social environments, history, ideology, subjectivity and truth. This is an important avenue for inquiry because, as I have argued throughout this book, non-fiction and particularly biography is currently a very important genre of children's literature. We perhaps understand, superficially, what the sales figures for these books indicate: that stakeholders like these books. Children, teachers, parents, librarians and so forth engage keenly with biographies for children. Adults are most likely the ones purchasing these texts. We might be cynical and reduce these books, their production and reception, to simple consumer products. But that will tell us little about what children think about books produced for them. And children's interpretations of literatures and cultures are just as, if not more, important than anyone else's!

When we are looking into non-fiction, the stakes and the investments that are made are different from fiction (as the children themselves raise in the book club). In reflecting on this, I consider Philippe Lejeune's 'autobiographical pact' as a useful place to start and invite the children to consider these stories as the 'true' stories of 'real' children. We discussed the effects of this in our book club dialogue.

I wanted the 'children-read-biography' book club that I established with the children to follow the lead of Skrlac Lo and Dahlstrom (2020), who reference 'transformative pedagogy', Paulo Freire and bell hooks as their inspirations (63). The aim of the book club is not simply to share information, but to think about the diverse ways we might work together to expand our knowledge and learning in a partnership (Skrlac Lo and Dahlstrom, 2020: 63). With an emphasis on playfulness and child-directed discussion, the goal is to disrupt the adult–child power dynamic (Skrlac Lo and Dahlstrom, 2020: 63). This works best outside of the rules and practices of the school, but might benefit from them (for instance, as I mention further on in this chapter, the way the children decided how we would signal different turns for speaking).

So, in this chapter I report the findings of a small pilot study engaging child readers aged eight and nine. How do child readers respond to biographies about children? Using guided reading and close-reading methodologies, we read *Kids Who Did* and focused on the representation of child heroes in the text. By combining literary and contextual analysis, and study of child readers, this chapter explores what these biographies might tell us about which lives and ways of living are valorized at this historical moment, and how young readers are responding to these representations.

## From *Tough Stuff* to *Kids Who Did*

Murray's book is an updated version of her 1999 book *Tough Stuff: True Stories About Kids and Courage*. On her author website, Murray explains:

> *Tough Stuff* was a book I'd dreamt of writing all my life, and it was jam-packed full of stories about people who inspired me ... When my publishers suggested I update the original stories for a new edition, I couldn't resist adding new stories as well as revisiting the old ones. Inspiring kids are born every minute of every day. (https://kirstymurray.com/)

According to the Author's Note in *Kids Who Did*, Murray discovered and selected the stories for her book through research and then conducted interviews with the children (mostly now adults) to complete the book.

It is not at all surprising that Murray was invited to update and republish her book twenty years later. The publisher, Allen and Unwin, is able to trade on the success of *Rebel Girls* (etc.) with its timely Australian version with a twist: the sole focus is children's lives. The cover art changed significantly between the book's publication and republication. The republication's use of colour and comic art aligns the book with its *Rebel* (and so on) predecessors.

According to Murray, the collection does not aim to present the stories of famous people. So, unlike the majority of the books discussed in Chapter 2, this book is not about revising histories. The focus of the book is 'kids who saved lives, came up with big ideas, survived terrible circumstances and believed they could make a difference'. As previously mentioned, its republication is not surprising after the rise of the *Rebel Girls* franchise and with the plethora of similarly styled books being published for this age group (discussed in Chapter 2).

These books are clearly well intentioned, however, as adult-produced texts, they are imbued with particular representations and values that adults (purchasing these texts) will likely find appealing – resilient children, spectacular childhoods and so forth. As discussed in Chapters 1 and 2, like other biographies for children before them, there are inevitable ideological agendas and stakes and after effects here regarding the moral and intellectual instruction of children.

However, these books also have the capacity to engage with children as social actors who have the potential to achieve amazing things from meaning-making and interpretation, creativity, bravery, activism and everything in between. We should not assume that children take books written for them at face value, that they make the most obvious interpretations. Children are active agents in choosing and interpreting literatures written for them (as studies by Benton, 1999; Harkin, 2005; and Hoffman, 2010 have found). As Hoffman's (2010) study of children's book clubs online asserts, 'Far from revealing an "essential" or passive child reader, this sample set bears witness to children's capacity to derive highly personal meaning from the text while simultaneously manifesting self-awareness about their status as children in a larger reading community' (Hoffman, 2010: 234). Children's book clubs offer a unique opportunity for children to experience and articulate various ways to make meaning from books.

Studies of child readers have found that children's preference is commonly for stories about children, and/or about children who reveal something about children's experiences. This approach is sometimes referred to as the 'mirrors, windows, and doors' approach to empathic reading and engagement: mirrors reflect their own lives, windows offer perspectives into the lives of others and 'doors' invite new interpretive perspectives (Bishop 1990; Botelho and Rudman, 2009). For example, in their study of Indigenous children's reading preferences, Susan Hill, Anne Glover and Michael Colbung found that children preferred reading stories that highlighted children's agency (Hill, Glover and Colbung, 2011: 83). Similarly, in their study of an after school book club with middle–primary-school children, Amanda Haertling Thein and Renita R. Schmidt (2017: 313), argued that 'deep engagement with literature is facilitated when students are encouraged to make connections between literary texts, their lived experiences, and the lives of others around them'.

## Notes on method

To ensure feasibility this study focused on child readers from a particular period of childhood: middle–primary-school aged children (and more particularly, year three where students are aged between eight and nine years). Children of this age group have comprehension levels, independent and collaborative reading skills appropriate for the biographical literatures I include for this study (Bargiel et al., 1997; Mantzicopoulous and Patrick, 2011). This is a significant transition period towards independent, autonomous reading and also a time when students still enjoy and practise various forms of interactive and collaborative reading (Merga, 2017; Ledger and Merga, 2018).

Interdisciplinary research argues for the positive effects of children reading socially and politically engaged books. But most of this research conflates fiction and non-fiction (Albers, 2016; Bargiel et al., 1997; Farris and Furhler, 1994; Martens et al., 2017; Strehle, 1999). This conflation overlooks the strong history and recent robust interest in particular types of non-fiction for children – particularly in the UK, United States and Australia (Abrahamson and Carter, 1992; Beckton, 2015; Brien, 2015; Coats, 2018; Onwuemezi, 2018; Rosen, 2015; Tang, 2017). There are fewer studies on children reading non-fiction, but this research (which is primarily from the disciplines of literary studies and educational psychology) points to a correlation between reading non-fiction and developing empathic skills; explores the pleasures in reading non-fiction; and offers methods for reading non-fiction (McCreary and Marchant, 2017; Alexander and Jarman, 2018; Sutcliff Sanders, 2017). The current project is different from previous research because of its particular focus on reading and interpreting biographical texts and their representations with children themselves. Recent studies have highlighted how biographical stories for children have myriad social, cultural and educational benefits. These benefits include literacy development, engaging with STEM and environmental sustainability topics, assisting children to comprehend demanding and sometimes traumatic public events, and helping to foster social cohesion and ethical global citizenship (Mantzicopoulos and Patrick, 2011; Gonen and Guler, 2011; Strehle, 1999; VanderHaagen, 2012; 2018). These stories are influential for young people's development and worldview (Bargiel et al., 1997; Mantzicopoulos and Patrick, 2011).

In my study of children reading biography, I recruited eight children from a local school's parents' and carer's information page on Facebook. The goal was not to offer any representative sense of how children read biography, but to provide a snapshot and trial methods in a small, but hopefully insightful, study. The children were from the same year level and the same school. Previous research suggests that focus groups with children of this age were more likely to be successful if the children already knew and felt comfortable with each other (Gibson, 2007: 476; Peterson-Sweeney, 2005: 106) and they are familiar with group or shared reading formats in school. The children who participated were nine years old: five were girls and three were boys.[1] Copies of books were distributed to children three weeks before the focus group. It was emphasized that it did not matter if the children read every story in the book (because I wanted to reduce the pressure on the task).

I encouraged them to choose stories that appealed most to them, but to read as much as they could.

The discussion group took place in a private room at a local café. We ate pizza for lunch first, then talked for forty minutes. Before we began, I again talked about the reason we were meeting (about my research). They asked if they could call this catch up a 'Kids' Book Club' and I said I thought this was a great idea.[2] I asked the children what they would like to do to indicate they would like to ask a question or make a point, and to ensure that everyone got to speak. The children said they would like to raise their hands like they did at school.

The focus group followed the 'reading-as-sensemaking' method that privileges children's abilities to comprehend and make meaning of a text based on a variety of skills and knowledge, regardless of conventional reading skills (see Aukerman, 2015: 56; Haertling and Schmidt, 2017). It was important to the ethos of this project that this discussion was child-driven. This was not a study of literacy or even comprehension and I emphasized this to the children on the day. It was not about who was the 'best' reader. The aim was to discover what they thought about the stories and the children in the books. This study, more broadly, has explored the plethora of biographical books published for children. And many of the books I have presented in this study have been aimed at the eight–ten years age group. So, this reading group, and indeed this chapter, is about turning to child readers to see what ideas and feelings these books spark in them.

I wanted to know what they thought was most important to talk about. However, when working with children, previous studies have suggested that encouragement, care and prompts may be required. As Diane Barone (2011: 3) notes, children's responses to book club discussions can be unpredictable and often stray from the book itself. And as Selina Van Horn (2015: 1) posits, it is hard to separate the personal from the professional when you see opportunities to really engage children as readers in exciting ways. Therefore, in line with what I had already learnt in this study about biographies for children, I had the following prompts ready for use:

- What happened in the book?
- Which stories did you particularly like?
- Did this book remind you of the world you live in? What was familiar, what was different?

- Did you like the character [name them] in the story? Are they like you?
- What do you think a hero is? Are there heroes in this story?
- Would you choose to read another book like this?

The discussion was recorded. The qualitative data generated through the focus group was transcribed by transcription software and edited by me. I used thematic content analysis (keywords) to look for patterns in the discussion.

## Discussion: Amazing kids

Though I did use the prompts above, the conversation was a free discussion driven by the children. For instance, I started the discussion with a very open-ended question: 'Does anyone have anything they would like to start off with? What was one of the things you thought was pretty cool about the book?' This also functioned as an acknowledgement that in reading biographies about children's lives, their own lives or worldviews were useful starting points for critique. This approach brought some fascinating, although perhaps also predictable, alignment with Murray's purported aims for the book. But my open-ended question also brought some unexpected discussion points regarding children's agency more generally to be social actors and enact social change. There was also some discussion (prompted by me) in which the children discussed how reading non-fiction has a different impact on them than reading fiction. My aim was to pick up, but not guide, the discussion points made.

Three themes that emerged strongly in the discussions were:

1. The child participants wanted to tell me what they liked about the particular stories and children in them. They did not shy away from difficult subject matter, in fact they gravitated towards it.
2. They found the stories 'inspirational' but particular themes were mentioned again and again.
3. They wanted to talk about how amazing kids can be and wanted to draw relationships between these heroic children and their own potential.

As I quote the children later, I have changed their names to give them anonymity.

## Theme 1. The child participants wanted to drive the discussion and tell me what they liked about the particular stories and children in them. They did not shy away from difficult subject matter, in fact, they gravitated towards it

The children spoke in depth about the stories in the books which included discussions of the Holocaust and death camps; child slavery; accidents, trauma, and rescue; environmental activism; child prodigies and other success stories. Their ability to engage deeply with the stories as biography, as recounts of children's life stories, was a significant finding of this focus groups. They remembered the children's names, ages, and could tell me a lot about what they each did and why. They understood the children's contexts (if they did not, they asked me, for instance, about the location of particular stories) but they were very good at locating the children in historical time and understanding that the lives, experiences and living conditions represented, for instance, were different from their own.

In relation to the stories about death camps, which was the first selection of stories they wanted to discuss, they talked about what they already knew about the context, then explored the individual stories. They understood that the experiences represented here were particularly harrowing, and they mentioned the strength and resilience of the children who survived:

*Demi:* Um, that, that was five death camps and that, um, that was one really hard one that I think Arek [Hersh] was like, one of the only kids that survived through all five of them. And he survived the hardest one, I think that was called Auschwitz.

*Madi:* Um, that he was cheeky because he snuck into one of the other lines and pretended to have a particular skill that would help him get a job and survive. He was resourceful.

*Claire:* He believed in himself.

*Andy:* He was confident.

*Demi:* He wanted to make his parents proud.

Though the children were particularly keen to recount the events in the stories (probably a hangover from school's focus on comprehension) their focus most often came back to what they perceived to be the qualities that enabled these children to be 'kids who did'. For instance, Demi's comment recognizes how incredible and unusual this feat was. Madi offers a very particular interpretation of how he managed to survive, pointing to particular things that he did. They enjoyed reading about the kids represented and engaged strongly with them, not just as characters in a story, but for their particular experiences and personal attributes. Without acknowledging the concept of biography overtly, they discussed what was valuable about looking into the lives of other children. They understood that these lives were being presented to them as examples of 'good' and 'heroic' lives. They articulated the knowledge gained from reading about the lives of others. They demonstrated empathy in their discussion of the character, the difficulties he faced, and the qualities he showed as part of his experience. The children were quickly able to demonstrate a strong relationship with the character and with the biographical narrative. As Dorinda J. Carter and Georgina M. Montgomery (2017: 44) posit, 'literature is a historical and contemporary medium through which children learn to read and name their world, "see" themselves in social justice dialogue, learn how to advocate for what is just, and understand how to resist the unjust'. We can see, in the children's comments above, that engaging with Arek's story meant engaging with history and injustice, and to closely consider what it might have been like to walk in his shoes.

## Theme 2: They found the stories 'inspirational' but one particular theme was mentioned again and again

The environment was mentioned over and over by the child readers. Though there is only one section and then a couple of separate stories earlier in the book that focus on the environment, as suggested in Chapter 2, at a time when Greta Thunberg is highly visible, and young people are engaged in environmental protests across the globe, it is perhaps not surprising that those children in *Kids Who Did* who were climate crusaders had particular resonances for the children in the focus group.

Sophie: It inspired me a lot. How people were trying to plant trees and to save the world and I think that's pretty cool.

Demi: Um, it was about this girl [Gitanjali] in America who found out that people were putting lead in the water, the tap water. So they always had

|        | to drink out of bottle water. And then she used strips to find test the water and realized they weren't working. So, she did experiments and won an award for a new way to testing the water for lead. |
|--------|---|
| Madi:  | 'Ocean Boy' made a machine to clean up the ocean. And after a while he got his first machine into the water, but it didn't work. It was meant to pick up rubbish … so he started making a new one because he had more people on this side now. So more people were helping him and he made a bin machine and it actually works. |
| Andy:  | We like these kids because they were life-saving, like they save their own life, or the environment. |

These responses reveal something of the effects of biography on the child readers. They have an expectation that this is a genre that will address the big issues. But they also accept that such remarkability is a part of children's everyday lives. This is the value of biography for them. For example, in speaking specifically about what the children did to enact change (plant trees, developed a water testing invention, making a machine to clean the ocean), they interpret the children's goals and strategies as feasible. This is likely the tone that book wanted to achieve: the children would need to easily comprehend the achievements of the children in the book, otherwise they might not want to read it. But they also needed to see the children as remarkable in line with more general ideas about who might be represented in a published book.

Further, there was a lot of talk in this section of our discussion about how the children themselves might enact change like those children did in *Kids Who Did* and also, the extent to which the world is a better or worse place to that depicted in the stories. I asked, did this book make you think about anything else?

| Demi:   | It makes me think about lots of things, because some, some of these things where a long time ago, it makes the world a bit of a better place now. |
|---------|---|
| Leila:  | Um, because a long time ago, these things actually happened and maybe you think how things would have changed from then to now. |
| Andy:   | We have got bigger brains now and we have thought of bigger stuff. |
| Claire: | Pollution. We tried to fix it. It hasn't changed. |
| Sophie: | Global warming, um, the PM hasn't done anything to help school global to go away. It wasn't helped in any way. It's up to us kids now because we have a better generation. |

The children consistently anchored the stories and children represented within the world they live in, for instance, in exploring the ongoing consequences of environmental degradation (as outlined in *Kids Who Did*), or optimism that the world was slowly becoming a better place because of the interventions of amazing children. In fact, the level of optimism on this issue, as can be seen in the comments of Demi, Leila and Andy, is as endearing as it is revealing. They explained that they understood the difference between non-fiction and fiction, and the potential for non-fiction to go places that fictional texts cannot go. This led us into a discussion of the relevance of these the 'kids who did' and their own potential.

## Theme 3: They wanted to talk about how amazing kids can be and (eventually) wanted to draw relationships between these heroic children and their own potential

I include this dialogue verbatim because it I want the children's voices to be visible throughout this chapter. It is very telling on the children's perception of how children are seen by adults differently to how they are represented in this biography for children.

*Demi:* This book is great. I think it's cool how amazingly smart kids can be.
*Kate:* Do you think adults don't always think kids are smart?
 Unanimous and loud YES.
*Andy:* 1000%
*Kate:* What makes you say this?
*Andy:* They don't listen to a thing we say.
 [other kids are giggling]
*Kate:* If they listened, what would they find out?
 That we are very smart
 That we know stuff.
 That we are different.
*Kate:* Well this book proves your point, that kids can do absolutely amazing things.
*Kids:* EXACTLY!
*Kate:* What's going to stop you from changing the world?

| | |
|---|---|
| *Madi:* | Um, lots of control can actually make a really big difference, but lots of people that don't have much control can't do anything. So they try to get help. But no one wants to do it. |
| *Kate:* | How do you get power and control? |
| *Andy:* | Elected to be the prime minister. |
| *Kate:* | And do you want to be prime minister? I'm going to ask everyone. |
| *Henry:* | Cause it's a lot of work. A lot of work. You might be really good at it. |
| *Andy:* | It's a job that goes for seven days a week. |
| *Madi:* | Like, you have to do all this stuff and then you don't get to do anything that other people do. Your schedule is always full. |
| *Sophie:* | You can't like, sit down with your family or go out. |
| *Leila:* | Uh, cause it's too much pressure and uh, like responsibility. Like if you've never done something like, like being in charge of like a classroom or something like that, you won't know what it's like and. |
| *Demi:* | I was fine with student parliament.[3] |
| *Claire:* | Um, you have to be like, you have to think about things that are coming up really carefully because a lot of them make a big impact. |
| *Sophie:* | You have to be aware of everything coming. And if it, if it says another couple of problems are coming, you have to get straight on to that, but you also have to try and do the other problem as well. And it's very hard. |
| *Demi:* | It's like with Covid if they like started making plans before it's gotten a lot, got a lot worse than it would have gotten. It was kind of, they had a lot of other stuff going on, like bushfires and they had to get that under control. And then under the Covid because they were kind of multitasking. If something big comes out, everyone's going to come and ask me first. |
| *Sophie:* | Um, well actually the prime minister will push for us. We're still going when Covid-19 started. And they were still very bad, but I didn't think the prime minister did much about it. It was like cancelling stuff because he doesn't believe in global warming. And it was probably because he didn't, he didn't believe in it. So he just, he just left it. |

There is a lot to unpack in this insightful commentary. The children consider the unenviable pressures on politicians and why they would not want to be one, but also strongly argue that the current Australian prime minister is something of an anti-role-model to them. This commentary works in direct contrast to the role models who have appealed to them, from *Kids Who Did*, who they see as keen social agents. Note the repetition in the children's comments above that our prime minister has not been effective on the big issues (bushfires, Covid-19, climate change). As Carter and Montgomery (2017: 44) argue, 'young children have a keen awareness of and passion for fairness at an early age. Whether at home, on the playground, or in the classroom, children often demand what is right and shun what is wrong'. We can see this in the comments about the prime minister and the children's observations about the problems affecting Australians during 2020 and 2021. They take on the position of sociopolitical commentators. But fascinatingly, in the conversation earlier, they make only minor links between the children in the biography and themselves. They take the opportunity to cite their potential as social actors ('That we are very smart; That we know stuff; That we are different') but suggest it is 'control', which is in the hands of the politicians, that allows people to enact change, and Australian politicians have not successfully done so.

So, this, I argue, is the potential power of biography for children such as *Kids Who Did*. The books might inspire children to see themselves and their own lives differently because of the children in the book, or, perhaps like the children in my study, they are only a small step away. They certainly admired the children in *Kids Who Did*. And they also saw themselves and their capacity to be marginalized and underestimated by adults. I took my opportunity, as book club facilitator, to ask them about this. I wanted to explore, as the book does, the possibility that children could make a difference (even if they did not want to become prime minister). I asked, 'What else could you do to create change?' Their responses seemed directly inspired by the stories from the book.

*Sophie:* You could create groups for a cause, so you can convince other people to do what we think is right. And we don't have to put all of the responsibility on the prime minister's shoulders we'll do it ourselves, but some people don't believe that. So we still have to be better.

*Henry:* You can work and make an own company and, um, help with the world or collect the rubbish from the ocean.

*Andy:* Um, you could save somebody from a life-or-death situation, then you would get some sort of an award.

*Demi:* Um, if you run a restaurant and you should be nice. If you see a homeless person out on the street and you just care about how much money you're making, you don't give them any food, then that could

| | |
|---|---|
| | keep world hunger still going. You could instead think about ways to use your money and leftover food to help people. |
| Sophie: | You can start and get more people to join your organization. And some people who don't want to actually have to join could donate money. And then you can make like a giant clean up along the beach. You could plant lots and lots of trees. |
| Henry: | Make your own ad about like something that you want to help with. |
| Demi: | It's like when we go to Banrock and we plant trees. So, it just helps out a little bit in the world. Then if everyone else did something like this too, then it can make the world a bit better.[4] |
| Madi: | You could organize a public speech so that you could announce that you'd like to make changes. Lots of people might come, like a protest. |
| Sophie: | You could sing a song with a message. |
| Sophie: | If we listen to our teachers we will become smarter and be able to have impact in the world ourselves. |
| Madi: | If someone's upset or lonely, you could go over there and comfort them. |
| Claire: | My friend got sand in her eyes and had to go to hospital. And, um, if someone just said like, don't throw sand, like it could help someone else from having that happen to them. |
| Madi: | Um, so I, um, found really amazing was how these kids just did it without thinking twice because, um, they didn't have as much power as people. |

These gentle prompts to the child readers helped them to consider the relationship between the events in the book and their own agency. The examples they gave are quite varied and reflect their broad thinking beyond, but prompted by the book. *Kids Who Did* inspired the children to think differently about their capacity to enact change, however small. For instance, they might stand up (publicly) for things they believe in, they might show small acts of kindness every day, they might act bravely and spontaneously in their everyday lives, they might be generous with their resources, and they might work hard to get an education as a means of gaining power in the world. Though the children's answers were clearly influenced and indeed narrowed by the stories they read in *Kids Who Did*, there are an equal number of answers that seem inspired, but not directly taken from ideas explored in the biography. There is evidence here to suggest that *Kids Who Did* enabled lateral thinking on the part of the children in terms of encouraging them to generate their own ideas on social change.

As Ní Dhúill (2020: 71) argues, 'biographies in the heroic tradition are marked by their masculinism, protagonism, and an apparently hierarchical disposition of the relationships between subject, biography and reader'. In a book like *Kids Who Did*, we can see, as Ní Dhúill (2020) predicts, an unsettling of this hierarchy in contemporary biography, in which the reader is invited to admire those represented, but not to see them as superior or to consider their achievements unattainable. However, that the biographical subject's achievements might seem attainable is not to say that the child readers will necessarily align themselves within those children represented in *Kids Who Did*. In the children's book club, we can see the myriad effects that reading this biography for children has had on the readers, not the least of which is a diversity of reactions. Reading the biography triggered their thinking about their micro and macro experiences of heroism and justice, and potently about power and their place in the world.

## Conclusion

The findings of this chapter remind me of the importance of engaging child readers whenever relevant in future research on life writing for children. Their ability to drive discussion and offer engaged comments was insightful and engaging throughout. The children's understanding of what biography is and does, and what heroes are and how this idea is culturally constructed and shifting, offered genuine understanding of what sparks children's attention when reading a biography like *Kids Who Did*.

Though the children demonstrated their robust skills in textual analysis and also in making links between the events in the text and broader social issues they were observing around that time, they needed some gentle prompts when it came to seeing themselves as having agency and potential as political actors – that they were capable like the children represented in *Kids Who Did*. This is perhaps not surprising, especially if they had not been in a book club before, or perhaps never read stories like these ones or thought about the issues. Children are not always included in such discussions, but when they are, good ideas tend to flow.

The limitations of this study are that it was a small study of children from one school and city. This does create the possibility of a homogeneity in responses, and it did seem, at times, one or two of the participants were repeating interpretations already tabled. One way around this in future would be to encourage children to take ideas further or deeper by way of gentle encouragement by the facilitator. Or, they might have worked in pairs to generate ideas from readings and brought their thoughts to the main group. Though the children did have their books with them and consulted them often, would a close reading of particular sections have been productive in this context?

In future research, I would like to take this chapter's methods and aims to different locations in Australia (and beyond) to investigate how children read biography, with the goal of discovering more about how diverse personal and geographical contexts might impact on children's interpretation of biography.

The children from this book club reappear in the next chapter. Chapter 4 considers biography's intervention into another significant subgenre of children's literature: animal stories. How have heroic dog stories become important to children's biography? What cultural work do such texts do around animal rights and child–animal relationships?

## Notes

1 I had intended to recruit four girls and four boys; I ended up recruiting five girls and four boys, but one of the boys was unwell on the day of the focus group.
2 I became aware that most of the kids in the group had mothers who attended book club and this is why they thought it would be fun to have a book club of their own.
3 Here Demi insightfully refers to her role on the Student Parliament at her school as similar to that of a politician.
4 Demi is referring to a tree planting, regeneration partnership between the children's school and a winery in South Australia's Riverland. The children and their families (in a particular year level) visit the site each year to support this programme.

4

# 'Tales of Trusty Hounds':
# Posthuman biography for children

Virginia Woolf famously argued that, 'anyone who has lived a life, and left a record of that life, [is] worthy of a biography'. Kimberly Hamilton's *Rebel Dogs: Heroic Tales of Trusty Hounds* (2019), like its prototype *Rebel Cats: Brave Tales of Feisty Felines* (2018), smartly rides the coattails of the *Rebel Girls* book series discussed in Chapter 2. The *Rebel Cats/Dogs* books look very similar to their *Rebel* predecessors from their book covers and shapes. They share the same structure, and work to engage a similarly aged readership. And, of course, these are not the first biographical text about cats and dogs for child readers. At the time of writing, Amazon lists eighty-eight results in a search for 'biographies for readers aged 9–12', including the search term 'dog'. Expanding the search to 'animals' includes over a thousand results, with biographical subjects including US presidential pets; animals that served in war and conflict; animals as muses for famous conservationists, activists, artists and animals engaged in therapeutic pursuits.

This chapter explores how these biographies work in terms of their status as children's biography, and their engagement with children on the issues of biographical representation and the lives of animals. How do they explore and explain the lives of animals to children, and how do child readers respond, for instance, in relation to the representations of animals that might already be familiar to them? Ideological agendas inevitably underlie these representations. This chapter draws on the work of critical animal studies and animal-biography scholars, alongside theoretical work on posthumanism and life narrative, to read a selection of heroic-animal biographies and consider how they are framed to do cultural work, whether individualizing or celebrating particular animal lives, to consider the relationship between children and animals or as literary activism, for instance. I argue that *Rebel Dogs: Heroic Tales of Trusty Hounds* tunes into and seeks to revise previous biographies of famous dogs in light of broader communal animal-rights activism and knowledge from animal studies and contemporary biography. The result is biographical representations that offer nuance, ambiguity and individuality to the dogs represented. Child readers are encouraged to read the dogs' rebelliousness into the representations made. But further, children come to think about their own relationships with animals, often identifying with them as the children reflect on their own position in social hierarchies.

## Biography and animals

In discussing contemporary non-fiction book about animals written for children, this chapter works at the intersection of interconnected disciplines: children's literature and the long tradition and, indeed, centrality of animal representation, biography and Critical Animal Studies (CAS). CAS is a fast-developing hybrid field of equal interest to science and humanities. Where animals were predominantly considered in relation to human lives and histories, CAS scholars seek to consider the individuality of animals, their role as historical and cultural agents, the impact their lives have had on cultures and the world (see the work of Herman, 2016; McCance, 2013; Nocella et al., 2014; Twine, 2015).

Animals, and more particularly, dogs have been the subject of wide and varied cultural representations, whether fiction or non-fiction, and for as long as representation has occurred. Their appearance in non-fictional genres has always been notable, and as Frederike Middelhoff (2018) states,

> Animal quasi-autobiographical stories have been distributed for more than 200 years. The genre stages animals as the narrators, or even writers, of their lives, retrospectively engaging with their upbringing, educational training, memorable developments, and experiences from a first-person perspective. The autobiographical animal narrator comprehensively and anthropomorphically narrates his or her life, while the animal protagonist, that is, the experiencing subject of the story, behaves 'naturally', neither metamorphosing nor using human language, as is the case in many fables, parables, or fairy tales. (57)

These representations reflect various desires including our wanting to know animals better, to imagine what goes on inside their heads, what they would say if they could talk, and so on. But as Middelhoff (2018) argues, this desire often resembles control and an inability to distinguish animals from humans. In such representations, human authors construct life narratives for animals – voices, personalities, perspectives and experiences. These life narratives may be understood as necessarily fictional and in the spirit of imaginative fun for child readers, but ultimately, they may deny animals their individuality and diversity. Susan McHugh (2009) also explores this idea in relation to the 'disappearing animal trick' that occurs when animals are represented in literature. Speaking animals often disappear or are revealed as humans in children's stories or exist as parables, and thus their value is only in providing lessons for humans (24). Middelhoff (2018: 57) explains, 'Considered as human representatives or "mere" literary motifs, animal narrator-protagonists become nonhuman signifiers for alleged signified human concerns'.

Joel Haeffner and Cynthia Huff (2012) argue that another example of this is the 'animalography', in which 'the human author ventriloquizes the animal's voice allegedly to tell his story. This common practice in the memoir boom of stories about heroic companion animals achieving bestseller status concerns ethical questions that have long troubled life-writing theorists, namely, 'who has the right to tell a story' (Haeffner and Huff, 2012: 279). Examples of such books include *A Dog's Life: Autobiography of a Stray*, by Ann M. Martin; *A Big Little Life: A Memoir of a Joyful Dog*, by Dean Koontz; *Soul of a Dog: Reflections on the Spirits of the Animals of Bedlam Farm*, by Jon Katz and *Rin Tin: The Life and the Legend*, by Susan Orlean (Haeffner and Huff, 2012: 155). In their review of critical posthumanism and the question of whether life narratives of animals are possible, Haeffner and Huff (2012) suggest that despite their prevalence, such texts, as they stand, are problematic. Despite technologies that might be used to consider animals' experiences (such as trackers or cameras on dogs), animals cannot access language for narration. They cannot speak for themselves or through ventriloquism. Haeffner and Huff (2012) propose that the only way such narratives might become possible is through posthuman praxis in which humans and animals interact in equal ways.

This argument is persuasive; what Haeffner and Huff (2012) and other critical posthumanists have observed regarding the production and circulation of life narratives of animals is problematic because it is human centred and serves particular investments that humans have made and continue to make in animals. However, when it comes to biography, the risk that we might run if we invest in this is the erasure of animal histories that have been recorded across various historical and memorial documents and spaces. What these histories have taught is exactly what critical posthumanists are arguing: that humans have mistreated animals horribly throughout history, but that animals have always and will continue to have meaningful lives, have individuality and have played important roles as social and cultural agents over time. While critical posthumanism offers a way forward, what do we do with the documents of the past? And this is particularly important when it comes to children's literatures; children are the future and represent a future in which we might feel more optimistically about human–animal relationships.

If animalographies, with their autobiographical fakery and human ventriloquism, are the problem, as Haeffner and Huff (2012) argue, is animal *biography* a partial solution, at least when it comes to the stories of the past that already circulate to tell stories about the lives of animals? As discussed in Chapter 1, as ideas of what biography is and does have evolved over centuries and particularly recent decades, this has paved the way for the rise of animal biography. Andre Krebber and Mieke Roscher (2018) note, it is a daunting task to represent animals' individuality (1). However, this is what many writers of animal life narratives have and are attempting to do. Krebber and Roscher (2018) explain how biography, though not without significant challenges, has emerged as the most stable form for presenting animal narratives. They note that while history is,

> dominated by attempts that try to standardize, de-individualize and automatize the behavior of animals, it also proves to be littered with records of the exceptional lives of unusual animals.
>
> A biography, it is hoped, projects, almost by definition, the possession of emotions, personhood – a self. Moreover, the personal element of the biography proves popular and promises to tie a knot between the biography's subject and its reader. (2)

As I have argued through the first three chapters of this study, biography, and more particularly biography for children, is a genre of growing potential. It has the capacity to show and represent a diversity of subjects for children's engagement. And through its potential for ethical and expansive interdisciplinary research and responsibility to the subject, it surely has the potential to achieve at least some of the aspirations when it comes to the representation of animals' lives, as a means of 'making visible and honoring animals as individuals externally, from historical sources, lived experiences, the bodies of animals' (Krebber and Roscher, 2018: 6). As Hermione Lee (2009) argues, we've come to accept that biographies are not definitive, but offer something of a life (18). And perhaps when it comes to animals, this point looms large in any representation of their lives. Further, in thinking about Caitríona Ní Dhúill's (2020: 11) idea about metabiography, we might see animal biographies as an opportunity to expand the methods required for constructing biography; they might 'unsettle what we think we know about biography and to find the tools we need for that task in biographies themselves, as well as in theoretical writings on biography'.

There has been a plethora of non-fictional representations of dogs including biographies of 'wonder dogs' such as Christina Hunger's *How Stella Learned to Talk* (2021), as well as many texts about dog behaviour, photo books of dogs in homes or travelling and so on and comics such as Gemma Gene's *Living with Mochi* (2021). Recent non-fiction books about dogs for children tend to focus on information about dogs: whether historical, behavioural or the biology of dogs; guides to particular breeds and books about engaging more deeply with dogs, for instance, books about communication. Depending on the genre of book, these books tend to cite the evidence on which the texts are based, for instance, scientific research. But when it comes to biographical representations of animals, the evidence and its use is necessarily different. The biographer sutures facts and assumed knowledge into an accessible children's story.

The emergence of *Rebel Dogs* is important in this space. The book contains thirty main narratives and a series of micro narratives which result in it being an expansive offering. The book is also illustrated by a diversity of illustrators who contributed to the biographical narrative through these illustrations. The stories are largely constructed around limited human knowledge: historical records and existing stories already in circulation such as adult books or films, for example.[1] But this also represents an opportunity – to revise and offer nuance to human knowledge of these dogs. In reading *Rebel Dogs*, children are invited to consider and understand these dogs' lives in relation to the dogs' individuality.

## *Rebel Dogs* and *Rebel Cats*

US author Kimberlie Hamilton, now based in Scotland, writes non-fiction for children and is an animal activist (author's website). In an interview, Hamilton explains that after having come across many incredible animal stories over the years, she wondered how many other amazing animal stories there were out there. She decided to write *Rebel Dogs* and *Rebel Cats* to give these animals the recognition they deserved (Q&A with Kimberly Hamilton, 2018). Hamilton explains,

> I love animals and I love biographies, and the thought of putting those passions together really appealed to me. So I started doing research and found some great stories about dogs, including many that I felt were 'under the radar' and deserved more recognition. One of my challenges was to narrow all my favourite stories down to a mere 30! I tried to make the final list as diverse as possible, featuring different countries, time periods, breeds and types of stories. (Interview with Sarah Farrell)

As Aaron Skabelund (2018) explains, 'the difficulties of telling the history of animals is similar to those faced in trying to retrieve the largely silent and invisible past of certain subaltern people' (85). Krebber and Roscher (2018: 6) concur; they suggest that when writing about animals, much like other marginal subjects, writers do not always have the sort of 'data set', methodologically, that might be drawn on to construct a biographical subject. They explain:

> More than the writing of human biographies, the writing of animal biographies then relies fundamentally on interdisciplinary efforts. Even though animals are present throughout the array of cultural documents and artifacts, at least within the last two or three centuries a lot of knowledge about animals has been collected within the natural sciences … the task

now ... is to submit this knowledge to new and critical analyses in order to perceive animals in new lights. (6)

Hamilton does not include much detail about her method in constructing the stories, but as many of these dogs' stories are familiar it is likely that Hamilton's primary goal here is to adapt existing materials and stories for a child reader. In his research on Hachikō, the famously loyal Japanese dog that also features in Hamilton's book, Skabelund (2018) writes:

> A biographer can find an extraordinary amount of source material about Hachikō that could be used to reconstruct his life. Many, many dozens of newspaper and magazine articles, a book, and songs about and photographs of him as well as the textbook story and the Shibuya statue were produced while Hachikō was still very much alive ... The station's office contains an archive of Hachikō-related materials. Among its holdings are business cards of those who made financial donations to build the statue, essays composed by grade-school children about Hachikō, and other ephemeral. In ōdate, the Society for the Preservation of the Akita dog displays a letter describing Hachikō's birth and first two months of life written by the (human) family into which he was born. And of course at the National Science Museum is the stuffed Hachikō himself, wearing the same harness and collar he wore while alive. There is no shortage of artifacts and textual sources to document this dog's life. (85)

Hamilton's motivations seem clearly positioned in relation to the positive potential of animal biography as outlined above. Krebber and Roscher (2018: 2) argue that biographies of animals aim to 'capture the individuality of animals' as well as increase their visibility as individuals. Such writings do not anthropomorphize. They do not attempt to read the minds or construct feelings or intentions for animals (Krebber and Roscher, 2018: 2). These texts have the potential to show animals' personalities and idiosyncrasies. Animal biography has the capacity to distinguish animals rather than emphasizing their similarities (Krebber and Roscher, 2018: 2). Authors, in writing biographies of animals, 'lend voice and recognition' to them and emphasize the important relationship that exists between humans and animals (Krebber and Roscher, 2018: 2). In such stories, humans are positioned as allies, but not central to the animals' stories.

Dogs have life experiences and stories worth sharing. In *Rebel Dogs*, these stories are inevitably framed within the genres and structures of children's books and biography, where animals are celebrated for particular recognizable qualities such as cuteness, bravery and loyalty, that are often uniform across different books. But, I argue, that *Rebel Dogs* goes beyond the sort of popular or humanist posthumanism discussed by Cynthia Huff (2017) in which animals are lauded by simply being given human status and/or being acknowledged within animal-rights frameworks. For Huff (2017), posthuman auto/biography should dismantle the centrality of the autonomous human self, asking radical and potent questions about the non-human. Huff (2017) explains,

> In a posthumanist imaginary, writing would be decentered and destabilized as a technology controlled by humans to gain mastery in favor of a more expansive concept of narrative relating. That concept would deprivilege sight – the sense with which humans most identify and the one they most use – and qualitative cognition by equally favoring touch, taste, smell, and hearing as well as quantitative thinking, all ways of knowing the world that are just as or more important for non-human animal and mechanical relationality. (279)

Using the example of problematic animal life writing projects, Huff (2017) explains that foregrounding the experiences and subjectivities of non-humans in telling their own life stories is very difficult because non-humans do not have access to human language as a starting point (280). Huff's (2017) way forward, for posthumanist life narrative is that

> scholars must counter ventriloquized representationality in favor of a politics of subjectivity that emphasizes relationality and process among disparate types of beings. Instead of life writing taking as its primary trajectory the autobiographer's life from birth to the telling of his or her story (likely emphasizing individual growth), a posthumanist life narrative would reject that story of progress in favor of those disrupting any linear narrative, telling, instead, a becoming together. (280)

Do books like *Rebel Dogs* offer any progress then? Though Hamilton clearly does not aim for a posthuman representation in the strictest sense, these representations of 'true' stories of dogs for children reveal a consciousness of a future relationship with animals that supersedes that of past representations.

Though *Rebels Dogs* represents the thirty dogs' lives most often in light of their relationship to humans and human constructs of loyalty, love, talent and trust (Hamilton, 2019: 13), the book also attempts to show and construct dogs' lives as distinct and individual from human lives. They are 'rebel dogs' who do rebellious acts like bite Napoleon, stow away on planes and insist on being taken to Sweden. Among the many stories represented are those that are perhaps expected: dogs in service (for instance, in war, in adventures, as helpers, for instance, Buddy the first seeing-eye dog) and dogs being physically remarkable (for instance, Bobbie who returned home to his family after walking 4,830 kilometres and Ashley Whippet the amazing frisbee dog). However, there is nuance to the representations, generally, that invites child readers to consider what lies beneath and beyond these stories. The dogs' lives are of value outside of their contribution to the lives of the humans around them. This is important when juxtaposed to the facts of their lives which were so often in the service of humans. In writing *Rebel Dogs*, Hamilton offers a challenge to readers: has our treatment of dogs historically been ethical? Readers are left with a feeling that the popular phrase 'we don't deserve dogs', is absolutely true.

For instance, *Rebel Dogs* offers the story of Antis, the dog who became a companion to Czech pilot Robert Bozdech in the Second World War. Bozdech found him in a farmhouse. In her biographical sketch of Antis, Hamilton explains how Antis was not trained for rescue work but rescued instinctively, 'after a nearby city was bombed, he raced to a collapsed building and began to sniff and paw through the rubble … [and] managed to find six survivors. Robert had to carry an exhausted Antis back to base, his paws torn and bleeding' (Hamilton, 2019: 18). Throughout this story, the emphasis is on Antis's unique skills and individuality, which is often superior to the humans he works with. Hamilton inverts the idea of a dog's service to humanity, for instance, in recounting how Bozdech and his colleagues had to make a custom oxygen mask after Antis stowed away on a flight (Hamilton, 2019: 18). The image of Antis, drawn by Andrew Gardner, foregrounds Antis looking up at three aircraft in the sky. Antis is drawn large and is the focus of the illustration. He is a beautiful, strong and healthy-looking dog. He is what is important in this image. His eyes are wide and bright, ears engaged, and mouth open. He appears happy and excited. Antis wants to be in the planes, as we have learned from the narration. This is my human reading of the human drawn image of Antis. But it shows Antis's individuality and desires in line with the aim of *Rebel Dogs*.

The story of Antis is followed by a list of animals that 'also served'. These narratives are roughly one-sentence long. It is clear that the author wants to be as inclusive as possible when it comes to the representation of animals that served in war. These animals have been the subject of exhibitions and anthologies such as Robin Hutton's *War Animals: The Unsung Heroes of World War II* (2019), '"A" is for Animal' at the Australian War Memorial, Animals in War at The Devil's Porridge Museum in Scotland and 'Animals at War' at the Imperial War Museum, London.[2] But the detailed recounting of Antis's story reveals an intention to show individuality through the inclusion of greater detail.

Like Antis, Arthur the Amazon Adventurer is also represented as a stray dog who chooses to be with a human. The unknown origins of such dogs, their unknowability, make for intriguing subjects; we would like to know more but never will. Arthur seemingly knows what he wants and makes it happen. He followed Mikael Lindnord and the Swedish adventure racing team through their incredibly rugged and dangerous race. His reward was Lindnord taking him back to Sweden (*Rebel Dogs*, 2019: 22). Arthur gets a two-page narration because he did his own thing. Is this human-defined remarkability or autonomy? It's still a human construct of a story, however, it seeks to centralize Arthur's autonomy and ability to express himself and his individuality. The image of Arthur shows a gorgeous mixed-breed dog. The illustration is simple, almost childlike in its shaping, lines and colouring. Arthur forms the centre of the illustration, taking up the majority of the page. His paws are dirty; his surrounds are grass and trees and there is a human leg at the side of the picture. The human presence reminds us how Arthur gained the attention of his new human companion. But Arthur's human is not as important to the story as Arthur is.

*Rebel Dogs* contains the wonderfully humorous story of Fortune who was the pug dog of Marie-Josèphe-Rose de Beauharnais (Josephine), who would become the wife of Napoléon Bonaparte. As the story goes, Napoléon was jealous of Fortune, but Josephine insisted that the dog would sleep in the marital bed and Fortune bit Napoleon when he challenged his position

(Hamilton, 2019: 46). Perhaps the most comic of all stories in *Rebel Dogs*, and accompanied by a cartoon-ish image, is Fortune's narrative that shows how a dog can outrank a powerful man; the story disrupts conventional hierarchies. The image of Fortune is a perfect accompaniment to the narrative. Little Fortune, 'Napoléon's bite-sized nemesis' is pictured sitting innocently on the royal bed which is beautifully adored in red and gold coverings. Fortune's head is cocked to the side, eyes wide, ears down, the pose suggesting he would not hurt a fly.

Children might already be familiar with the story of Hachikō, who, after the death of his human companion, continued to go to the train station where he would meet him after work, for ten years after his death. Reading it in this context we are invited to consider this loyalty, as a human construct, as something that dogs redefine. This is an issue that resonated strongly with the children in my book club and a point that I return to later. Similarly, the story of Laika, the 'first canine cosmonaut' who was sacrificed by the Soviet space programme. She was sent into space to test the space craft. Those who sent her knew that they had no capacity to bring her back. Hamilton explains, 'Many people felt this was wrong and it sparked a big debate about the humane treatment of animals' (Hamilton, 2019: 68). Her concluding paragraph asserts thus:

> Laika's courage inspired books and films, postage stamps and pop songs. There's a statue of her at the cosmonaut training centre, she's featured on the Monument to the Conquerors of Space in Moscow and NASA named a Mars Landing site after her. Laika was a genuine hero and her memory should never be forgotten. (Hamilton, 2019: 68)

We might read this now and see Laika not as 'courageous' or as a hero, but as a victim of human's cruel disregard and destruction of animals. But perhaps it is reassuring to construct her in this way for a child reader, and invite that reader to empathize with Laika's plight. The narration of Laika's story in *Rebel Dogs* intersects with biographical representations that have gone before. There's a suggestion here that biographical narration can become a means for reparation. As the same story becomes adapted over time and for different readerships, its potential to offer nuance and indeed criticism is crucial in expanding our sense of what biography is and can do, particularly when it comes to presenting stories to children. What better way to acknowledge the mistakes of the past than to get children on board to redress these mistakes and work towards better shared futures for humans and animals?

In *Rebel Dogs*, the picture of Laika is adorably cartoonish. She smiles, reassuringly at the reader from what seems like the porthole of the space craft. She appears happy and safe. One way to interpret this might be that this is a childish representation seeking to soften the blow for the child reader. Laika is not drawn as realistically as some of the other dogs in *Rebel Dogs*. Another way to read this image is that it might (should?) intensify our sense of injustice of what society did to Laika. This Laika looks like other cartoon dogs the children might be familiar with. It provides a point of connection and understanding for the child reader who might be familiar with animal stories and animals in fairy tales. But also, presenting this subject functions as an assertion that children can and should read about difficult subjects and injustices like this one, a point I return to in Chapter 5.

## The Kids' Book Club

The children from my book club (as introduced in Chapter 3) deserve the final critical word on this text. The children read this book in their second, follow-up book club session. In the introduction to this chapter, I hypothesized that 'child readers are encouraged to read the dogs' rebelliousness into the representations made'. Was this the children's reading in the Kids' Book Club?

The children and I discussed their favourite stories and what they liked about them. We discussed what, if anything, they found surprising about the stories in *Rebel Dogs*. I asked: did the stories change what you thought about dogs and what dogs could do in the world? They unanimously said 'no', and that they expected dogs to do amazing things like those represented in *Rebel Dogs*. They were not surprised that the dogs got their own books like the *Kids Who Did*; 'Why wouldn't they?', asked Andy.

Children appreciate clever and otherwise remarkable dogs. Such dogs are part of their cultural lexicon. The children said they were familiar with seeing dogs' lives represented in movies and so understood that there were things to be learned about dogs' lives that they did not already know. The children in the book club live at a time when celebrity dogs are commonplace. As Margo DeMello (2018) notes,

> the biggest celebrities of all, like Grumpy Cat and Lil Bub, have public personas which are as carefully cultivated (by their human handlers/ PR specialists) as those of Tom Cruise or Beyonce. And yet the millions of followers of these celebrities are happy to ignore the fact that there is a human (or sometimes a marketing team) behind the persona. We are only interested in the animal. (248)

Children are familiar with dogs being amusing on YouTube and TikTok. They are aware of dogs having their own Instagram pages. They are used to seeing biographies of animals in the public sphere, for instance, at the zoo, or in activist or adopt-a-pet campaigns. So, perhaps, these stories might not seem so remarkable to them because they are at an age, and living at a time, where they understand dogs to be remarkable and are not surprised to read about their rebellious and accomplished histories. Children are also familiar with sad animal stories, for example, in films such as *Hachi: A Dog's Tale* (2009) and *A Street Cat Named Bob* (2016), even *The Lion King* (1994), and suggested that it was okay that there were some sad stories in *Rebel Dogs* but were relieved that it was not just sad stories.

What the children did notice and emphasize in their discussion was the potential superiority of dogs to humans, and the ways in which the rebel dogs surprised adult humans with their actions. The children were drawn to particular aspects of the dogs' lives represented: skills that dogs have, that humans do not, dogs doing unexpected things like surviving under challenging circumstances, dogs having superior fitness to humans, dogs' ability to accomplish more than people, dogs' outstanding intelligence ('where humans often think dogs are dumb'). I asked, why do some people not value the lives of dogs or dogs' having distinguished lives? Demi suggested, 'because humans can be jealous'. Andy stated, robustly 'dogs are better than people' and the children agreed unanimously.

Such comments are not surprising when considered more broadly in light of representations of animals in children's books. As scholars such as Tess Cosslett (2002) and Zoe Jaques (2015) have argued, anthropomorphized animals in children's stories often stand in for 'the child' as fellows lowest in the power hierarchy. So, the children in this study might well be reading these texts in light of such fictional representations. The child readers' responses, therefore, might have an element of identification in them. We can interpret their engagement with animals' stories at least in part, as an attempt at self-understanding and a more general concern about social power hierarchies and who is undervalued in our world.

The children explained,

*Andy:* Dogs are more affectionate than humans.
*Demi:* Dogs are more forgiving.
*Sophie:* Dogs can do inspiring things.

The child readers pointed to the 'heroics' of the dogs and the rebellious things that they did. For instance, stories like that of the Japanese Shiba Inu dog Mari who survived with her pups after they were left behind after an earthquake in 2004 when all humans were evacuated. After her human family returned two weeks later, Mari and her puppies were still alive. Also, Taro and Jiro, the Sakhalin huskies, survived in Antarctica for eleven months after they and seven other 'snow dogs' were left behind by researchers after a snowstorm.

The children emphasized that the skills the dogs showed were not just limited to their ability to serve humans. Madi explained 'the book is a bit about what we already know about dogs, but a lot about what we don't already know. It's about challenging people to think better of dogs and what they can do'. Some of the qualities that the children saw the dogs as having, that were superior to humans included: 'swimming and physical stuff'; 'loyalty in friendships', the ability to 'cure human's anxiety', the ability to 'help others in need, such as those who are blind', 'taking risks', 'surviving' and 'making sacrifices to help others'. Again, we might consider these comments as interpretations of injustice; why does our society undervalue the skills and contributions of some of its members?

For example, Madi argued, 'like we know dogs are loyal, but this book takes us to the next level in showing *how* loyal dogs actually are. It's bigger and better than we thought'. Sophie explained that the dogs in the story are 'heroic because of all the cool things they did' but they were 'rebels' because they did unexpected things too: 'Sometimes naughty things like the pug who bit the emperor because he didn't want him to sleep on the bed', but, as Adam stated, also good things that were not dog-like: 'when Oddball protected the penguins on Middle Island, Australia where we might have thought he would just eat them. I asked, "why are these dogs 'rebels'"'? Claire explained: 'because they are sometimes naughty to adults, but really it is because their lives are special'. Demi continued, 'all dogs lives are special, but not everyone gets a story told about them. Maybe if people read this book they will like dogs more'. The potential of biography then, for the children, is that it goes beyond representing the lives of some animals. Though these dogs' lives are compelling reads, but also function as consciousness-raisers on the rights of dogs and animals more generally. The children's comments also lean into social injustice more generally, and why a hierarchical approach to the value of life is problematic. The biographies encouraged the children to reflect on these issues and speak about them more widely, beyond the book. Thus, Lee's argument that biography is 'always an index of its time' (9) is useful in thinking about the possibility that *Rebel Dogs* reflects broader cultural shifts in the way animals' lives are perceived and represented, and the ways in which children might see their lives in parallel to animals when it comes to seeing and interpreting socio-cultural power balances.

## Conclusion

Krebber and Roscher (2018) remind us that those constructing biographies of, or for, animals face similar challenges to those constructing biographies for human subjects:

> Biographies can be smooth and uneventful, but they can also be broken, fractured, fragmented and fragile … For some individuals or even groups of individuals, biographies can be comprehensively recoverable, but they can also be partial, interrupted and sketchy … the real and the fictional always and necessarily pervade each other. It is the task of the biographer to organize the remnants into a coherent story; it is he or she who creates. (6)

But organization is never without agenda. In constructing biographies of dogs in *Rebel Dogs*, Hamilton assembles their histories in new ways that consider what we now know about animal histories in relation to posthuman theories, animal rights and CAS.

Biographies remain imperfect cultural constructs, whether of animals, humans or objects. They are enabled and limited by the plethora of social, cultural, political and methodological elements that affect their production. But what animal biographies have the capacity to do, for instance, in comparison to other discourses that represent their lives, is they give these lives individuality, colour and shape. The same questions apply to animal biography and biography in general. Who gets a biography and why? What is it supposed to tell us? Who will it be of interest to at this time and why?

What's productive at the intersection of children's literature and biography for animals is a sense of what biographies of animals for children aim to do for child readers. In the instance of *Rebel Dogs*, it is clear that, much like those biographies of marginal subjects introduced in Chapter 2, we see a desire to insert these narratives into history in meaningful ways. The short biographies in *Rebel Dogs*, a combination of narrative and illustration, build on existing knowledge of these subjects, but shape and colour the life story to engage a child reader. There is a sense from the author and animal-rights activist who is reproducing these stories to children that this reproduction represents an opportunity. It is an opportunity to engage children with true stories about animals where they might be very familiar with fictional-animal stories. It is an opportunity to gently introduce animal-rights activism and social justice more generally, to children via biography.

We can again see didacticism at work in biographies for children, however; in this instance it is much less overt than the moralistic histories explored in Chapter 1. Here again, we can see biography's potential for inserting marginal subjects into mainstream storytelling. But as posthumanist scholars remind us, we should also be mindful of the limitations of animal biography. These remain human constructs that imagine animals in certain ways and for particular human agendas. *Rebel Dogs* addresses this criticism within its pages. In constructing its biographies, the book makes obvious what we cannot know or cannot see from reading these stories, and in doing so, invites child readers to see the limitations of biography.

The interpretations made by the Kids' Book Club readers offers an optimistic conclusion for this chapter. The children gained a lot from reading these stories, but in particular, appreciated the potential of these biographies as consciousness raisers. They were excited about the possibility that reading these stories would grow readers' understanding of what dogs are capable of and the unique contributions they make to the world. They read these biographies as both confirming their own general understanding of dogs as equal or even superior to humans and providing particular knowledge of the lives of certain dogs in history.

In Chapter 5 I extend this discussion of biographies for children as texts that aim to engage children politically. I look at two children's picture books that engage the mode of speculative biography to represent the experience of asylum-seekers for children. In aiming to make the lives of child refugees visible to child readers, these biographical picture books reveal something of the perceived value of sharing trauma narratives with child readers, and a sense of children's capacity to comprehend these biographical narratives.

## Notes

1  There are citations at the end of the text that point children to 'Fur-ther Reading' – mostly books on the dogs represented, but also some websites. The websites range from dog adoption sites through to information about dogs, and charity and activist sites. The back matter of the book also contains a call to action, '10 Ways to Help Hounds in Need' and a 'Rebel Dogs Timeline' showing the history of dogs.
2  *A is for Animals*. (2010), Australian War Memorial, Exhibition. Available online: https://www.awm.gov.au/visit/exhibitions/animals; *Animals in War Exhibition*. (n. d.), The Devil's Porridge Museum, Exhibition. Available online:https://www.devilsporridge.org.uk/animals-in-war-exhibition; Animals at War. (n. d.), Imperial War Museum, Exhibition.https://www.culture24.org.uk/history-and-heritage/military-history/art38557

# 5

# Children's picture books as collaborative biography

In 2017, Alexandra Alter wrote a piece for *The Guardian* titled 'Why Children's Authors Are Taking on the Refugee Crisis'. Alter notes an exponential growth in children's books about the asylum seeking the previous two years. Though some of these books are fiction, notably, many are non-fiction and draw on texts and methods from life writing, for instance, picture books based on true stories, actual testimony or interviews with asylum-seekers and refugees and archival research. For example, Suzanne Del Rizzo's *My Beautiful Birds* (2017) is based on a true story of a Syrian boy living in Jordan in the Zaatari refugee camp who had tamed wild birds; Atia Abawi visited Lesbos, Greece, to interview Syrian refugees to research for *A Land of Permanent Goodbyes* (2018) and Francesca Sanna's *The Journey* (2016) draws on the story of two girls that Sanna met in a refugee camp in Italy and other interviews she conducted with refugees, to create a 'collage' of personal stories.

This engagement with children's stories aligns with global concerns about children's displacement more generally. Many of those affected are children. According to UNICEF

> children are dramatically over-represented among the world's refugees. Children make up less than one third of the global population, but almost half among the world's refugees in 2020. Today, nearly 1 in 3 children living outside their countries of birth are child refugees; for adults, the proportion is less than 1 in 20.[1]

As parents and teachers consider ways they might approach these issues with child readers, authors and illustrators of children's books develop methods for remediating this knowledge for children. As we have already seen in Chapters 2 and 3, contemporary biographies for children are facing up to the big issues of our time, seeking to revise problematic histories and insert marginal subjects into the public sphere, all the while, trusting child readers' abilities to engage with this knowledge.

This chapter considers *My Beautiful Birds* and *The Journey* as examples of children's books that offer biographical narratives as source of historical, social and cultural knowledge on the experience of child asylum-seekers. These books aim to make the lives of child refugees visible to child readers. Within the contexts of displaced and disappearing migrant children, these picture books seek to tell stories and share testimony that might otherwise disappear. How do these texts draw on life-narrative methods (such as oral testimony and interviewing) to construct life-narrative texts for children and to authorize these texts, more generally? I argue that these biographical picture books – their authors and illustrators – become witnesses to, and conduits for, the circulation of asylum-seeker testimony. In their construction, they reveal something of the perceived value of sharing trauma narratives with child readers.

## Biography, picture books and the big issues

At the time of writing this book, Francesca Sanna's children's picture book *The Journey* (which she wrote and illustrated and was published in 2016) had 4,122 reviews on the popular reader-review site *Goodreads*, for an overall rating of 4.4 stars out of 5. Here is one of them:

> This one didn't work for me, the illustrations are lovely but I feel that the story line would be confusing and all together too scary for the young.
> 
> The story shows a happy family who enjoy everyday life until war comes, their father is taken and they have to leave their country. Their father isn't seen again. There are some scary characters and scenes of their mother crying alone in the woods whilst giant guards reminiscent of creatures from film the Yellow submarine look down from the sky. There is a boat crossing where wave droplets become fairies and then the family are on a bird's neck migrating with the birds. I didn't like the mix between reality and fantasy, I think if I were a child reading this I would feel confused which parts of the book actually reflected the experiences of the refugees, and as this families

[sic] situation is scary enough anyway, I think their [sic] could be better ways to explain this. I could imagine some children would find this upsetting.

The reviewer gave it 2.5 stars out of 5.

This one short review centres on some of the core debates affecting children's literature now. Children's picture books are a popular literary genre, and as discussed in Chapter 2 of this book, non-fiction picture books are experiencing a rise in both sales and in critical acclaim. Recently, there has been positive attention given to biographical picture books for children: in the representations they make, and their perceived role, for instance in educating children. Biographical picture book authors and illustrators now have a mandate for representing timely social and political issues, such as environmental change, family diversity, equal access to health and education, and representations of diverse cultural and national identities.

Children's literature scholar Evelyn Arizpe (2015) discusses the power of children's picture books, 'there is something about the way both word and image are brought together in these highly crafted picture books that doubles the impact – on our minds, our emotions and even our bodies' (xvii). Like published literatures from other popular genres, children's picture books are multiply mediated texts. They arrive to children via authors, editors, publishers, marketers and various other gatekeepers of good or appropriate literary taste. But children's texts are subject to further layers – perhaps most notably, adult stakeholders – such as teachers and parents. What children are reading, or should be reading, and how they are shaped by the books they read is always a hot issue. As Perry Nodelman (2015: 33) argues,

> children's literature as a whole is a category built on restrictions; special books for children would not exist if adults did not believe that children want or need to know less about their world than there actually is, and so, children's literature … is almost by definition, a literature defined by what it leaves out. Inevitably, however, different adults have different ideas about what needs to be left out. (33)

Reading impacts not only upon childhood literacy, but also on social and cultural development, and identity formation. But when children's books are about 'challenging or controversial' (to borrow the title of Janet Evans's 2015 research book on the subject), subjects, the responses to picture books shift.

When children read about trauma, for example, it is confronting to adults because it challenges notions of childhood and what children can comprehend intellectually and emotionally. This is despite the fact that, as Evans reminds us, 'in the early nineteenth century, the Grimm brothers were recounting stories such as these traditional folktales that reflected life as it existed at that time. Subjects such as murder, cannibalism, incest, child cruelty, sex and violence were all significant elements' (Evans, 2015: 11). As Sandra L. Beckett (2015: 49) notes, many contemporary picture books 'have their roots in the time-honoured tradition of folk and fairy tales, cautionary tales, and nursery rhymes'.

Though such texts are not without controversy for the representations they make, contemporary books for children have an immediacy in their representations that might be more threatening for adult's perceptions of what children can safely read. In writing about the here-and-now world that children occupy, non-fiction-picture books for children such as those I discuss in this chapter have a transparent agenda to educate their readers about the contemporary world. As Arizpe (2015) contends, contemporary ideologies about children and childhood pervade these representations. She posits that

> the argument about protecting children from particular realities is a hard one to resolve, given that definitions of 'child' and 'reality' are continually modified as the historical boundaries between childhood, adolescence and adulthood are constantly being redrawn. Often this urge to protect seems to be an unconscious way of dealing with the guilt we adults feel about having made the world such a dangerous and endangered place for children. (Arizpe, 2015: xviii)

Arizpe's (2015) comments here are persuasive. The debates she points to are about content and thus relate more to the relationship between children's literature and civic literacy and knowledge about the world than they do to discussions of children's reading and literacy skills. Many scholars of children's literature and more particularly of biography for children argue that children's books are an ideal site for introducing children to difficult subject matter. Roni Natov (2018: 4) argues that, 'fears are an everyday and important part of our lives and stories … Literature provides a way of approaching them at a safe distance'. If a child has read about a difficult subject in a book, it might help them make sense of it should they ever encounter this issue in the real world

(Natov, 2018: 4). Representing difficult subject matter or conflict in biography for children assumes an intelligent reader who can decode information and engage in interpretation. Linda Walvoord Girard (1990: 1) argues, 'perhaps the greatest enemy of biography is not didacticism, but the lack of any theme or interpretive activity at all, a book in which "nothing happens"'. Here, Girard rightly argues that children are likely to value narrative tension and power in a book as much as adult readers might. She continues:

> Surprise is close to the heart of biography. Children like surprises, liveliness, victories won and causes served. They like to be inspired … Surveys of children's choices in reading show that they handle almost any kind of trouble or conflict if the overview is hopeful. (Girard, 1990: 1)

It seems highly unlikely that even when representing difficult subject matter an author of children's biography would do so without hope; it is unlikely that such books would not be published. Natov (2018: 58) offers a similar position in suggesting that trauma stories can give children hope, 'a recognition that this terrible thing has happened to others and that they have survived … The reader bears witness'. The effectiveness of a trauma representation within children's biography, then, lies in the telling, and in this chapter, we will see some of the strategies that children's authors and illustrators deploy in this spirit.

* * *

In this chapter I consider Suzanne Del Rizzo's *My Beautiful Birds* and Francesca Sanna's *The Journey*. Both books fit within different genres: children's picture book, folktale, a life narrative, a collaborative biography and testimony. In looking at De Rizzo's and Sanna's texts, I consider how each works as collaborative biography. These is another subgenre of biography for children that invites us to think differently, more broadly, about the limits of children's biography. This mode again reminds us that it is most often adults who take up children's stories, who author them, who find these stories their readership. In these instances, adult author/illustrators become witnesses for children's life narratives where children might not be able to speak publicly. Both authors assert a commitment to locating and sharing the child's voice in an authentic and ethical way, and this creates particular challenges for us, as readers, in terms of our acceptance of this as true and valuable. In these examples, neither author intrudes inside the text in obvious ways. Both attempt a first-person narrative, mimicking the autobiographical. But the adult authors remain the named author, the biographer. So, we recognize the limits of this mode in terms of foregrounding children's voices. But perhaps we might also recognize the value of adults using their voices and skills to empower children. Looking at examples like Ben Quilty's *Home: Drawings By Syrian Children* (2018) we can see the emergence and potential of children more often authoring their own auto/biographical narratives.

In examining these two books, I consider how the authors, in their method, style and content, present a trauma narrative for child readers, and what assumptions are made (within the text) about readership and interpretation. How do *My Beautiful Birds* and *The Journey* work as sources of historical and cultural knowledge on the experience of child asylum-seekers? And, as a non-fiction picture book for children, do they face up to the concerns expressed by our *Goodreads* friend, quoted earlier? Should they? If so, how?

## *The Journey*

Life-narrative texts have been crucial in exploring and raising awareness of the global asylum-seeker crisis: non-fictional genres including documentary, social media, diaries, memoirs, letter-writing projects and so forth. These texts have sought to draw attention to the experience of asylum-seekers and refugees, whether through foregrounding first-person experiential testimony, or through as-told-to texts by second-person witnesses and writers.

*The Journey* is an award-winning book aimed at readers aged five–seven.[2] The book aims to make the lives of child refugees visible to child readers. Within the contexts of displaced and disappearing migrant children, this picture book aims to tell stories, and share testimony that might otherwise disappear. The author's website explains:

> *The Journey* is actually a story about many journeys, and it began with the story of two girls I met in a refugee center in Italy … I began collecting more stories of migration and interviewing many people from many different

countries. A few months later, in September 2014, when I started studying a Master of Arts in Illustration at the Academy of Lucerne, I knew I wanted to create a book about these true stories. Almost every day on the news we hear the terms 'migrants' and 'refugees' but we rarely ever speak to or hear the personal journeys that they have had to take. This book is a collage of all those personal stories and the incredible strength of the people within them. (Penguin, 2016)

In an interview, Sanna explains how she felt a need to 'do something' with these stories (Jurich, 1972, 'Interview with Francesca Sanna'). Sanna felt an obligation to those children she met, and so sought out other narratives that she might include in her project. Her method, as outlined above, is to present children's real-life experiences of displacement and asylum seeking for a child readership. So, Sanna's book is a biographical 'collage'. We might refer to such texts as collaborative or as-told-to life narrative.

As suggested above, in thinking about such texts, we should also be mindful that this is still an adult writer and illustrator at the helm. Whilst the children's voices are not absent, children are not the authors of the text. There are much larger questions we might ask here about how authors and indeed critics might work to make the child more present in the creation and in the interpretation of such texts, and this is something I speak on in Chapters 6, 7 and 8 of this book. Maybe a further problem is the extent to which we can or cannot hear the children's voices (that Sanna interviewed) in *The Journey*. Like other types of collaborative life narrative texts, there are obvious power differentials in as-told-to narratives like *The Journey*. This considered, is this picture book something we can recognize *as* biography within the context of this study?

I am going to argue strongly: 'yes'. In this project I have sought to show how biography for children now exists as a highly diverse genre. What has traditionally plagued or limited the genre: overt and problematic didacticism, a lack of diversity in representation, the absence of children's voices in the creation and interpretation of texts, is slowly changing. Each of the texts and case studies in this book reveal something about the dynamics of the genre now, as it changes shape for the twenty-first century.

Rather than focus on what came before displacement, or the experiences after relocation, Sanna's focus is 'the journey' – a story that she feels might be overlooked but should not because of what it reveals about people's humanity and strength. That the book is endorsed by Amnesty International reminds us of the perceived power of literature and what it can achieve in the world. The book's promotional material focuses on the book's truths and timeliness and its likely impact upon readers:

> With haunting echoes of the current refugee crisis this beautifully illustrated book explores the unimaginable decisions made as a family leave their home and everything they know to escape the turmoil and tragedy brought by war. This book will stay with you long after the last page is turned. (*The Journey*, 2016)

When I completed my close-reading of *The Journey* for this chapter, I did so with my (then) seven-year-old daughter. This seemed like a superior method to reading it alone (and a step towards the sort of social-reading-reader research I ultimately completed in Chapters 7 and 8 of this book (though I wrote this chapter first). My daughter saw a lot that I did not see, and I saw things that she did not, for example, she was particularly tuned into the hidden animals on the pages that follow the family through the story. They seemed to her mysterious and like animals in fairy tales. I reflected with melancholy on the family having to leave family, friends and animals behind during forced migration. The book works effectively on these different levels. Through the child narrator, *The Journey* allows for different disclosures for different-aged readers, and thus alternative meanings to be made. This is, of course, a common strategy in picture books, but, particularly important to observe in non-fiction-picture books which purport to offer true stories and engage current events.

Sanna's is a beautiful book. It is easy to fall in love with all aspects of its style and subject. As Arizpe (2015) reminds us, though the politics of such books might overwhelm other observations, we should not side line the aesthetics of picture books and pleasures of reading (xviii). *The Journey*'s first-person narration establishes its simple, accessible plot: an unnamed female child tells the story of her family's post-war displacement: the death of her father and her mother's strength and courage in leading her family (two young children) on a very long, perilous and frightening journey to a new home.

The text's style is described by Sanna herself and reviewers as 'folk art' – art that aims to showcase particular community traditions, folklore and cultural heritage (Glaveanu, 2013: 153). Sometimes referred to as 'naïve art', folk art is usually characterized by bright colours and childlike perspectives. Folk art is not conventionally associated with elite forms of art but speaks to different classes and cultures (Harper, 2019). This genre is important to children's picture books because of its use in illustrating folk tales – real life stories that have been passed through generations. The style works for Sanna; she wants to tell 'true' stories that illuminate local cultures, lives and experiences.

Though we are given some clues, we do not know where the family is fleeing from or to. Sanna's visual ambiguity is not reductive; it shows her commitment to this communal biography project. She aims to represent the distinct experience of the children she interviewed, and in doing so, presents a scene that will also be intriguing to a curious child reader. The scene might look unfamiliar, but the illustrative and narrative style might be recognizable from other folk stories they have read. *The Journey* begins at a family beach holiday. The colours, the fashions and the buildings give the scene a paradoxical location (which at once symbolize a real city close by, and one made of very elaborate sandcastles by the girl and her family at the beach) that seems concurrently in the past, but also from an imaginary world. The rounded peaks of the buildings might signal a Middle Eastern or southern European location. In the opening picture we see a mother and father and two children, one of whom, the young girl, is our narrator.

The sea is black – which we might interpret as the Black Sea, but the colour black also works conveniently within the scheme established in the opening page. The colour of the sea is juxtaposed with the mother's and brother's hair and encroaches ominously on their physical space as they relax and play. Though the opening pages depict a beautiful family story, there is already a sense of foreboding that is further established by the narrative: 'I lived with my family in a city close to the sea. Every summer we used to spend many weekends at the beach. But we never go there anymore, because, last year, our lives changed forever'.

The narrator tells us that 'the war began'. The war is not named. Black shapes that look like hands creep over the right-hand-side of the page. Like a lapping ocean that destroys the children's hard-built sandcastles at the end of the day, the large hands, like tentacles, scatter the castles (into 'chaos'), symbolically representing the destruction of the city that the family live in. Ambiguity is important here – is the dangerous force human? Is it a monster?

In an interview, Sanna explains that she intended the hands to represent 'the world' and the way it takes things away from people. Children's stories often work at the intersection of the real and fantastical, and Sanna's narrative shows how life narrative for children can incorporate different stylistic and literary traditions to construct a biographical story. The ambiguity (over who or what is responsible for the traumatic event) is important in communicating the story to the child reader. The child reader might interpret the scene as real and human inflicted (if they are ready to) or as a fairy-tale monster (if they are not).

The family retreats quickly; their shadows chase them. This page is followed by a double black page that is almost blank, except for her father's glasses and some tiny, scattered objects: plants and buildings from the previous page. We learn that 'and one day the war took my father'. Sanna's narrative builds towards representing grief and loss in realistic ways. There is no ambiguity here; the child reader will understand the full implications of this representation.

Is this representation problematic? Such questions relate to both the perceived limits of life narrative and what are acceptable representations in children's literatures. As Beckett (2015) summarizes, many contemporary picture book artists agree that 'it is their duty to tell young children some terrible truths even if this causes horror and distress' (67). And Maria Tatar argues that 'children love fairy tales precisely because they speak the language of pain, suffering, loss, and torture with a candor they often do not encounter in real life' (quoted in Evans, 2015: 67). These images and their ambiguity persist: the child explains that everything has been 'darker' since her father died and her mother 'has become more and more worried'. This (again) is symbolized by the large, tentacle hands which envelope the page and seemingly mock the family hug that they encircle. The family picture to the right reminds us of the family's trauma. Circling back to the question, is this representation problematic? For now, perhaps it is less important for us to make a judgement on this than it is for us to understand Sanna's methodology for representing the real for her perceived dual readership of children and adults.

The remainder of *The Journey* represents the family's passage towards asylum. In a domestic scene where two women are drinking tea, we gain knowledge of a potential escape. It is depicted through a speech bubble from her mother's friend: it shows a mountainous place where buildings remain intact. The town is drawn in whites, creams and greens – in contrast to the darkness of the previous scenes. On the right side of the page we see silhouetted people, with suitcases, running away. The image looks like it belongs in a spy thriller, again reminding us of the myriad genre crossings Sanna wants to engage in *The Journey*. It is important to note the representation of ethnic diversity here: her mother's friend wears a veil where her mother does not (reminding us that though people may live in the same place, they are not all the same).

Over the pages that follow, with more vivid colours, we see the bookish mother (surely a sign of experience and intelligence?), her children subsumed by the large page. Their diminutive stature matches their lack of knowledge, their persistent questions about the place they are going to. The picture to the left of the bookshelf shows the mother and children inside of the books: 'She shows us pictures of strange cities, strange forests and strange animals until she finally sighs, "we will go there and not be frightened anymore"'. Books are a common way in which children acquire knowledge so, this symbolism is important here. Books equal agency for the children. We see the family packing up an unrealistic amount of luggage – signifying what it is like to pack up your whole life (we see their belongings become smaller and smaller the further along they progress in their journey).

These are 'strange animals' to the children in the story, but they are not necessarily strange to the reader. The reader is positioned as knowing and perhaps feels reassured on behalf of the children, that they will be okay in this new location. The mother is a powerful force, and she physically moves her children and their life. Consider the double page in which the children lie in the forest in their mother's arms; her hair envelopes them, offering a safe bed to sleep on. Their arms and legs circle around each other so that it is difficult to tell where one person ends and the other begins.

In the second image, the child cannot see what the reader can. As she says, 'but mother is with us, and she is never scared' we can see the mother crying streams of tears. This is one of the most powerful elements of *The Journey*: the story brings the reader (whether adult or child) into its confidence, as we understand something that the child narrator does not: the mother too is very frightened and sad. This scene also offers recognition of the social nature of children's reading, and the possibility of adults and children engaging in collaborative reading and interpretation, especially when it comes to difficult subject matter. As Arizpe (2015) notes, the majority of recent studies on children's picture books that represent trauma show that children have a way of coping with and interpreting the material within:

> Children not only enjoyed these encounters but were motivated to search for their own answers and reflect on their interpretations, acting with sensitivity and independence ... [The] problems of suitability arise when adults condemn a book before taking the time to read it carefully, to think about it or discuss it with children ... it is adults, not children who have come up with the labels 'controversial' and 'challenging'. (xviii)

It is clear that Sanna, like other authors for children before her, sees the value in communicating this particular story for a child reader. In *The Journey* Sanna has to find ways to communicate cultural difference and traumatic experience to children.[3] Perhaps also, she has to convince adults that it is okay for children to be reading about these subjects, and so the representation of the mother's tears is a good example of how Sanna works towards intergenerational and intercultural empathy. But it is also important here to consider the importance of animals more generally to folk and fairy tales; in these stories animals are often protectors, even heroes. In *The Journey*, the animals are not given mystical powers. But Sanna subverts what we might know as villainous animals. For instance, the fox, often a trickster in fairy tales, is friendly.

The family arrive at the border, in darkness; it is 'an enormous wall and we must climb over it' (is the wall symbolic of another infamous proposed border wall?). The colour shifts starkly now to earthy red, and the 'angry guard' is a very large, red-bearded man. It is significant that he is Anglo-Celtic in appearance, demonstrating who are the usual gatekeepers to save havens. Also, this giant seems reminiscent of the giant in *Jack and the Beanstalk*, a recognizable perpetrator thus linking *The Journey* to more traditional fairy tales. Further in the story, it is a different giant – one with an insect-like appearance, that picks the family up and drops them over the border. In fairy tales, insects (such as ants) are often symbolic of industrious endeavours, but also of self-interest. Here, the giant ant-like insect hints at people smugglers.

The family's journey does not end here:

> We have boarded a ferry with so many people!
> There is not much space and it rains every day.

But we tell each other stories. Tales of terrible and dangerous monsters that hide beneath our boat ready to gobble us up if the boat capsizes!

The boat rocks and rocks as the waves grow bigger and bigger. It feels like the sea will never end. We tell each other new stories. Stories about the land we are heading to, where the big green forests are filled with kind fairies than dance and give us magic spells to end the war.

The travellers console themselves with folk stories – reminding the reader of stories' (particularly life stories') capacity to heal? *The Journey* does not conclude with a promise of safety or asylum, but a hope, 'I hope, one day, like these birds, we will find a new home. A home where we can be safe and begin our story again'. Sanna's choice, to focus on 'the journey', allows her to tap into some of the traditional themes of children's stories: family relationships, friendship, adventures, courage, the heroic quest, justice and injustice, and also to bring these themes into the potent, real-world context of displaced persons

## *My Beautiful Birds*

Canadian Suzanne Del Rizzo was an award-winning illustrator before *My Beautiful Birds* marked her debut as author–illustrator in 2017. Del Rizzo's style, in her illustrations, is polymer clay and acrylic paint, which creates a strong child-like-creations aesthetic which is important to how the narration develops. Del Rizzo explains that 'my art director, Rebecca Bender also suggested I used a limited colour palette, which I think worked very well' (Gayleen Rabakukk, 2017). These stylistic choices each contribute to the beauty of Del Rizzo's complex art which masquerades as children's art.

In an interview, Del Rizzo explores her motivation for writing *My Beautiful Birds*. Del Rizzo echoes others (writers, teachers, parents) who speak of the importance of finding age-appropriate ways for introducing children to difficult subject matter. It is not enough to simply shield children from this knowledge. They may encounter child asylum-seekers and refugees at school or in activities such as sports. Children might be exposed to representations of displacement in the media. We want children to respond with empathy. Del Rizzo explains that the Syrian Civil War was in its sixth year. Her school-aged children had questions from things they had seen on the news. Del

Rizzo searched for child-friendly information; she wanted to make sure her kids would be left feeling 'empathetic and reflective yet informed' (Rabakukk, 2017). Del Rizzo states,

> I came across some good articles and information including a short article featuring a young boy who was raising a variety of wild birds in the Za'atari refugee camp. I thought to myself how important it was to have picture books that act as windows into the world, providing a safe opportunity for children to learn about other children's circumstances and issues. (Rabakukk, 2017)

Del Rizzo's rationale here is persuasive and matches what theorists of children's literature cited earlier in this chapter who have asserted the potential of picture books to provide a safe space for children to encounter difficult subject matter for the first time. In my close reading of *My Beautiful Birds*, as with *The Journey*, I want to look at the literary and visual strategies Del Rizzo employs to share a trauma story with young readers. But more context is needed first.

The choice of non-fiction, and more particularly, biography, is important here. As with Sanna in *The Journey*, Del Rizzo chooses to draw on real-life people and their stories in writing *My Beautiful Birds*. As I have argued throughout this project, child readers, like adult readers, have a notably different relationship with fiction and non-fiction. Non-fiction for children promises something different to fiction. It establishes a pact between author and reader. The author posits that the story is 'true' or based on real-life events and people. The reader agrees to approach the text according to the rules of non-fiction, for instance, believing that the people depicted are real and that the events happened. But children, like adults reading non-fiction, have the critical capacity to understand that 'true' stories can never be 100 per cent truth. Child readers understand that authors creatively (re)construct stories to make them accessible and enjoyable for a reader.

So, Del Rizzo's choice of genre: a biography 'based on a true story', is important here. There is significant cultural cache in non-fiction, as I have hopefully established throughout this study so far. Del Rizzo, in seeking to write an important, timely and needed book for children, likely understands this cache. As with *The Journey*, but perhaps more pressingly so, there is a larger question of ethics here. Is it acceptable for an author to draw on documents from life (in this instance, an online magazine article) to construct a story without the permission of the biographical subject? As with most ethical discussions around life narrative construction, the key issue is potential benefit versus harm. Del Rizzo benefits from telling the story because she has a published, award-winning book. It is not clear whether the original author benefits at all. However, it is possible that Del Rizzo's story has myriad potential benefits beyond the author or subject, for example, benefits for readers who learn about the Syrian Civil War and its impact upon asylum-seekers including children. As Del Rizzo argues, 'I hope my story helps to encourage readers to be thoughtful and kind, to look past the external difference of clothing and so forth, and remember that inside kids are kids; to reach out and help refugee newcomers feel welcome and make new friends' (Rabakukk, 2017).

Del Rizzo explains why she wanted to tell the story of Sami to other children:

> *My Beautiful Birds* was inspired by that little boy, his struggle with displacement and the universality I think all children have with their affinity to animals.
>
> Displacement is something many children face, from forest fire evacuation, to moving house, to fleeing war, and the struggles they encounter to reacclimate can be very hard.
>
> Likewise, all children, regardless of nationality, gender, or religion they all love to play, learn and make new friends. It is my hope that these commonalities presented in *My Beautiful Birds* resonate with all children.
> (Rabakukk, 2017)

Del Rizzo's words here sum up the responsibilities and risks that come with writing biography for children. Her mandate is to discover how to construct a trauma story for a child readership. She must do so in a way that encourages the child reader to develop empathy for the subject, a displaced child, but does not have a negative emotional impact upon the child reader or else their parents or carers will probably not allow them to read it (teachers and librarians will not recommend it and so forth). It is a tricky balance. Arguably the biggest challenge for Del Rizzo, as evidenced by her comment above, is the risk of not universalizing the child subject in reductive ways that deny the child's diversity and the particular traumas they are experiencing, because 'moving house' is not the same as losing your home in a violent war.

But we must also acknowledge that love it or hate it, today's children have grown up with the concept of 'relatability'. We should respect their critical capacities to use this concept as a helpful starting point for deeper analyses. As Del Rizzo argues,

> I knew I wanted to explore and relate a child's innate strength, hope and resilience, which I believe all children possess, even during hardships such as displacement.
>
> Children are smart and very inquisitive about what is going on in the world; they are our leaders and humanitarians of tomorrow. I hope this book may act as a gentle yet realistic introduction to the Syrian refugee crisis but also may serve to remind us all that even during our hardest times, there is always hope and beauty to be found. (Kalb, 2017)

She is aware that child readers need an entry point when reading about trauma. In an interview, Del Rizzo explains,

> My publishing team at Pajama Press and I were very deliberate in our decisions about how to depict the scarier moments, in the book. For example, in the pages depicting Sami escaping during the bombing of his village, we decided to put the village and plumes of smoke and fire in the background to give some visual separation from these images to ensure even the most sensitive of readers would feel safe and secure.
>
> Artistically, because many aspects of the book speak to the main character's connection with the sky and his birds, I chose to illustrate in a more painterly style to evoke this emotional connection on a subconscious level. (Rabakukk, 2017)

In *My Beautiful Birds*, Del Rizzo uses symbolism (animals, play) to create these moments for her child reader.

In *My Beautiful Birds*, Del Rizzo finds an aesthetic for representing trauma to children, and as argued above, it involves constructing points of connection for the child reader. For instance, the book's back and front inside covers are filled with children's paintings: handprints, houses, love hearts, people, creatures, flowers and rainbows, all in bright colours. We do not know until the end of the story that these pictures recall those drawn by Sami and his new friend, and it emphasizes happiness and normality replacing feelings of anxiety and alienation. This childish style is immediately contrasted with Del

Rizzo's sophisticated 'original art created with polymer clay and acrylic', which leaps from the opening page, appearing three-dimensional. Del Rizzo uses few colours to highlight the clothing of characters, objects and the limited greenery in the characters' spaces. However, the effect of the children's drawings is not to highlight the sophistication of Del Rizzo's own work against the children's, quite the opposite. The goal is inclusion; the children's artwork is worthy enough for inclusion in this book for children; it forms part of the narrative as it links Sami's childhood to those of the children whose visual narratives adorn the inside covers. These drawings are a point of reassurance that the story within this book is one that children will understand and develop empathy for.

*My Beautiful Birds* is narrated in the first person by a young boy Sami who is recognizable for the blue hoodie he wears throughout the story. It is one of only three times the colour blue appears in the book, so Sami is always centred in the visual narration.[4] One the book's first double page (Figure 5.1), Sami's hand is being held as he and his family and community form a single line walking up a steep hill. The babies and children in this image are each protected by adult figures, held close. There is little vegetation, save trees scattered here and there. It is rough, rocky ground. This unforgiving terrain simply symbolizes the immense difficulties faced by Sami and his family as

**Figure 5.1** From *My Beautiful Birds*. Courtesy of Pajama Press, 2017.

they flee their city in search of refuge. In the background, far in the distance, in the top left corner of the page, we see a city engulfed in flames. 'The ground rumbles', the book's opening explains. We see that they had to evacuate quickly, this is evident as Sami wears slippers and carries a tiny backpack. Del Rizzo explains, 'I wanted to let my illustrations do some of the "heavy-lifting" when it came to showing the more distressing imagery such as emotional moments and the city's bombing' (Kalb, 2017).

The book's focus is introduced immediately as Sami explains, 'father squeezes my hand. "It will be okay, Sami. Your birds escaped too", he repeats'. The reader learns that Sami has had to leave behind his pigeons when his family evacuated their home. He wonders what has become of them, but his father tells him that they too have escaped, and Sami believes in the strength of his birds.

On the book's fifth page the style shifts from double-and-full-page images to three parallel images on the page, to represent the time the journey takes. It is day, it is night, 'I count footsteps, never wanting to look up again'. The gutter shows footsteps going under and through each of the panels. The images depict people initially in the foreground, then a little further away, then far in the background of the picture. Children reading this page will gain a sense of how long and far this family has walked to find safety. In the page that follows, we see the family's arrival at a camp, characterized by large tents with washing hanging from the tent poles. Sami explains, 'We made it. We are safe'.

The birds are a potent symbol in the book as Sami reflects on the life he has left behind. Pages 9 and 10 juxtapose Sami in the present, blue hoodie, hand over face with one eye closed and his hood up, with Sami in the past: red jumper, brown curly hair visible, face happy as he feeds his beautiful birds by hand. Sami tells the reader, 'I wish it were like it used to be, just me and my pigeons on our rooftop with the wind and boundless sky. Happy. Free'. Sami's birds are symbolic of the happiness and freedom that he has lost, his connection with his previous life, his experience of joy. The book represents Sami's feelings of alienation and loneliness in his new world. He cannot connect with activities that he previously loved (playing with his cousins, soccer and painting). As he tries to paint his birds, he smears the page with black paint and tears his painting up. The colour contrast here is stark and reveals Sami's bleak feelings in his new world. He has no hope.

He runs outside and has an epiphany. The sky is beautiful bright with intense yellow light with purple lines. The ground is illuminated in an extreme and powerful violet. Sami explains, 'at the top of a dune, I stop in my tracks. "Is this my sky from home?"' The shared sky is a symbol of the global community – a point of connection and optimism for Sami. He asks the sky to look over his bird and keep them safe. He sees a vision of his birds in the yellow and purple of the clouds. From here, he not only dreams of his birds but encounters new birds to watch over: a canary, a dove, a rose finch and a pigeon. Like feathered brushes they paint the sky with promise and hope of peace'. He imagines that they are 'far from home too' and offers them protection. There is a strong message here, of our capacity to have empathy and to look after those more vulnerable than us, regardless of how vulnerable we are. And Sami's own displacement, and his experience with the birds prompts him to recognize this fear in another child, a young girl entering the camp, 'a shy smile warms my cheeks as I move quietly close and gently hold out my hand'.

## Conclusion

In an age of 'fake news' and mass information, children face considerable challenges when it comes to negotiating facts and competing representations of the world. Research in early-childhood education has found that non-fiction picture books play a key role in supporting children's literacy skills and civic education (Mantzicopoulos and Patrick 2011). Authors and illustrators like Del Rizzo and Sanna believe in the power of picture books to engage children with non-fictional stories that take up some of the most pressing global issues of our time. In *The Journey* and *My Beautiful Birds*, Sanna and Del Rizzo find a positive and productive way 'in' to difficult cultural terrain: how to represent a story of traumatic cultural displacement to a child reader and, in association, to adult readers who might be sceptical of the value of children reading such stories. They authors show that through a productive fusion of genres and styles, authors and illustrators might tell a collective biographical story such as this. The method allows these two books to find a truth that is widely recognizable without being culturally or politically reductive.

As we well know by now, life narrative texts commonly seek to blur the boundaries between fiction and non-fiction – or extend the means for representing reality. Sanna and Del Rizzo each find innovative ways to think through and represent lived experience. Communal biography isn't a new thing – many auto/biographical traditions work this way. But Sanna's and Del Rizzo's multi-generic, visual/verbal methods offer something genuinely exciting for life-narrative scholars, like me, who want to consider how life-narrative genres might become meaningful to child readers.

I wanted to conclude this chapter by going back to the issues raised at the beginning of this paper, by the *Goodreads* review. The reviewer proposed that (1) *The Journey* might be too scary for child readers – and (2) it isn't clear which parts are 'real'. Maybe the first point is more difficult to address than the second one. Such judgements require context; but I expect that in this chapter I have made my position clear on why I think child readers might benefit from reading books like *The Journey* and *My Beautiful Birds*. If we want to face up to global issues directly affecting children – to move towards more sustainable, equitable cultural and political futures, it makes sense that life narrative, as a wider form, should engage child readers.

In Chapter 6, and the two chapters that follow, the focus is on children as creators of biographical texts. These chapters seek to hear children's direct voices and read their narrations in light of issues affecting children which have been discussed in this book. Chapter 6 extends the discussion of child asylum-seekers begun in this chapter to consider children's testimony of displacement and detention as auto/biography. In considering the inevitable blurred boundaries between different life narrative modes (in this instance, testimony, autobiography, biography) Chapter 6 looks at children's drawings from the Australian Human Rights Commission (2014) as they function as auto/biographies of asylum-seekers, biographies of a detention centre and biographies of an imagined Australia and Australians.

## Notes

1   UNICEF (2021). Available online: https://data.unicef.org/topic/child-migration-and-displacement/displacement/

2 *The Journey* has won various awards and accolades including Winner of the 2017 Ezra Jack Keats New Author Honor and New Illustrator Honor Awards!
Selected as an ALSC Notable Children's Book of 2017
Selected for the 2017 USBBY Outstanding International Books List
Included in CCBC Choices 2017
A *The New York Times*'s Notable Children's Book of 2016
A *The Wall Street Journal*'s Best Children's Books of 2016
A *Publisher's Weekly*'s Best Books of 2016
A *Kirkus Reviews*'s Best Picture Books of 2016
A *School Library Journal*'s Best Picture Books of 2016
A *The Guardian*'s Best Children's Books of 2016
A New York Public Library's Best Books for Kids 2016
An All the Wonders' Best Picture Books of 2016
A Let's Talk Picture Books' Best Picture Books of 2016
A Chickadee Lit's Picture Books to Celebrate Kindness
Available online:
https://www.penguinrandomhouse.com/books/585963/the-journey-by-francesca-sanna/9781909263994/
3 As previously flagged, *The Journey* aims to raise awareness by encouraging conversations in home and educational settings between children and adults. Amnesty's promotion of the book, even has a guided reading booklet, help to support children's reading of *The Journey* and address any issues that might arise from their reading it.
4 The other is in the dove and the pigeon.

6

# 'Biography of a Detention Centre': Children's drawings as auto/biographical testimony

'Drawing by a fourteen-year-old, made in the Darwin Detention Centre in 2014' (see https://www.flickr.com/photos/23930202@N06/albums/721576 45938124048) was solicited as part of *The Forgotten Children Report: National Inquiry into Children in Immigration Detention* in 2014.[1] The drawing had a role to play in the national inquiry: as evidence of experience, as testimony and as a confrontation to those who read the report. As I discuss this drawing now, in this book, as an example of children's auto/biographical creativity, I am bringing this drawing into a new context, where we might think about the cultural and political spaces that children's first-person narratives occupy, particularly when it comes to advocacy.

For us, here considering this image, seven (or more) years on, an image like this will provoke many questions – perhaps mostly relating to how best to respond and to interpret it. As discussed in the previous chapter, there is a sense that children should be reading about the experiences of other children such as refugees and those seeking asylum. Children's picture books have become a global site for the circulation of this testimony. However, other discourses have also been crucial in this space. Children's own testimony of their refugee- and asylum-seeker status is vital in the wider circulation and reception of knowledge of the asylum-seeker or refugee experience, and this has been particularly true in the Australian context. Various genres and discourses, from charitable organizations through to mainstream media, government and literary publications, have published children's life narratives of displacement. The circulation of child asylum-seekers within cultural texts is usually to bring attention to asylum-seeker rights more generally, but also increasingly, to showcase children's agency as they stake a claim in debates about their lives. This chapter marks a shift in this book: from thinking about children as readers of and respondents to non-fiction, to our witnessing children as authors and illustrators in non-fictional projects. Starting with a significant twenty-first-century archive existing within the Australian national context, this discussion moves (in Chapters 7 and 8) to local, topical examples of small archives of children's life narratives assembled during this project. What these latter three chapters have in common is evidence of how children's engagement in life narration, and more particularly, biography, shows their desire and ability to engage with these life-narrative practices.

In this chapter, I consider a testimonial project that has sought justice for child asylum-seekers in Australia: *The Forgotten Children Report*, which contains thirteen drawings by detained asylum-seekers aged between four and seventeen. I consider how we might juxtapose these child-authored, self and life narratives with the biographies for children considered in the previous chapters. Though children's literature has become an important site for the exploration of non-fiction stories relevant to and about children's lives, in what cultural spaces and public discourses do children get to author non-fictional stories? When are children invited to speak publicly about their lives? In what forms do we see children's auto/biographical practice? This, broadly, will be the focus of the next three chapters of this book.

As I bring these testimonial images drawn by child asylum-seekers into this chapter and book project, more generally, I am defining and locating them *as biography*. In the previous chapter I argued that texts like these, as in the children's picture books, cross various genres. At once, we are looking at children's drawings, trauma testimony, legal testimony, historical documents, autobiography, biographical representations of family members, but also, importantly, as observations about place and space – in this instance, detention centres. In using a broad definition of auto/biography as an umbrella term (as discussed in the introduction of this book), this chapter looks at the ways that the drawings become multidimensional, relational life narratives of detained people and the institutions that hold them.

These drawings and their status as auto/biographical testimony reveals a cultural shift in the public sphere representation of the traumatized, asylum-seeker child in the Australian context in the 2000s. These representations ask us to think differently about child asylum-seekers. Being located in National

Inquiry, the child authors are afforded the opportunity to participate in political discussions about their lives. Their perspectives are significant, their voices powerful. They are less victims now than agents of political change. I conclude my discussion by briefly exploring ethical methods for reading, witnessing and analysing children's life narratives of this kind. It is important to note that adult, second-person witnesses are likely the intended addressees of the children's drawings but, this is not to say that the children have not anticipated readers of different ages as they draw and narrate their testimony.

## Asylum-seeking, childhood and the Australian context

Australia's shameful history of detaining child asylum-seekers dates back to the 1990s and reached its peak in 2012. In 2006, I researched representations of asylum-seeker children within activist contexts and projects of the early 2000s. This was a time when the child figure, particularly photographic images of individual children, had 'become central to the debates surrounding asylum seeking in Australia:[2] from news and documentary footage of innocent children being held in detention centres, to the ambiguous images of "children overboard"' (Douglas, 2006: 39). In my study of these life-narrative texts – which included anthologies, letter-writing projects, documentary and testimonies from the ChilOut organization, I found that (perhaps predictably) it was children's stories and images that were being foregrounded in these campaigns (Douglas, 2006: 39). At this time, the figure of the child and children's life narrative had become so 'emblematic in the asylum-seeker cause in Australia' it was rare for any other type of narrative to emerge (Douglas, 2006: 41).[3]

The centrality of the child, and indeed the child photograph in these debates and campaigns, was not so surprising, as Lindsay O'Dell (2008) reminds us:

> the notion that children need to be saved from harm and the concerns of the adult world is strongly embedded in (modern) Western ideology and practices.
>
> 'Lost children', child saving and 'stolen childhood' are common imagery and icons in liberal western imagery. (385)

Such child-saving practices have always focused on certain children more than others – for instance, children from low socio-economic backgrounds, or immigrant children (O'Dell, 2008: 385). These photographic images of child asylum-seekers would be interpreted within the 'symbolic system' in which they occurred, amid a range of existing photographic images of children such as missing person photographs, advertisements for children's charities, or for children's products' (Douglas, 2006: 49).

But, since my 2006 study, we are seeing fewer photographs of child asylum-seekers in advocacy projects. There is an obvious move away from representations of children that frame them as passive victims of trauma. In the Australian asylum-seeker context, we are listening to the first-person testimonies of children more and more, and drawings are important in this space for the ways in which they bypass language barriers. This shift is in line with more general socio-cultural tendences to listen to children. As I have discussed elsewhere, in my work on youth activists such as Bana Al Abed, Isadora Faber, Emma Gonzalez, Malala Yousafzai, children and youth are prominent in activist spaces (Cardell and Douglas, 2020b, 2020; Douglas, 2017; Douglas and Poletti, 2016), these young activists have provoked genuine cultural change as their voices and stories have circulated across various media and powerfully into the public domain. Auto/biographical testimony has become a means for individualizing children's experiences where they have too often been universalized and reduced to stereotypical notions of innocence and inexperience.

## *The Forgotten Children* (2014) and the cultural role of children's drawings

This 324-page report released in 2014 was presented by Gillian Trigg, the President of the Australian Human Rights Commission, and offers detailed information about the children in detention and their families, for instance their ages, how they came to be in detention, an assessment of their well-being and so much more. Ten years prior there had been another National Inquiry into Children in Immigration and Detention. At face value, these two reports look quite similar, but there is one very notable difference: the 2014 report includes testimonial texts by children in the form of drawings. So, what happened between 2004 and 2014 to prompt the inclusion of child-authored life-narrative texts in this second report?

Globally, there's a stronger sense now, more than ever, that children have the right to tell stories about their lives and to have the stories heard and taken seriously. This is a guiding principle of the Convention on the Rights of the Child, to which Australia is party. Article 12(1) of the Convention provides that: 'States Parties shall assure to the child who is capable of forming his or her own views the right to express those views freely in all matters affecting the child, the views of the child being given due weight in accordance with the age and maturity of the child'. There's also a deepening sense, internationally, of the importance of children's first-person life narratives. Children and youth engage prolifically in life-narrative practices – whether through drawings and recounts at school, engaging in oral storytelling with friends and family, taking photographs, making media or engaging in social media (and I will return to some of these practices in Chapters 7 and 8).

Children's drawings have become a significant feature of human-rights advocacy – for instance Eva Maagerø's and Tone Sund's (2016) research compares the drawings of Norwegian and Palestinian children, and Serap Özer and colleagues conducted research with Turkish and Syrian children where they asked them to make drawings of war and peace. I am also thinking of Australian artist Ben Quilty's (2018) work with Syrian children that is showcased in the book *Home: Drawings by Syrian Children*. Such projects remind us that new social and political contexts 'generate new forms of visual-verbal witness' (Hilary Chute, 2016: 5).

Here's what we know about the method for acquiring the drawings for *The Forgotten Children Report* (2014), and I quote from the report:

> As part of the National Inquiry … staff visited immigration detention facilities to speak to children … During these visits, staff gave the children paper and textas and asked them to draw something about their life. These drawings are the children's submissions to the inquiry. Staff asked the children for their permission to publish their pictures.

The report aimed to explore the effects of detention on the 'health, wellbeing and development of children', the 'Inquiry assessed the impact of detention on children currently detained as well as seeking the views of people who were previously detained' (*The Forgotten Children Report*, 2014: 41). The interviews were supported by 'independent paediatric and/or child mental health specialists' (*Forgotten Children Report*, 2014: 43). The report considered the experiences of 1,068 children (*Forgotten Children Report*, 2014: 51). The findings, generally, were that detention was a very negative experience; 'While they feel safe from physical harms they escaped in their home countries, they describe detention as "prison-like", "depressing", and "crazy-making"' (*Forgotten Children Report*, 2014: 51).

When children's narratives are solicited, there is always mediation which needs to be considered. But, I argue, being overtly attentive to mediation or the possibility of manipulation can reduce the potency of children's testimony. So, whilst a critical eye is important, unless we have evidence to the contrary, we should be reading these texts as first-person testimonies of trauma.

As Anna Poletti and I have found, children's life narrative contributes to children's agency and cultural participation, and their capacity to have social and political influence over issues that affect their lives (Douglas and Poletti, 2016). Where language is a barrier, drawings can function as testimony. As Maagerø and Sunde (2016) have found, drawing is one of the first meaning-making systems children learn. It is an early means for self-expression and for children to show their ideas, thoughts and emotions about their lives and the world. (Because drawings are commonly shared with friends and family; parents often display these drawings on their fridge or workspace).

Children's drawings have become important tools in various cultural spaces including therapeutic contexts for instance, art therapy (Cumming and Visser, 2019; Farley and Tarc, 2014) in paediatric health and in legal contexts. For instance, in Darfur, children's drawings have been used as legal testimony: 'In 2007, children's images entered into a legal forum when the nongovernmental (NGO) Waging Peace submitted five hundred drawings to the International Criminal Court at The Hague. For the first time in history, children's drawings were recognized as evidence in international law' (Farley and Tarc, 2014: 836). Margaret Mayhew notes that, 'paediatric psychology has a long history of encouraging children to generate drawings of traumatic events, and children's drawing have also been used in legal cases' (n.p.). Caroline Lenette, in her discussion of art therapy as a method for working with children, argues that

> art therapy as a form of communication through drawings has the potential to effectively convey children's experiences, and is mainly used with children who have experienced trauma and consequently suffer from mental illnesses or social, emotional, learning, and behavioural difficulties. (2017: 6)

In their research, Laura V. Loumeau-May and colleagues (2014) explored how art therapy was effective as an intervention into children's experiences of mass terrorism in violence. They document how art therapy has been used in the US schools to work with children experiencing psychological distress, for instance, after being exposed to traumatic media coverage, such as of school shootings (Loumeau-May et al., 2014: 97). Farley and Tarc (2014) present different human-rights projects that demonstrate the positive impact of children's drawings. Julie Gross and Harlene Hayne (1998) argue that when it comes to gathering testimonial evidence from children and encouraging them to share their experiences, drawing can make a useful intervention when interviewing might be too confronting. Drawing can be conducive to the retrieval of memories, for organizing memories into a narrative, to gain mastery over an experience, or to gain distance from it (Cardell and Douglas, 2020). As Wendy Sue Looman (2006) contends, drawing can 'help children externalise complex feelings … [and] gain symbolic control over events that are confusing and frightening' (158). It is a means by which a respondent or second-person witness can come to understand children's experiences of trauma. Looman (2006), however, adds a crucial caveat to her argument, 'Children should be asked to provide an explanation for their drawings when possible, because it acknowledges the importance of their perspectives and the personal meaning that is expressed in the drawing' (165).

Scholars have argued that we might do more with children's drawings as meaningful cultural texts. Guy Austin (2007) suggests that, 'children's drawings are often conceptualized as belonging to the realm of therapy rather than constituting objects of cultural study within trauma theory'; Richard Jolley (2010) agrees that that children's drawings have not been given the interdisciplinary academic attention they deserve. So, there's space for life-narrative scholars to make an interdisciplinary intervention here in giving more attention to children's drawings *as* life narrative.

In previous research Kylie Cardell and I considered closely the work of Ben Quilty who solicited drawings from Syrian asylum-seeker children to publish in a book. As we can see by the research cited above, Quilty is not the only public figure to have worked with artwork by displaced children in order to document their experience and enable their voices to be heard, or as therapy. These projects recognize that in the twentieth and twenty-first centuries, large numbers of children have been displaced across the globe. Mary Tomsic (2019) reminds us that 'the United Nations High Commission for Refugees (UNHCR) reported at the end of 2016, there were 65.6 million forcibly displaced people world-wide and fifty-one per cent of those were under eighteen years of age' (138–9). As Tomsic (2019: 139) argues, this has brought greater attention to the particular experiences of children.

Our findings, in studying Quilty's project, was that the children's drawings ultimately worked not only as powerful testimonial narratives, but also as important works of art. Quilty, famous and charismatic as he is, had to work hard to remove himself and his intentions from view. In *Home*, Quilty sees his role as bringing these child-authored texts into view which might not otherwise be seen. As Johanna Einarsdottir, Sue Dockett and Bob Perry (2009) note, children are used to having their drawing facilitated and influenced by parents, teachers and peers (219). And through this mediation, value is placed on children's drawings. Though this mediation is now without problems, *Home* adds a new layer of understanding to the ways that such projects can promote children as 'full historical subjects in their own right' (Tomsic, 2019: 141). We argued that projects like *Home* (Quilty, 2018)

> advance child-centred art, life narrative and research … [and] our reading has looked to ways that these child-authored texts construct art with facets, themes and qualities not necessarily anticipated in the text's curation and construction … the child-centred and child-driven contexts that emerge from within the narratives become crucial to how we can read these narrative and are essential to what good they might do in relation to the realities of trauma and displacement, of war and terror, that these children are also embedded within. When the children present their interior lives, prior to the war, they show us scenes that we could otherwise never see. They reveal

information about their personal lives that are necessarily embedded within the larger political and traumatic events and contexts affecting their lives, they do the work of life writing. (500)

Tomsic (2019) reminds us that although drawings 'cannot provide transparent, direct access to children's voices', they do hold considerable 'evocative power' (138). Considered within their contexts (for instance, social institutions), we can draw meaning from them, when carefully read (Tomsic, 2019: 138). That drawings by children are interspersed throughout *The Forgotten Children Report* sends a clear message of their importance and asserts the value of this type of first-person testimony in legal and human-rights discourse more generally. The drawings situate these 'forgotten' narratives into the official discourse that has come to narrate children's experiences for them. Though I am not able to reproduce the images here, I will speak to them (in different levels of detail), observe some important themes and offer interpretations in light of what we know about children's drawings as trauma testimony. And I am mindful, as Tomsic (2019) argues, that there are limitations on what I can 'possibly know about the children's intentions in creating them' (142).

These testimonials are given (always anonymous) catalogue-style references offering them status as curated art: for instance, 'Drawing By Primary School Aged Child, Darwin Detention Centre, 2014' ('Drawings by Children in Immigration Detention'). The representation of life in detention (throughout the drawings) is often symbolized by fences, barbed wire or cells that engulf the child figure. This particular image is both autobiographical (of the young illustrator) and biographical in that it represents their image in context, within the detention centre that is represented simply as bars. This easy symbolism becomes a powerful representation. The accompanying text from a different narrator, 'Unaccompanied 17-year-old' states: 'My hope finished now. I don't have any hope. I feel I will die in detention' acts as written trauma testimony to affirm the image. The detention centre becomes personified as potential murderer of the children. The lack of complex details in this text and image sets up a simple victim–perpetrator binary, reminiscent of what we might see in children's fairy tales, and we might also compare this to images in Sanna's *The Journey* which attempts to show readers recognizable victims (who are also heroes) and villains. No nuance is offered or required when considering the context of the image, to consider the impact of detention on children (*Forgotten Children Report*, 2014: 41). The representation conveys an experience which is not to be doubted.

Tears are also a common representation in these drawings, as in this image and also 'Drawing By a Primary School Aged Child, Christmas Island, 2014' ('Drawings by Children in Immigration Detention') and 'Drawing by 7-Year-Old Girl in Detention, 2014' ('Drawings by Children in Immigration Detention'). Tears are a clearly recognizable symbol; and the tears become the focal point of the images (the self is a simple drawing or stick figure; so again, the self is not the focal point of the image, but what the child is doing). Crying is something children explore the meaning of with their parents and other adult figures. When children cry, it is a cry for recognition, for empathy and understanding. Like the previous image, the detention centre is central to the drawing and thus the representation of the child's experience. The barbed wire encloses the child, and it is just child and barbed wire that are represented in the picture. This style and theme are also present in 'Drawing By a Preschool Age Girl, Detained 420 Days, Christmas Island, 2014' ('Drawings by Children in Immigration Detention') and 'Drawing by 16-Year-Old Boy, Christmas Island, 2014' – show just children behind the wire. These are the only representations that we need to see to understand the child's experiences.

In 'Drawing By Primary School Aged Child, Christmas Island, 2014' ('Drawings by Children in Immigration Detention') the focal point is again the sad face of the child. The drawing represents a child with hands wide, as if wanting to be embraced but is alone on the page. This image is accompanied by text written by a different child to the one who drew the picture: 'Unaccompanied Child, Nauru Regional Processing Centre' ('Drawings by Children in Immigration Detention') who writes,

> My country and my religion is target for Taliban. There were many bomb blasts and always big wars and terrible attacks. Shia people have arms, legs, noses hacked off, necks slashed, plus there is a rocket fire and missiles. This is because I am Shia. All this means no one is safe and now because I escaped I am in detention. ('Drawings by Children in Immigration Detention')

The juxtaposition of the image and text is important here. These are the testimonies of two different children, but united by trauma and loss, and despite this, detention. There is a strong sense of alienation within both narratives. The reader/witness is invited into these children's imaginary embrace. Similarly, 'Drawing By Child, Christmas Island, 2014' ('Drawings by Children in Immigration Detention'), depicts a child with a sad face and tears (104). The child's arms are outstretched similarly to those discussed above. But what is most fascinating about this image is that the child has drawn another child next to the first. This second child's face is not visible. It either has its back turned, or the child's face has been coloured in black. It is not clear if this is the same child (the child illustrator has drawn themselves twice, representing two different aspects or moods of the self), or whether this is a different child, symbolic of something else to the child illustrator. Whichever, it is obvious that this is not a happy image, it is a representation of a traumatic experience.

Other drawings are very detailed and complex, for instance, 'Drawing By a 14 Year Old, Darwin Detention Centre, 2014' ('Drawings by Children in Immigration Detention'). In their analysis of this image Caroline Lenette et al., (2017) argue that 'the focal point of the illustration is the saddened, young child with her/his face pressed against the fence; due to its salience, this may suggest that this is a personal depiction of the child who drew the picture' (51). I agree that the image creates the impression that it is auto/biographical. It appears experiential and deeply personal on the part of the illustrator.

In this biographical illustration we can see a juxtaposition of detention camp life with a depiction of life on the outside. Where those in detention exist within confined, ordered spaces, imprisoned in barbed wire, those on the outside drive cars, walk dogs, play with their children, seemingly oblivious to the detention centre close by. The detention centre is given a very close reading by this drawing. The rooms are small and numbered, suggesting order and little flexibility or change. The grounds space is also very small but well populated, suggesting little freedom for those within. At a time when most Australians likely knew very little about life in detention, and very few images were in circulation, such drawings become authoritative.

As Lenette et al. (2017) suggest, this representation reflects what the child believes that life on the outside is like for Australian children (51). Those detainees at the fence are highly visible; the child has drawn them out of scale with the rest of the picture, and yet they are still not seen by those passing by. Overall, this is a very powerful image as it explicitly confronts the issue of

Australians being oblivious to those in detention, and how this ignorance is causing significant harm. As in the previous two images discussed, there is a strong sense of loss and alienation affecting children in detention.

'Drawing By Primary School Aged Girl, Christmas Island, 2014' ('Drawings by Children in Immigration Detention') offers a similar juxtaposition of detention life compared with everyday Australian life. In this drawing, the child represents life on Christmas Island and compares it to an imagined Australian mother's and child's life. The child in detention (we might assume this is a self-portrait in line with the report's invitation for children to represent their own experiences) is drawn in black and white. She is behind bars, and she is almost the same size as the cell, suggesting confinement and a sense of claustrophobia. As in many of the images I have looked at in this discussion, this child is crying. In contrast, the Australian mother and child (who are notably blonde and Anglo in appearance) are drawn in colour. They are smiling. The child has a speech bubble, which says 'sinema'; the child in detention imagines a particular life filled with fun activities for the Australian child (including visits to the cinema with her mother). These images work as a powerful statement about injustice, questioning why one child has a better life than another. This plea echoes the Universal Declaration of Human Rights and the Convention of the Rights of the Child which assert basic universal rights for all children regardless of background. The children's drawings and pleas are testimony to Australia's failure to adhere to these conventions.

Some drawings offer direct calls for action, in 'Drawing By a 16-Year-Old Boy, Christmas Island, 2014' ('Drawings by Children in Immigration Detention') we see a self-portrait of a boy behind the wire. Though his pose appears strong and heroic (a bit like Superman), but the caption states 'I am 16, HELP!' which asks us to think differently about this image. Instead of making assumptions about a young man's strength and resilience, this image reminds us that even though some boys might look like men, they are still children under the law. They are inexperienced in the world and vulnerable. That many of these images are drawn by unaccompanied minors is a stark reminder of how many children are displaced from family or are orphaned by war. We know from the National Inquiry that these drawings were part of the interview process, so, that many drawings were a call-to-action is important.

They anticipate a sympathetic second-person witness who might be able to help them.

Similarly, in 'Drawing By a Primary School Aged child, Christmas Island, 2014' ('Drawings by Children in Immigration Detention') we again see a tearful child who has drawn themselves with their head in one hand, the other hand is on their hip. Though it is not clear, it seems the child is positioned in front of a drawing of trees in a forest, a world that they are not part of. The caption below the child says 'waitin'. As in the previous image discussed, the child anticipates an empathetic second-person witness who will see that this child's life is in a state of limbo. 'Waitin' suggests that the child, like 'Drawing by a 14 Year Old, Darwin Detention Centre, 2014' and 'Drawing By Primary School Aged Girl, Christmas Island, 2014' and '(discussed earlier; 'Drawings by Children in Immigration Detention') anticipates that a different, better life is possible in Australia. Similarly, in 'Drawing By a Primary School Aged Child, Christmas Island, 2014' ('Drawings by Children in Immigration Detention') we see a perhaps very recognizable image of a young girl with long hair, standing on what might be a half moon and looking at the sun and clouds. Reminiscent of a fairy tale image, this child imagines a better life. These drawings speak positively to the methods of the inquiry because the children seem to anticipate that their drawings will be seen and draw an anticipated, receptive audience, capable of enacting change.

So, it seems that the child illustrators have knowledge of where these drawings will go – who their audience will be – and, in collaboration with those constructing the report – are able to use this platform to powerful effect. As Margaret Mayhew states, children's drawings are 'accessible and compelling'. Where

> photographs of children are discomforting [ ... perhaps because they seem too real].
>
> By contrast, drawing is deemed as a safe and therapeutic activity for children to engage in, akin to play, and less tainted with the coercive implications of written or oral testimony.
>
> The value of drawings is less as visual evidence of the conditions of child detention, and more as testimony of the emotional response to detention. (2015)

Another risk with photographic representation is, as O'Dell (2008) notes, in representing children as 'permanently damaged victims'. Such representations are reductive and problematic for children's future, particularly if this image is still in circulation as they grow into adulthood (390). Comics theorist Hillary Chute (2016) found, in her early work on drawings, that people often struggle with the idea that drawing, 'and its attendant abstractions' could be a non-fictional genre (2). But, as Chute (2016: 2) reminds us, the visual medium of comics 'calls overt attention to the crafting of histories ... suggests that accuracy is not the opposite of creative invention'. In November 2015, Greens Senator Sarah Hanson-Young was pictured holding a drawing created by a child living in detention. In doing so, she aimed to bring a child's perspective into the parliamentary context, but this act also suggested the importance of such drawings in creating a sense of urgency for the cause (Lenette et al., 2017: 45).

## Conclusion: An ethics of witnessing

As Tomsic (2019) asserts:

> In examining children's expression in drawings, we need to think critically about how children as a category are understood. Symbolically children have currency as direct tellers of apolitical truths. But children are part of culture and children's voices and expression are part of social and political worlds. This is not to diminish the importance and carefully listening to what children (and all people) have to say – but to more fully understand the assumptions that lie behind the everyday use of categories like 'adult' and 'child'. (154)

The inclusion of children's drawings in *The Forgotten Children Report* an example of how children's drawings become life narratives, and how these narratives come to circulate in the public sphere. Where once, human-rights campaigns relied heavily on the static image of an innocent, traumatized child to bring attention to children's experiences of human-rights violations and consciousness-raise for social justice causes, in the 2000s, human-rights campaigners, educators and children's advocates have increasingly sought children's own testimony as the primary means for supporting children's rights. This move away from deploying children's images for symbolic use reflects an increasing awareness of the potential damage such methods might cause. A movement towards the use of other types of testimonial texts, in these instances, children's drawings to illuminate the testimonies of children, demonstrates a growing understanding of the relationship between human rights and personal storytelling, and the importance of hearing children's own voices on global issues that impact their lives.

Though the meanings of children's drawings are not always transparent, where language, age, trauma and context are impediments to communication, drawings reflect a positive step towards communication, participant and agency for children. Drawn life narratives become a means for better understanding children's capacity to articulate their understanding of their own lives. Children's voices become more central to discourses about them. Further, this chapter has explored how these drawings provide insight into the experiences of children, but also offer relational representations. Illustrative representations of their own lives quickly and potently become representations of imagined Australians living superior, more comfortable lives, and significantly telling representations of sites of detention. These biographical representations are powerful because they implicate Australian second-person witnesses as complicit in the experiences of asylum-seekers. Children's drawings function as a robust reminder of the 'slash' in auto/biography – the inevitable intersection between autobiographical and biographical representation – which is particularly present in children's life narrative. This is an important consideration for Chapters 7 and 8 of this project.

As scholars, approaching these texts requires an ethics of reading. As I have argued in previous research, the ethical circulation and reception of children's life narratives is crucial in allowing us to comprehend and value children's perceptions of their own lives and the world around them. Such understanding, of children's perspectives and knowledge, can only enrich our understanding of humanity, cultures and politics more generally, because of children's significant contribution. Life narratives add depth and nuance to wider cultural narratives. As *The Forgotten Children Report* chooses not to foreground children's images, but instead to showcase children's creative, life-narrative texts, the more recent campaigns add complexity to the issues, refusing to reduce the cause to singular representations or truths.

As these social justice campaigns about asylum seeking respond to cultural shifts, so should we as critical respondents and as children's allies. We *have* to look at these drawings. We have to read children's life narratives about asylum seeking and cultural displacement however they reach us, and in the various modes they take. And we have to do so with an open-minded curiosity and generous-reading practices that attend to their potential contribution to life narrative, to culture and to a better world.

The next two chapters move this discussion away from the political public sphere engagements that children might make in their consumption and production of biography, taking this research into the private spheres of family and relational life narrative. Chapter 7 looks at another space in which children write publicly, albeit within intimate publics, about their own lives in relation to the lives of those closest to them. We are quite accustomed to seeing children's biographical writing and drawing, for instance, in fun listicles on popular news sites such as *Buzzfeed* where children's innocent drawings become a source of humour for adult's consumption. Children are not only readers of biographies, but produce them, readily and often, in their everyday lives. Chapter 7 reports the findings of a small study into biographical texts children have made at school of their mothers. What do these texts tell us about how children practise biography? What do they tell us about children and how they construct relationships via biographical practice and representation?

## Notes

1 Unfortunately, I was not able to secure the rights to reproduce the images from the report for reproduction in this chapter. The images are available for viewing at: https://www.flickr.com/photos/23930202@N06/albums/72157645938124048and https://humanrights.gov.au/our-work/asylum-seekers-and-refugees/publications/forgotten-children-national-inquiry-children
2 But I found that further this focus on the child could be contextualized within a historical preoccupation with the figure of the 'lost' child in the Australian context. In his book *The Country of Lost Children: An Australian Anxiety*, Peter Pierce (1999) traces this representation through Australian literature and history,

beginning with 'nineteenth century representations of lost settler children, which typically connect childhood innocence and naivete with an unforgiving landscape' (Douglas, 2006: 44), and continuing through an exploration of Stolen Generations and the 'Orphans of Empire' (the post-Second-World-War-British child migrants to Australia), and the deaths of Azaria Chamberlain and Jaiden Leskie in the 1980s and 1990s respectively. He argues that the lost child is a symbol of socio-cultural guilt in relation to settlement, racism and poverty, but equally, the child figure is emblematic of Australia's future potential.

3  ChilOut (short for 'Children Out of Immigration Detention') was formed in 2001 in response to a Four Corners television special on six-year-old Shayan Badrai who had been detained with his family in Villawood and Woomera detention centres for two years (ChilOut). The organization was central in campaigns in the early 2000s to move children and their families out of detention and into the community for processing, and in political lobbying when a change of government brought a renewal of off-shore processing around 2010. In 2013, the number of children in detention in Australia had reached a record high (ChilOut). ChilOut closed their campaign in late 2018 when all the children were evacuated from Nauru.

End Immigration Detention for Children. (2022). Available online: https://endchilddetention.org/global_network/australia/ (2022)

7

# 'Five Reasons My Mum Is the Best': Children and biographical practice

Popular news sites like *Buzzfeed* commonly offer listicles that showcase children's seemingly hilarious, often inappropriate drawings. '13 Kids Who Did Not Intend for Their Drawings to Be X-Rated' (2018), 'Only a Parent Can Guess What 6/8 of These Kid Drawings Are' (2019); 'These Kids' Drawings of Their Moms Will Make You Laugh and Their Moms Cry' (2018), are just a few examples.[1] These renderings of children's biographical art reveal a perhaps predictable cultural predication to find humour in children's innocent mistakes. But in the context of this book, the proliferation of these drawings reveals much more intriguing knowledge of the myriad contexts in which children produce biography.

Children are not only readers of biographies, but also produce them, readily and often, in their everyday lives. Though it is impossible within the limits of this book to offer a comprehensive survey of the diverse ways in which children make biographical texts, I hope that this section of the book offers a meaningful reflection on some significant examples. This chapter draws on interdisciplinary theories of childhood, for instance, on children's writings and children as creative, social actors to read some biographical texts (indeed, ante-autobiographical texts, to borrow Claire Lynch's 2013 concept) produced by children.

The chapter also reports the findings of a small study of biographical texts children have made at school of and for their mothers. I believe that the presentation of these texts reveals some fascinating trends at work regarding how biographical practice has become embedded in pedagogy. Children are routinely required to draw and/or write about their family members – for instance, as a 'getting-to-know-you' activity at the start of the school or on days like Mothers' or Fathers' Day. In this study, ten parents of primary-school-aged children were asked to share biographical texts produced by their child; seven of these texts are reproduced in photographic form and analysed in this chapter. How were these texts produced (for instance, what were the aims, contexts and prompts?) I argue that these practices reveal something fascinating about how children write about their mothers, and something about children's skills and knowledge of how biographical practice works. I also explore how children and adults interpret these texts and how these interpretations might contribute to our knowledge of biography as a genre.

## Children as (life) writers

As Julia McMaster (2001: 277) argues, 'when a child takes the pen in hand, that child is taking a determined step toward the control of language, of representation, of power. The child ... has a lot to gain by wresting the means of representation from the adults.' It is important to note that children did not start writing biography in the twenty-first century. As Christine Alexander and Julia McMaster (2006) note, children have been engaged in writing for centuries. We just have not always been paying attention. Alexander and McMaster (2006) point to the many famous writers such as Jane Austen and Virginia Woolf who also wrote juvenilia. But these writings only came to attention long after they became famous writers. Peter Cumming (2017) similarly examines juvenilia in asking, why are children's writings often only considered in light of the canonical author the adult becomes? (5) The writings could not have been seen, would not have been noticed as valuable in themselves at the time of their writing. Kimberley Reynolds (2011) observes that '[h]istorically, children have not written what has been published as children's literature because they had little access to the equipment necessary to do so and ... it was generally assumed that they had too little experience of the world or the craft of writing to have anything to say or to say it interestingly' (24). When children did write, their writing was most often heavily mediated, as Clémentine Beauvais (2019) explains, children who write, whether in fiction or in reality, are never left in peace. Child-authored texts released into the public realm have typically been escorted by vast quantities of critical, paratextual and editorial adult additions. Like an army of prying aunts, with a mixture of loving admiration and disbelieving curiosity, adults read over the shoulders of child writers, commenting, analysing, comparing, marvelling about their works. (62)

Beauvais argues that this has ramifications for researchers who may find it difficult to locate the child's voice historically within literature because of these layers of mediation. Mediation happens because the child's voice is not trusted or seen as meaningful or comprehensible. Adult readers and writers made these writings intelligible.

Despite this, children did write, and scholars seeking to find the child's voice in literary history have found many examples of children's desire to tell stories about themselves and their lives. Siân Pooley (2015) in 'Children's Writing and the Popular Press in England 1876–1914' explores children's contribution to provincial newspaper columns in England during the nineteenth and twentieth centuries. Poole explains that the rise of the literate, leisured working class led to an increase in popular, provincial publications, many of which were aimed at children and provided opportunities for children to read and write outside of the classroom. Much of these writings were auto/biographical in nature, including writings about parents and siblings. Poole discusses the impact that the children's socio-economic backgrounds had on their writings. As Poole argues, these writings are important because they allow us to learn about children's contemporaneous experiences of their own lives and relationships with others:

> Young actions and beliefs do not matter solely when later interpreted as having affected the adults that children grew up to be. The young were complex, diverse and changing; we need sources that allow us to begin to understand how boys and girls interpreted themselves when they thought they were children. (Poole, 2015: 75)

Poole explains the pride in which children took in seeing their writing in print (80). However, 'like every historical source, the texts submitted by children were subject to writers' words which exist only as published' (Poole, 2015: 81). As discussed earlier, we know that these texts were likely heavily mediated by editors, so we cannot know which words were the children's own. But in the absence of knowledge on this issue, these texts exist as examples of children's voices and experiences of the time. As I have argued elsewhere, in my research on young life writers/activists such as Bana Al-Abed and Malala Yousafzai, presumptions of adult mediation is not a reason not to listen to young people's narrations, and not a reason to assume that we do not have genuine access to their voices.

In her discussion of the juvenilia of Marcel Proust, Beauvais (2019) suggests, 'By the late nineteenth century, the Western – particularly Anglophone – world was hungry for children's words' (65), however mediated, or perhaps because of this mediation and how it positioned children in relation to adults. For example, Beauvais notes

> it is difficult to overstate the role of the Romantic poets in presenting child figures as inspired interlocutors for adults, and the experiences of childhood as the origin of poetic creation. Children in the late eighteenth and early nineteenth century were seen as holding greater truths, though with insecure grasp (65).

Beauvais cites the example of nineteenth-century Scottish writer Marjory Fleming, 'Pet Marjorie', who started writing in notebooks every day from age six. The childhood writings were published as a 'highly fictionalised retelling' in 1847 by H. B. Farnie. Scottish doctor John Brown published another version in 1863, and writers Lachlan Macbean (1905) and Kayla Wiley (1909) offered further retellings (Beauvais, 2019: 65). But these publications contained very little of Fleming's direct words from her childhood. It was 115 years before Fleming's diaries became available as a complete transcription. Thus, the 'hunger' for children's words was not a genuine engagement with children themselves, their words or their experiences. This desire for children's stories was heavily inflected with adult notions of what children's stories should be. Beauvais (2019) summarizes:

> The story of Marjory Fleming is exemplary of the ways in which a child-authored text can find itself, paradoxically, both unearthed and buried by sprawling, celebratory, invasive adult discourse, layering over, restraining and denying access to the original text of the child while seemingly making it available. (65)

This engagement with children's voices did evolve somewhat towards the end of the nineteenth century in line with changing cultural perceptions of children and childhood. Beauvais explains, 'the notion that children were privileged holders of greater truth had firmly become part of the cultural and literary discourse surrounding childhood, and triggered unprecedented interest in the internal lives and cognitive faculties of children' (66). This prompted the publication of a plethora of apparently child-authored texts during the Victorian and Edwardian eras including 'nine-year-old Daisy Ashford's novel, *The Young Visiters* (1919) and prefaced by J. M. Barrie' (66). As Beauvais argues, adult mediation persisted, as did stereotypes and symbols of children as ingenious, pure and spontaneous (66).

Children's writings were thus largely positioned based on what they offered adults, for instance, satisfying nostalgic desires for their own pasts or idealizing better futures. But what of children's creativity as valuable for children themselves? And how might we read these texts considering their contribution to literary history? Peter Cumming (2017) argues for a broader consideration of children's literature *as literature* worthy of study. He explains that 'in this digital age, children and youth may well have unprecedented opportunity, access, and control in publishing their writing … life writing, zines, and slash fanfiction … an app enabling children to publish their own books' (5). Diane Mavers (2010) concurs in arguing:

> Much of children's everyday text making is apparently unexceptional: a swift drawing dashed off in a few moments, a routine classroom exercise, exchanging messages, copying from the class whiteboard … Ordinariness masks richness and complexity, routine features that pass by largely unnoticed are not at all trivial and commonplace 'errors', even if not overlooked, are replete with meaningfulness. (1)

In the twentieth and twenty-first centuries it has become a staple for children to practise life writing in primary school contexts and also outside. Mothers', Fathers' and Special Persons' days are commonplace at school, as are 'About Me' and family-tree-style assignments to a new school year. In her study of family letter writing in kindergarten, Kathryn Pole notes the potential of such exercises in building intergenerational bonds and building authentic learning experiences for children. Inevitably, much of the letter writing that happens in this context was auto/biographical. Not only do children write what they know on impulse, but they are also encouraged to do so because it is an authentic way of developing literacy skills. Julia Wollman-Bonilla (2000) reports findings from a study of first graders using journals to write home to their families about what they did in school that day. She found that the process enhanced children's abilities to recount and reflect on people and events from school and home, whether recent or from the past.

Biographical texts are commonplace in the teaching plans of primary school educators, especially when it comes to teaching writing skills (Cottrell and Woods, 2018; Dollins, 2016; Koutsoftas, 2018; Meyer, 2010; Tompkins and Jones, 2018; Wollman-Bonilla, 2000). Whether children are asked to write about family members, celebrities or classmates, writing lives is thought to have pedagogical and social value. Depending on the child's age, and their abilities to write auto/biographically which might differ, they will gain different outcomes from life writing activities, for instance, older children might develop a sense of identity, or a different perspective on the world and so forth, from engaging in life narrative practice (Habermas, 2010). Cynthia A. Dollins (2016), researching in the US context, notes an increased commitment to teaching elementary school students to read and write non-fiction. In her research she found that children's creative writing skills, their understanding of what non-fiction writing is and does, progressed significantly by reading and writing in different non-fiction modes.

Biographical writing skills and practice are also seen as valuable in community projects that aim to connect children intergenerationally or intercommunally. For instance, Francis Kaemaek and Beverly Logas (2000) discuss writing workshop exercises between primary school students and senior centre residents. These workshops became a book called *Across Generations* where the children would write biographical profiles on their older writing partners. And Kathleen Olmstead and Bobbie Kabuto (2018), in their study of young children writing narratives, found that writing was a means for children to explore their emotions and social environments; they explain, 'as soon as children put writing tools to material they are in the process of organizing their social worlds and writing their identities' (102). Again, much of this writing was biographical – about parents, grandparents and pets, for instance.

Other research has shown the potential for children's biographical work to promote cultural diversity and inclusivity. For instance, in her discussion of children completing their family tree as a classroom project, Patricia Vreeland (1998) explains, 'as a teacher of such a diverse student population, I wished to construct a classroom language community in which the heritage of my students' primary language communities is respected and built upon' (17). The students conducted interviews with family members and reviewed documents to construct this biographical snapshot of their family members. On a similar note, Tracey L. Flores (2019) presents her findings from a family writing workshop for children in grades three and four and their families. In this project, Flores (2019) aimed to, 'to imagine a family writing workshop that could revitalize and sustain family language and literacy practices within a restrictive state and educational context' (60). The result, in terms of the writings produced, was largely auto/biographical writings. Flores (2019) summarizes, 'Collectively, we worked as writers and storytellers to make sense of our lives and to honor each other's voices and histories while building *confianza* or mutual trust … through the sharing of personal stories' (68). For Flores (2019), the power of sharing life stories lies in their potential to be culturally empowering at a time when dominant cultures aim to erase or homogenize cultural expression in the United States. And I want to add that this is particularly important for children who might find themselves doubly marginalized because of their status as children with limited access to cultural expression.

So, it is clear that children have been engaging in non-fictional modes of writing for as long as they could read and write. The forms of life writing that children have engaged in is highly diverse. However, when educators complete studies on children's life writing in the primary-school age group, it is most often with the aim of assessing their capabilities as writers. As Anthony D Koutsoftas (2018) argues,

> Writing provides children with a means to share what they know about a topic, to express ideas about the world around them, and to make sense of complex phenomena they learn in school. Writing is also an important skill necessary for achieving academic success the elementary school journal during compulsory education, leading to entrance into higher education and gainful employment later in life. (632–3)

But as I have asserted throughout this study, I am less interested in such assessments and more interested in how children produce life-narrative texts with or without structures or templates. There are many potential payoffs beyond children's intellectual capacities in us learning more about how children engage with and create tasks. For instance, what motivates children to write what they do? And because previous chapters have focused on drawings, this chapter focuses exclusively on children's writings to provide a different discussion point on what texts children write and share about their lives. Such 'little archives', or collections of children's writings and drawings, likely exist in domestic storage across the globe. They are what Claire Lynch (2013) refers to as 'ante-autobiography'. Lynch (2013) explains:

> Although only a small proportion of people will compose and publish a full-length autobiography, almost everyone will, inadvertently, produce an archive of the self, made from public records and private documents. Here, such works are seen as providing access to writing both about and by children. (97)

Such texts may provide children an opportunity to speak for themselves, to speak about their own lives in ways that are meaningful for them. Lynch (2013) posits that

> in cultures where childhood is now relentlessly documented, the first portrait obtained in utero, followed by diligent parents writing, photographing, filming, and uploading, young lives are recorded in greater detail than ever before. From the private archives of family photograph albums to the official collation of medical records and census returns, children's lives are perpetually narrated by adults. While we are familiar in the age of new media with older children and teenagers engaging in self-narration through Facebook, Twitter, PostSecret, and so on, younger children's autobiographical impulses are, perhaps understandably, often overlooked. (106)

Studies like the present one, and those cited above, offer attempts to look at children's life writing in supportive, child-centred and responsive ways. My aim in looking at children's writing was to find new frameworks for analysing children's life writing as self-expression and parents' practices as informal curators of their children's art. This is important at a time when we are increasingly understanding the important role that children play in society and cultures as storytellers. Their contribution to knowledge about family life and history is important.

## Method: Biographical texts your child made[2]

I made a post on a Facebook primary school parents' and carers' page advertising my research project. I invited ten parents or carers to share one or two items that their children had written, drawn or made about them. I wrote,

> I am completing a study on the types of biographical texts (writings, drawings, digital projects) that are created by children about parents/carers during school. What sorts of biographical texts do children create? And what makes these texts valuable to parents/carers? What do parents/carers save and why? What meanings do children and parents/carers attach to these texts?

Permission was sought from both the parent/carer and the child to produce the text. I explained,

> I want to urge you to respect your child's privacy during this process. If your child does not want you to share certain items with me (for instance, they are embarrassed because they produced them when they were much younger), please exclude these items and seek their permission for those they consent to you showing me. Please assure your child that their artwork etc is not being judged or mocked; quite the opposite. I am looking to learn as much as I can about how children produce biographical texts about their parents.

The first ten respondents to my post were invited to participate in the study. I interviewed ten women, all mothers of primary-school-aged children ranging from reception to year four (five to ten years old). All parents and children were connected and attending (respectively) local public primary schools in middle-class socio-economic suburbs close to the city of Adelaide. It is clear from our conversations that the women and children were from middle-class families and that the women I interviewed were the primary carers of the children (even though half of them worked full time as their partners did). In all instances, the mother had more than one child.

The interviews were conducted individually at a local café. We discussed the items over coffee, and I took photographs of what the participants brought. Prior to the interviews, I asked the parents/carers to ask the children what the item meant, as I aimed to gather both the perspectives of the biographical subject and creator. This information was also shared at the interview in the form of 'artist statements'.

With hindsight I might have sought out a diversity of parents or carers rather than being pleased with the first who volunteered. Each were women, and informal discussion revealed a mix of working and stay-at-home mothers; not all, but the majority were in heterosexual marriages and each of the women had more than one child. But rather than see such homogeneity exclusively as a limitation of the study, it also offered me a means for containment. I could consider this a snapshot of a time and place when it came to children's representation of their mothers.

The women presented me with many (many) texts to consider. It seemed as though the participants liked doing 'show and tell' when it came to their children's representations of them. This is interesting in itself and fuelled ideas for future research. During my meetings with the mums, there were laughs and misty eyes. Of the many texts shared, the texts that I chose to include in this discussion were those that centred on the theme of the 'best mum'. I chose these texts for two main reasons: first, because every one of the participants brought something on this theme which meant that I could include something from all participants in my discussion (though I have not been able to include images from all participants); second, because this theme allowed for some detailed storytelling by the children about another person that they knew well and were interested in telling stories about, and so could be classified as biographical representation. These texts were narrative-rich (where others were image-based) so this became another focus. As the previous chapter focused on drawings, and the following chapter considers life narrations that are image-and-text-based, these texts allow this chapter to focus on children's biographical writing. These texts also had strong 'writers' statements' attached to them. The focus on the child–mother relationship would also provide a point of containment in terms of the issues it might raise for biographical representation. Biographies and memoirs of mothers by their (usually grown up) children is a subgenre of life writing (Henriksson,

2021; Kellond, 2020; Nash and Pinto, 2020). These texts encompass all kinds of representations, but perhaps the most infamous of these are those at the extremities of representations: books that represent perfect mothers and books that represent flawed mothers. Though it is not within the scope of this chapter to discuss this subgenre in a meaningful way, it is a useful place to locate these narratives of mothers by their children. It is likely that the children who write these biographical texts of their mothers do so with the expectations of genre in mind.

## Findings: Best mum!

Most of the texts I collected as part of this project were completed as gifts to parents. As all of the people who participated in this study were women, the majority of texts were produced as Mothers' Day gifts, or as introduction texts at the start of a new school year. I am not sure if this is a particularly Australian practice, but it is certainly very common in Australian primary schools. This being the case, it is not clear if this is something children desire to do in terms of creative activity, or something that is largely imposed upon them.

In her research on children's drawings, Wendy Sue Looman (2006: 165) rightly argues that 'children should be asked to provide an explanation for their drawings when possible, because it acknowledges the importance of their perspectives and the personal meaning that is expressed in the drawing'. In developing this study, I was keen to make sure that the children were able to comment on their own narratives and I have included these statements as 'writer's statements' below the narration. Their interpretation foregrounds that made by their mother and by me, the researcher. As I argued in Chapter 6, when children's narratives are solicited, there is always mediation which needs to be considered. But being overtly attentive to mediation can get in the way of accessing and considering these texts as a contribution to biography.

*Writer's statement*

*I wanted my mum to see that she was the greatest and the best at supporting me to do the things I want to do. I know that sometimes she is busy, but she always helps me.*

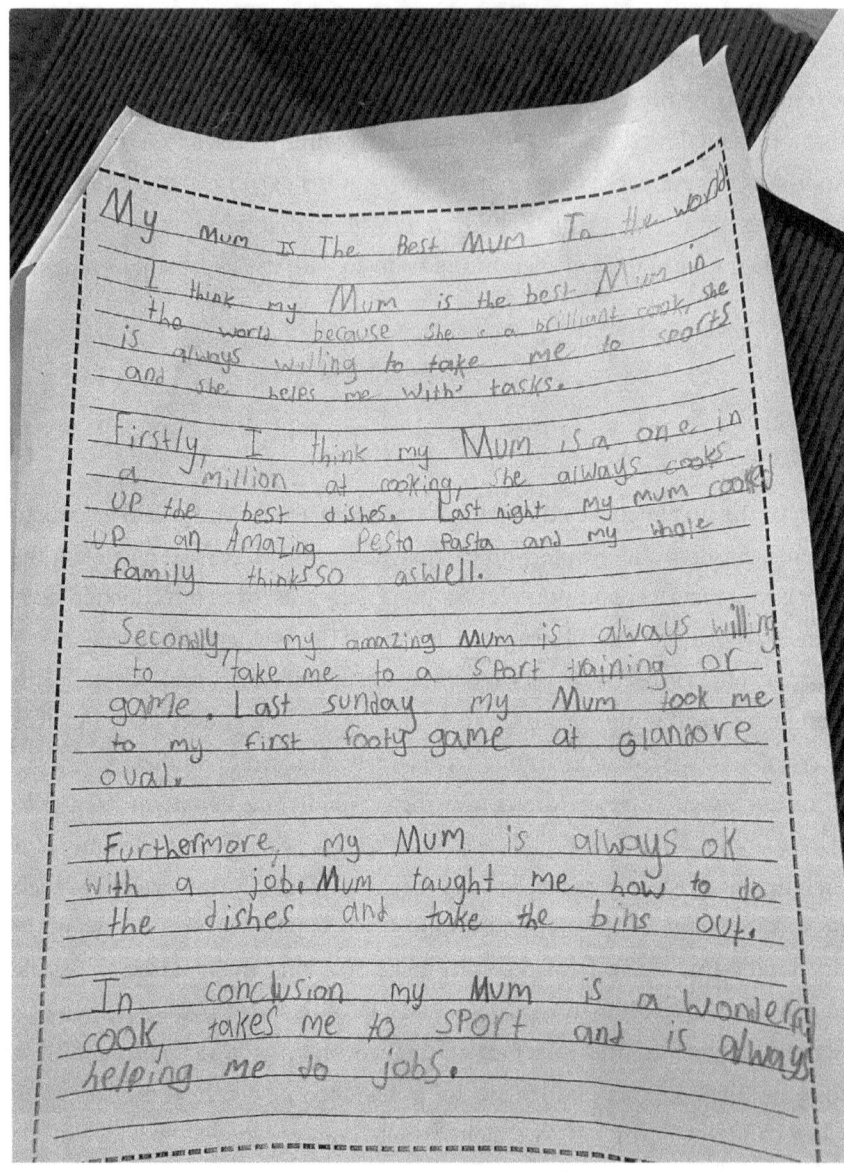

**Figure 7.1** 'Best Mum'. Courtesy of the author.

For example, Figure 7.1 is a piece of persuasive writing that doubles as a biographical sketch for Mothers' Day. Aiden (aged nine) was asked to explain why his mum (Christine) is the best mum in the world. He writes about her cooking, her willingness to take him to sports and how she teaches him to do jobs around the house. Aiden explained to his mum Christine that he thought that these were the particular qualities that she would like him to mention, because all mums want to be good at cooking and helping out with sports. They also, according to Aiden, want to make sure that they support their children to be better at jobs. Christine joked about being surprised about how much her son liked her cooking (because this did not always seem evident) and about learning how to complete jobs around the house. She laughed and suggested that Aiden's words had inspired her to 'lift her game' when it comes to cooking. Christine and I also had an amusing discussion of how this biography puts a spin on the sorts of arguments we might have with our children about doing jobs around the house. In this text, Aiden positions these arguments differently – they are opportunities for him to learn.

*Writer's statement*

*I wanted my mum to understand that she is special in a way that no one else is. She is a hero and always helps me do what I need to do.*

Similarly, in Figure 7.2, Amelia (aged six) offers a 'listicle'-style Mother's Day testament for her mum Jules, in which she outlines the reasons why Jules is the best mum in the world. These reasons include putting her to bed at bedtime, standing up to her and giving better hugs than dad. In my conversations with Amelia's mother Jules, we saw the humour in this – the preference of one parent's hugs over another and the positive responses to parental discipline which tends not to be well received normally. But when Jules asked Amelia to tell her about this representation, Amelia explained that even though she might not always like it when her mum tells her what to do, this is one of the things she knows is a strength of her mum's, so she wanted to mention it. Jules particularly enjoyed the focus on what made her different to dad, and she felt appreciated by Amelia's words here.

**Figure 7.2** 'Mothers' Day'. Courtesy of the author.

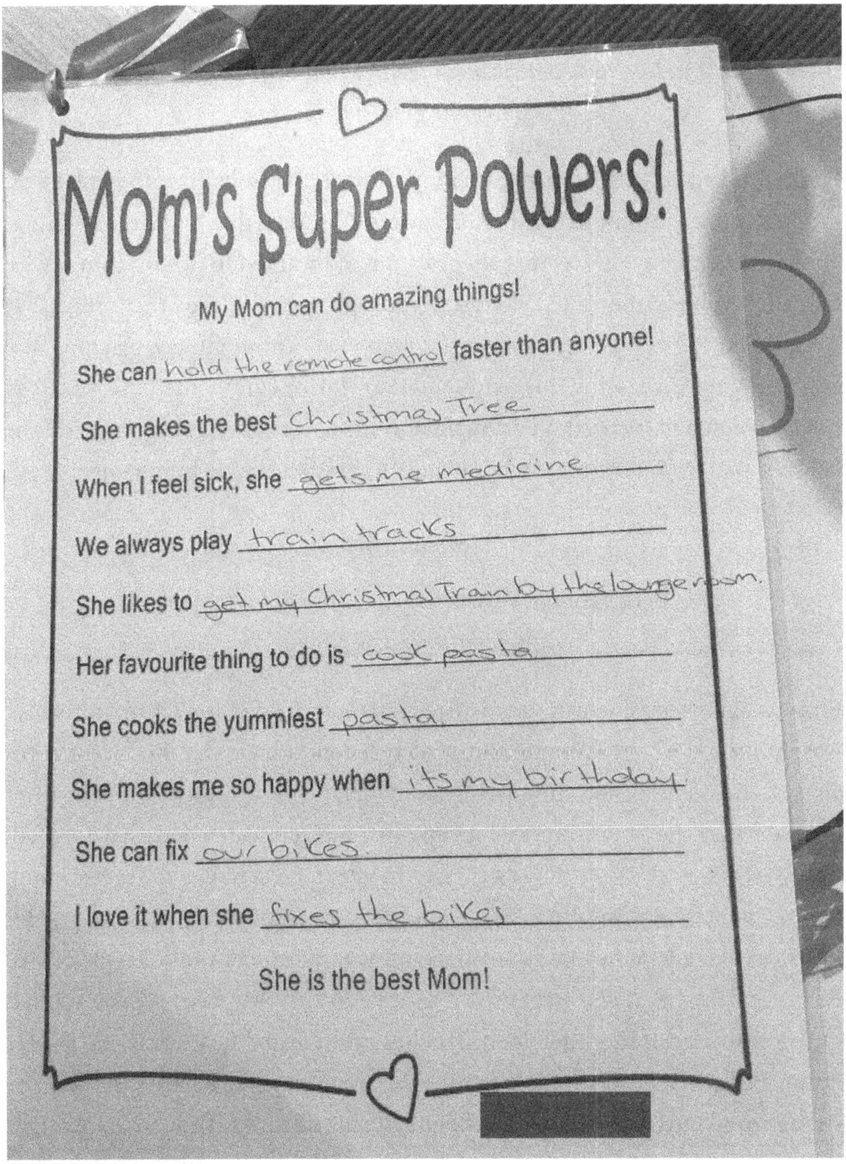

**Figure 7.3** 'Mom's Superpowers'. Courtesy of the author.

*Writer's statement*

*Mum and I do awesome things together and I love it. I want her to know how great she is.*

Hayden (aged six), is working with a proforma that asks him to explain his mother's 'superpowers' in Figure 7.3. Hayden explained that his favourite things about his mum Taylor was that she was fun and wanted to do fun things with him all the time. Amongst Taylor's superpowers were, like the other mums, her cooking talents and her ability to bring happiness through play, teaching and service. When discussing this representation, Taylor commented that she liked how Hayden had focused on a couple of things over (bikes, toy train) and she enjoyed that his reflections on her related to how she made him happy.

*Writer's statement*

*We were asked to write these at school so I wrote what I thought would be good.*

Eliza's acknowledgement in her artist's statement for Figure 7.4 that this task was guided at school is important in that it reminds us that life narrative is almost always mediated, no matter the context. But it also shows that Eliza is aware that she is writing to conventions and templates and that this will necessarily impact on what she writes. In this text, Eliza writes about her mum, Holly. Holly, according to Eliza, is affectionate, comforting and clever. Her mum can 'juggle many things at a time', answer questions and solve problems. Eliza explained that she wrote the narrative in this way because she wanted others who read it to understand who her mum is and how great she is. Her mum, Holly, reflected that it was nice that her daughter commented on her strength and intelligence as well as her nurturing qualities. Though there might be a tendency (even invitation in such tasks) to focus on stereotypical mother qualities, there is also room for movement, particular if this is the inclination of the child author, to write what it is they want to write about their mother.

*Writer's statement*

*I wrote this because I love you both so much. I didn't get any help from the teacher. I structured it this way because I thought it would work this way and*

# Children and Biographical Practice

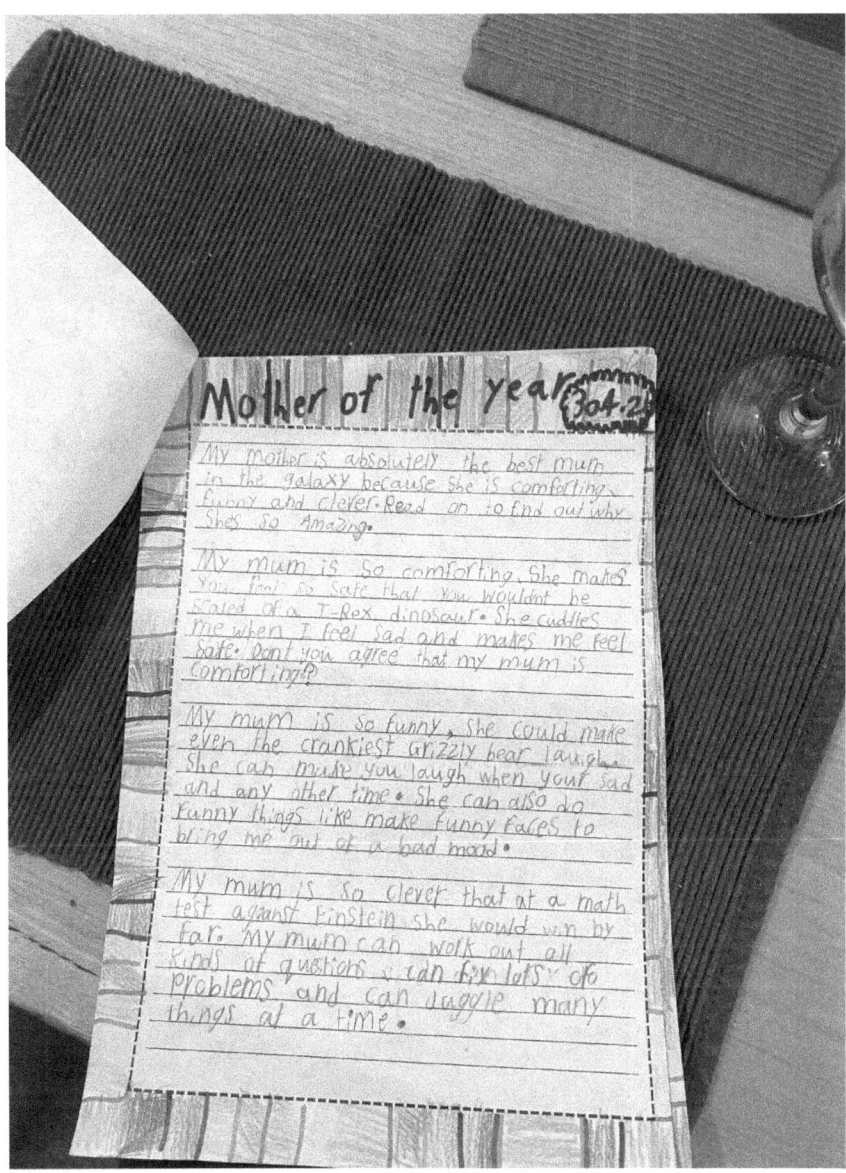

**Figure 7.4** 'Mother of the Year'. Courtesy of the author.

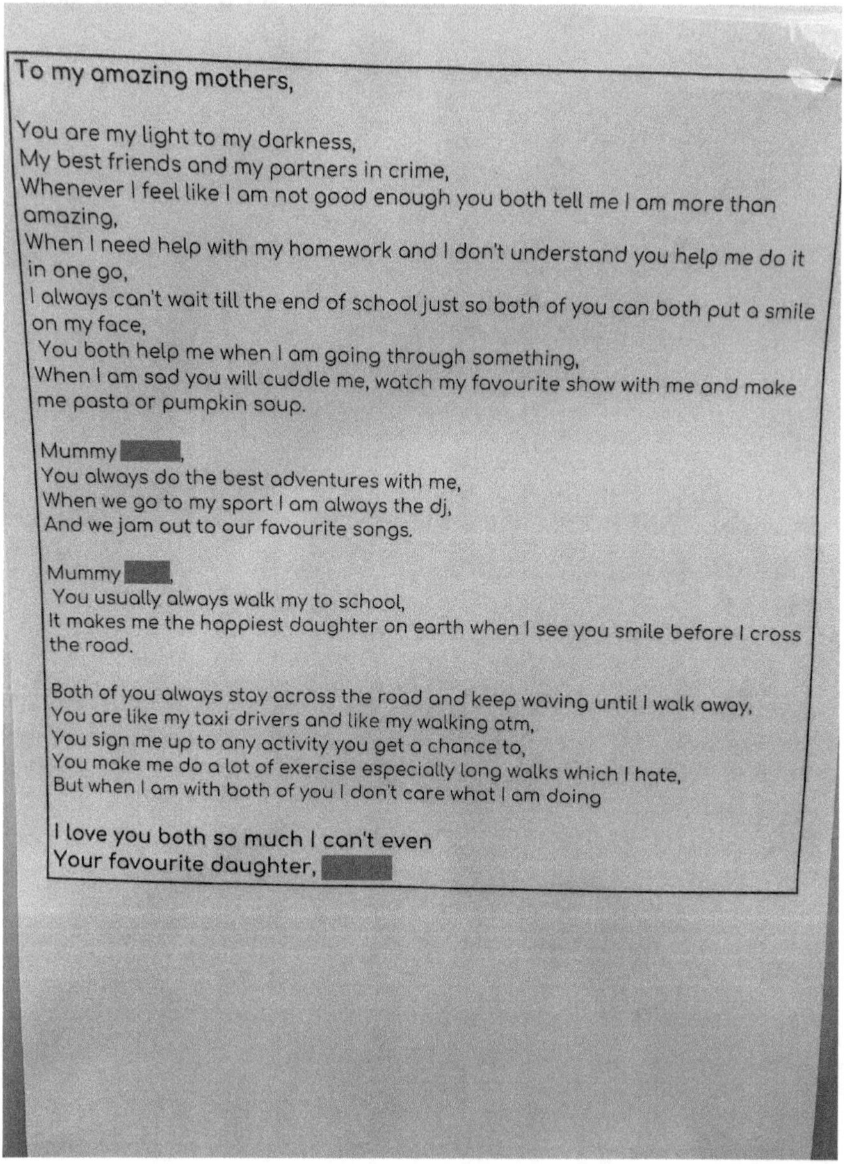

To my amazing mothers,

You are my light to my darkness,
My best friends and my partners in crime,
Whenever I feel like I am not good enough you both tell me I am more than amazing,
When I need help with my homework and I don't understand you help me do it in one go,
I always can't wait till the end of school just so both of you can both put a smile on my face,
You both help me when I am going through something,
When I am sad you will cuddle me, watch my favourite show with me and make me pasta or pumpkin soup.

Mummy ▆▆▆,
You always do the best adventures with me,
When we go to my sport I am always the dj,
And we jam out to our favourite songs.

Mummy ▆▆▆,
You usually always walk my to school,
It makes me the happiest daughter on earth when I see you smile before I cross the road.

Both of you always stay across the road and keep waving until I walk away,
You are like my taxi drivers and like my walking atm,
You sign me up to any activity you get a chance to,
You make me do a lot of exercise especially long walks which I hate,
But when I am with both of you I don't care what I am doing

I love you both so much I can't even
Your favourite daughter, ▆▆▆

**Figure 7.5** 'To My Amazing Mothers'. Courtesy of the author.

*I knew I had to write about two mums. Most kids only had to write about one mum. So, I wanted to make sure I had a good structure that would mean I could say all the things I wanted to.*

This portrait by Dacey (aged nine) in figure 7.5 for her mothers Kayla and Diana, offers many reasons why Dacey loves her mothers which include offering support, help with homework, giving affection, cooking favourite meals and watching favourite television shows. Dacey explained that she completed this piece of writing as a Mothers' Day gift. She wanted to tell her mothers that she loves them so she thought about what she loved most about her mothers, and what she thought about the most when she thought about them. These are the things that stand out the most, Dacey said. These are the most important things. Kayla was not surprised by Dacey's focus, 'she always compliments me on my cooking and how she loves that I pick her up from school and take her to her sports. I like that it is my time she values, because this is what I find most challenging about being a mum'.

*Writer's statement*

*This story is about how my mum is the best and I love it when we do special things together. I hope she knows how much I love her and the things we get to do.*

In this representation (Figure 7.6), Lacey (aged seven) explains why her mum Tam is the best: she is the best cook, and she takes her places. She loves her and is also always available for hugs when Lacey is feeling sad. In our discussion, mum Tam, commented that she liked that Lacey mentioned her cuddles and her cooking, but even better that she enjoyed going out with her. Sometimes she thinks her kids do not enjoy spending time with her, so it is good to hear. Lacey said she wanted her mum to know how much she loved her and thought she was very special.

*Writer's statement*

*We were asked to think about this for Mothers' Day and I thought about it and my mum is the best and these are the things that mean she is the best.*

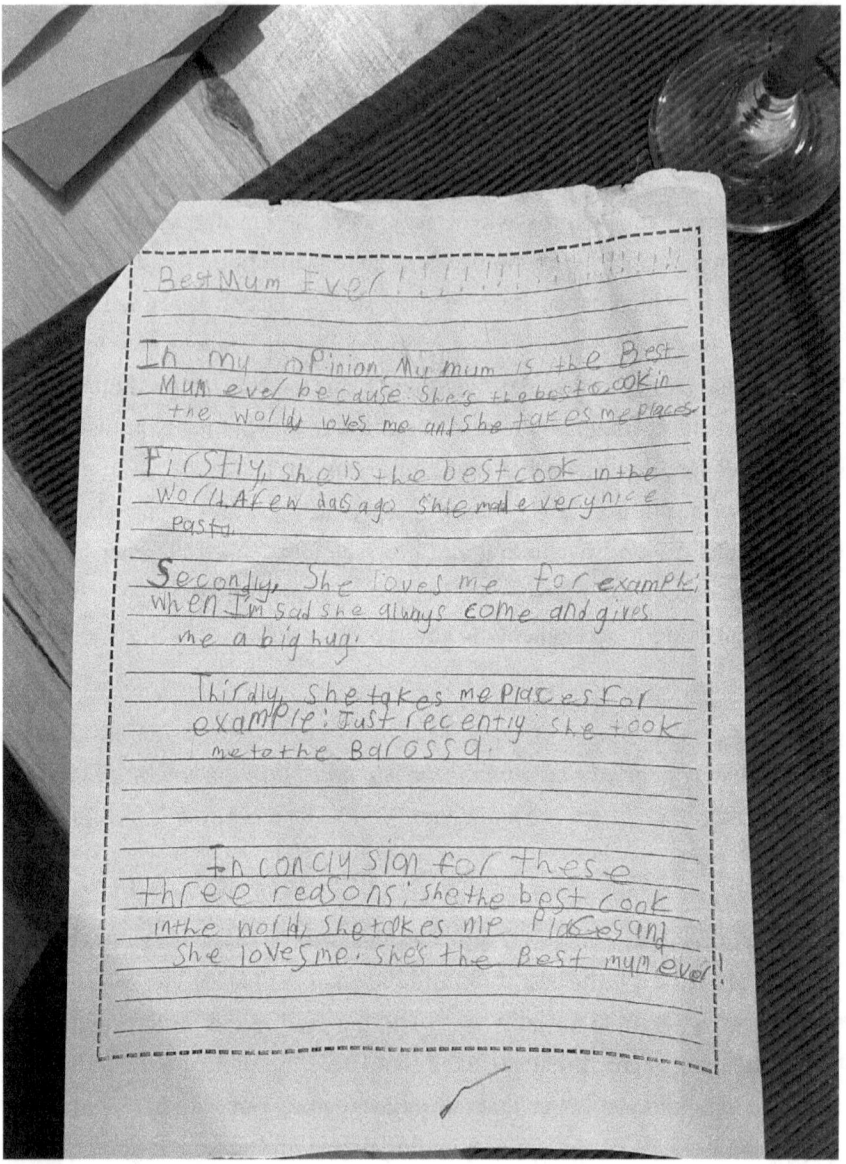

**Figure 7.6** 'Best Mum Ever'. Courtesy of the author.

Poppy (aged seven) in Figure 7.7 explains what makes her mum (Kris) the best is the advice and support she provides. She puts this first in her list but follows it up with the (now expected) cooking food and comfort provided. She completes her list with the warm feelings she has when seeing her mother

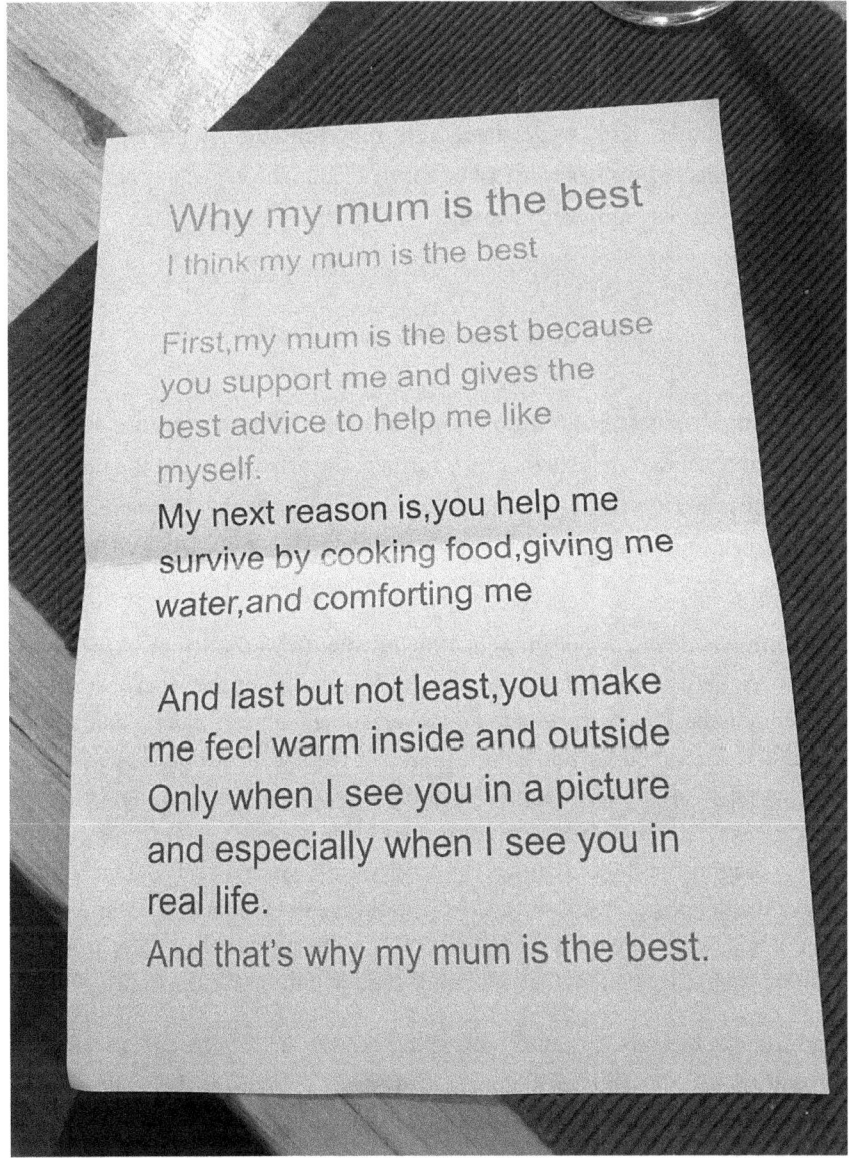

**Figure 7.7** 'Why My Mum Is the Best'. Courtesy of the author.

(whether in a photo, but even better in person). Poppy explained how she thought there were things she had to mention about what her mum did every day for her, but also she wanted to explain the things she thought were special too. Her mother, Kris, appreciated this representation, enjoying how her daughter reflected on her role in her survival! But she especially thought the final two sentences were very sweet.

## Discussion: Simply the best!

Lynch (2013) writes about finding some of her childhood creations stored in a box and coming to realize that they formed an early version of life narration which she refers to as 'ante-autobiography', or autobiography that was produced without prior knowledge that it would ever be received as such. Lynch (2013) explains,

> The theme of this paper grew, at least in part, from the happenstance of discovering a box of artifacts from my childhood. Among the usual nostalgic memorabilia, I was surprised to find several documents in which I had, as a child, written about myself. For the most part these were mediated by adults, the product of activities designed to develop literacy, handwriting, and other skills. Nevertheless, they also seemed to form part of a wider project of encouraging the child to construct a developing life narrative. Dates indicate that the documents were written between the ages of four and eight, and the contents range across the factual recording of height and hair color to the more subjective matter of favorite smells and ambitions for the future. (99)

Framing such texts *as* auto/biography is not a convenient means for retrofitting texts to be useful objects of study. It recognizes the usefulness of auto/biography as cultural frameworks for celebrating children as significant sources when it comes to perspectives and knowledge of life experiences. If we listen to children, we can better include them and their knowledge about life in decisions and practices around social justice and children's literacy, for example.

I felt very privileged to be able to discuss these biographical texts with the children and their mothers. There are various aspects of style and theme I might discuss in this section; I will focus on what the children achieve in relation to their perception of what biography is and does, stylistically and thematically, and speculate on why they wrote what they did. What I cannot comment on here is the probable extent to which the child biographers were influenced by what they read, for instance, the biographies they might read at home or at school. As discussed in Chapter 2, children read biography and have knowledge of what the form is and does. And as discussed earlier in this chapter, children are used to writing according to templates and teacher instructions. Mediation is ever present, but not so easy to measure. As Mavers (2010) argues,

> representation and communication are never ideologically neutral ... What and how children draw and write are framed by what is valued, and what is valued in one social environment might be denigrated, ignored or reconfigured in another ... This is highly political because what is acknowledged shapes how young people are positioned, whether as social agents or as developmentally deficient, or whatever else ... Societal and educational discourses and practices have far reaching implications not only for what it means to be literate, and more broadly an assured text maker, but also for citizenship and social justice. (3)

So though I will speculate, I will also try and focus on the texts themselves and value them as examples of children's creative engagement in biographical practice. As Lynch (2013) persuasively contends,

> while there are, self-evidently, differences between autobiographies written by children and adults, they should not be understood as weaknesses. Those who would question children's capacity to narrate their own experience are at risk of missing the representative power of the text as well as unfairly undermining the author's agency. (100)

Lynch (2013) discusses the work of Peter Alexander as it might help us to see the value in children's writing, and to understand it better. Acknowledging children's writing and other creative outputs has the opposite effect to assuming children's powerlessness and silencing children.

The children write about their mothers' 'great qualities' and there are common themes in these representations: nurturing qualities such as investing time, instilling skills, service – such as supporting children's activities such as games and sports, teaching discipline, offering advice, providing sustenance through cooking and giving affection. But also, lots of personal qualities are listed such as strength, intelligence, skills in making things and the ability to multitask. Fascinatingly, these representations do not, on the whole, conform to the sorts of gender stereotypes that we might have once expected of mothers, and this might reflect changing times but also the demographics of the group of children and mothers included in this study. It is beyond the scope of this research to explore this variable in any depth but would be a point for attention in future research.

The other theme to emerge strongly in these representations, and it is very much prescribed by the genre in which they are writing into, is the representation of 'greatness' – why my mum is 'the best'. As discussed in Chapter 2, children are used to reading about heroes and thus it is not surprising that in writing biographically about their mothers, they position them as everyday heroes. These descriptions are likely in line with what children might think biography is meant to be. The higher the platitude, the better and they are not wrong. This tendency also aligns with the aims of persuasive writing, for example, as mentioned earlier, Figure 7.1 is a piece of persuasive writing that doubles as a biographical sketch for Mothers' Day; when it comes to children's biography, there is an obvious and convenient relationship between these two genres. In this narrative, Aiden is compelled to argue why his mum is 'the best'. As Brett Healey and Margaret Merga (2017: 199) note, 'to support student achievement in writing, educators need to understand how children experience the act of writing. Surprisingly, little is known in this area'. It is perhaps not surprising that so much of the writing that is requested of children in the early years of school is life writing. Children's writing stems from their experience of the world. Similarly, Lynch (2013) argues that children's life writing is

> typically produced in an educational environment and, therefore, instigated and monitored by adults. As a result, the work may be shaped and influenced by the teacher's guidance at the same time as being dependent on the child's developing skills of self-expression and limited by the time allocated to the task and the author's patience. (100)

As we can see in the biographical sketches in Figures 7.1 and 7.2, where a child might normally criticize their parent for asking too much of them, or for being too much of a disciplinarian, biography requires that they 'spin' this information in a different way. This of course is reminiscent of one of the main criticisms of biography, generally, that it is largely a genre of compliments where criticisms might be underlying. But it also could reveal children's awareness of genre, and perhaps also the ways in which the forms of biography prompt deeper reflections on the part of the writer.

The elephant in the room here is – what if these statements are not 'true'? What if what we see here is nothing more than an expected biographical performance, and these words do not reflect the relationship between the child and mother at all? There are ethical stakes here regarding the ownership of these biographies. Though the children created these texts, it is the mothers who own and now circulate them. They play a significant role in the text's interpretation, and this is indicative of the more general ways in which children's writing is mediated when it reaches the public sphere. The women in this study did bring in some texts that were not complimentary like those I have included. For example, one of the mothers brought in a card which said 'Happy Mothers' Day Mum. I love Dad'. Other texts offered 'feedback' on things their mothers might be better at. We laughed at these; they echo some of the texts in the *Buzzfeed* articles cited at the outset of this chapter. When mothers do circulate these texts, they likely do so from a position of security. They see the humour. Though these were not representative of the texts generally that the mothers brought in, there is scope for future research on this.

In Figure 7.3, Hayden is working with a proforma that asks him to explain his mother's 'superpowers'. He has an explicit biographical mandate and structure. The notion of the superpower is fascinating for its obvious relationship to what biography is about, and more particularly what biography for children is thought to achieve. As we have learned throughout this study, biographical subjects for children are held up to be examples to follow. This is what is at work in Hayden's biographical representation of his mother, but also in the form and task assigned for Hayden to complete.

The other theme that is obvious and recurrent in these biographical representations is relational biography. Though each of the texts focus primarily on 'mum', the relational life of the child is central to the representation of the mother. This is perhaps not surprising given the developmental age of the child and the likelihood that they see themselves as central to their mother's worlds. They also understand (and perhaps prescribe) that this is each woman's primary identity with the limits of this task: mother. Each woman has a biographical life and potential representations outside of this identity, but this is not the children's mandate nor is it within their capability for this task (this is fascinating in itself and another point for future research). So, we learn about the child as we learn about the mother, and the texts might thus be another example of auto/biography, again affirming that this is the central life narrative genre in which children write.

## Conclusion

Though the conclusions I can draw here are limited by this being a small study, but, as Sidonie Smith and Julia Watson (1996) reminded us over twenty-five years ago, we can learn a lot about the expansiveness of auto/biography as a cultural practice by considering its everyday uses. Qualitative interventions are not the norm in literary or in studies in life writing. Nor are considerations of child authors. And this is where I hope this research may find traction: at the intersections of everyday life narrative studies and childhood studies.

This chapter offers insights into how children use biographical practice to construct and celebrate relational lives, in this case their relationship with their mother. It explores how they negotiate the limitations of genre. Sometimes we might read this as acquiesce, other times as subversion, and everything in between. Children seem well aware of being coaxed by these tasks, and perhaps the extent to which they are willing to play along or not, or value-adds to end product that we see. The biographies exude love and regard; they are creative and thoughtful. They work within the 'great man' mode of biography but subvert it in telling stories about their mothers and their everyday heroics including a veneration of domestic life not seen in other biographical representations in this study.

Chapter 8 aims to give the final word in this study to child-life narrators, bringing together knowledge from the previous two chapters on children's biographical drawings and writings, to look at children's diaries written during Covid-19 lockdowns. Continuing on with the small-archive approach of Chapters 6, 7 and 8 consider how the written and visual elements of these diaries construct auto/biographical representations. These three chapters considered together offer new frameworks for analysing children's auto/biographical production.

## Notes

1. *Buzzfeed*. (n.d.) Available online: https://www.buzzfeed.com/kristatorres/13-kids-who-did-not-intend-for-their-drawings-to-be-x-rated; https://www.buzzfeed.com/mikespohr/can-you-figure-out-what-these-kids-were-trying-to-draw; https://www.buzzfeed.com/kristatorres/these-kids-drawings-of-their-moms-will-make-you-laugh-and
2. This project has been approved by Flinders University's Human Research Ethics Committee (Project ID 4239). I am incredibly grateful to the children who made these biographical texts, and to the women who shared their children's narrations for this research and also shared their time and thoughts with me.

8

# My lockdown diary: Childhood biography during Covid-19

## Introduction

In their historical research on child writers, Christine Alexander and Juliet McMaster (2006: 1) posit that 'for centuries children have been taking the pen into their hands and writing ... The child's expression of his or her own subjectivity is there and available for us, if we will only take the time to pay attention'. Through this study, I have argued that life narrative is one genre in which children have written, historically through to the present, for private and public readerships. But children's life narrative has often been marginalized or is missing from official histories and accounts of childhood. This is despite the fact that, as Diane Mavers (2010) passionately explains,

> children are prolific makers of a range of texts. As they go about their everyday lives, they draw and write for a multiplicity of surprisingly diverse, and not mutually exclusive, purposes to solve problems, to demonstrate learning, to explore ideas and feelings, to create imagined worlds, to greet, to plan, to document their experience, to communicate with others, and so on. Subject matter is wide-ranging, and includes places they have visited, objects or living things that intrigue them, things they have done, people they care about, issues that concern them. (11)

This final chapter offers an example of children's life writing – lockdown diaries produced during the Covid-19 pandemic by South Australian primary-school children. During this time, most school children were away from their extended families and friends, schools, sports and so on for an extended period of time.[1] 'My Lockdown Diary' was produced by New Zealand artist Stephen McCarthy and released as a free, downloadable tool for children to make a record of their experiences during lockdown. In reading examples of 'My Lockdown Diary' we have an opportunity to hear children's voices and document their experiences at a significant point in recent history.

When examining a selection of these completed diaries, there is potentially much qualitative data to mine. Because there are various elements to these diaries, they could be read within different registers: for instance, as diary, as auto/biography, as social history, even as socio-political commentary. However, as this is a study of biography and childhood, my aim here is to focus on the biographical expressions made in the lockdown diaries. As argued in the previous two chapters, children's lives are necessarily relational: they imagine and construct their life stories in relation to those of their families, friends and pets. And as we will see, 'My Lockdown Diary' actively frames its activities in this way, likely anticipating that this is how children's life narrative works. So, in this chapter I again interrogate the 'slash' in auto/biography, as I have done in the previous two chapters, to consider how seemingly autobiographical, diaristic representations quickly become biography when it comes to children's life representations.

I read the diaries to gather qualitative data with the aim of understanding more about how children make biography, and how they write and draw relational lives during a period of considerable change and potential social isolation. In light of scholarship on children's drawings, on children's life narrative, and biography, this discussion aims to produce new frameworks for analysing children's biography as self-expression, as social history and as political engagement. I am mindful, as Emese Hall (2015) argues, of examining these texts in a child-centred way. Hall (2015) states,

> Researchers have their own agendas and these agendas may not always have children's needs and interests at their heart. I argue that, although children should be recognised as expert informers and witnesses regarding their own experiences and perspectives ... the 'use' of children drawings in research can, at times, be restrictive and tokenistic. (140)

I aim to consider what is specifically informative about these diaries as children's biographical testimony. To what extent do children exercise power in their construction of these texts? For example, in spite of prompts for autobiography, what does it mean for children to default to biographical representations in making these lockdown diaries? What does this say about children's relationship to biographical production and their particular engagement with relational life narrative?

## Children's drawings; children's life narrative

As discussed in Chapter 6, in which I examined an archive of asylum-seeker children's narratives, children's drawings have been variously considered across disciplines, for what they can reveal about the way children see and engage with the world. It reveals knowledge on their perceived agency and the extent to which they believe their drawings might impact on those who read them. Educators ask children to draw and interpret their own drawings as part of children's development. Drawing is a means for children to communicate prior to and following the acquisition of writing skills (for instance, see research by Baroutsis et al., 2019 who focus on how children communicate their classroom learning through drawing). Drawings allow educators to understand how children interpret their experiences, people and relationships, the world and events (see Bland, 2012; Gernhardt, Keller and Rubeling, 2016; Kaplun, 2019; Knight, 2013; Maxwell, 2015; Soundy, 2012). Children draw in therapeutic contexts, as icebreakers or in making psychological health or well-being assessments (Katz and Hamama, 2013; Linder et al., 2018. Researchers have looked to children's drawings as documents of their experiences of warfare, trauma and displacement (Cardell and Douglas, 2020a; Nuttman-Shwartz, Huss and Altman 2010; Oztabak, 2020). Children's drawings have been used in political campaigns and to inform education policy (Bland, 2012). And children's drawings reveal and assess children's diverse creativity and the development of their visual literacy (Hopperstad; Knight, 2013; Watts, 2010). Drawing can offer a link between children's visual, written and verbal literacies as children develop these varied ways of communicating.

Educators have commonly looked to children's drawings to provide 'evidence' of children's learning experiences and outcomes at a time when schools are looking for tangible means to measure these (Darling-McQuistan, 2017: 281). As Bland (2012) notes, though researchers might evaluate children's drawings to assess children's creativity, creativity is difficult to measure (235). When children produce creative, visual artefacts, researchers do not always know what to do with them in terms of how they might inform our knowledge of children and childhood (Bland, 2012: 235). Just as we might struggle to interpret art produced by professional adults, children's drawings can 'present visual researchers with rich data; the process of analysing what can be ambiguous and very subjective' (Bland, 2012: 235).

Throughout this book I have argued that there has been little scholarly attention paid to life narratives created by children. This is despite the fact, as discussed in Chapter 2, that there is a proliferation of life narratives produced for children to read. And when we consider children's life narrative in the abovementioned contemporary education contexts, perhaps this makes sense. It is ethically tricky terrain if we are asking children to make life-narrative texts so we can learn more about how they engage in the practice of life narration. And historically, children's narratives have largely been marginalized, so this explains the absence of scholarly attention. However, if scholars of life narrative, are genuinely engaged in a broad push for inclusivity when it comes to who gets to read and write life narrative, then where do children fit in to our sense of life narrative's cultural purposes and resonances?

Catherine Kaplun (2019: 392) summarizes recent research on children's rights and capabilities. She reminds us that children are 'capable of reporting their ideas and opinions on subjects and activities that are important to them'. They are well practised at expressing their hopes and dreams, their fears and sense of the world they live in, for instance, through drawing. Children are diverse in terms of their backgrounds and their capabilities, and this presents urgent challenges for those researching with children (Kaplun, 2019: 392). For instance, researchers should look for ways to collaborate as much as possible with children on research projects in which children are subjects. Researchers also need to embrace acts of resistance by children, or respond positively if children seek to exercise control over research (Kaplun, 2019: 392).

When it comes to advocating for children's life narrative, it is important to remember that voice is not something stable, to be searched for, but dynamic and contextual. Children require multiple forms of expression. This is a researcher's 'teachable moment', when we can observe genuine collaboration with children in research affecting them. In this book project, I have asserted that children are prolific life narrators, and particularly accomplished when it comes to writing biographical texts, but mostly in marginal contexts. It is one of these marginal contexts that I consider here.

## Method: 'My Lockdown Diary' as a tool of life narration

While in lockdown, I was working from home while my eight-year-old daughter did her schooling from home. While completing my daily doomscroll on social media, I began to notice a plethora of helpful lockdown materials being shared on parents and children pages on social media. People in the community, notably artists and educators, recognized the challenges of entertaining children at home and the difficult balances faced by working parents. These shared activities included creative activities such as cooking and making things, reading challenges, worksheets and games. But significantly, and perhaps not surprisingly, there was a strong focus on encouraging children to record their experiences of lockdown. As discussed in the previous chapter, children are used to doing personal, creative recounts at school as they are perceived to have educative, civic and personal value.

One example of lockdown activities is Stephen McCarthy's 'My Lockdown Diary'. McCarthy released this on his artists website, with free access (he asked for a small donation for its download and use).[2] The diary is twenty-eight pages long and contains a range of different activities that put a positive spin on the experience of lockdown for children. In an interview with Vicki Anderson (2020), McCarthy explained how he had the idea four days into New Zealand's initial month-long lockdown; there are four weeks of activities in the diary. He wanted to offer something that might help out children and parents during this difficult time. He sketched the book in a day (Anderson, 2020: n.p.).

McCarthy did not want the activities to be too prescriptive. As Anderson (2020) explains, McCarthy created the diary with a mix of 'prompts' and a 'careful use of blank space'.

> 'I didn't want it to be too constrictive so there are lots of blank spaces for children to record their experiences which are different to those of us oldies,' he said.

> Children sometimes find it hard to talk about what they're feeling and drawing is a way of accessing that. Get the crayons out, do something tangible and away from digital distractions. (n. p.)

As someone who illustrates for children, McCarthy is likely aware of the debates that surround children's activity books or worksheets and children's creativity. Kirsten Darling-McQuistan (2017) argues that 'drawing is an everyday feature of primary school classrooms. All too often however, its role within the classroom is limited to a "representational" one, used to demonstrate the accuracy of children's images and representations of the world' (281), for instance, rather than trying to document or demonstrate children's experiences in a more open way. As Marilee Ransom and Maryann Manning (2013) note, teachers have long debated the usefulness of prescribed 'worksheets' in the classroom, as they can become a one-size-fits-all model for learning or expression which do not allow children to collaborate in the learning or to demonstrate their creativity (188). If we are to move beyond such default positions, as childhood studies scholars such as Allison James and Alan Prout (1997) have long argued, we much engage with children as critical subjects who are able to create knowledge, who are not just objects of study.

McCarthy's 'Lockdown Diary' seems far from the prescribed worksheets described above. Its prompts are very open to children's 'hacks' – for instance, its length and variety of prompts mean children can (and did, in my experience) skip certain activities in favour of those that were more meaningful to them. In this way, the book reminded me of the *Wreck My Journal* books described in Chapter 2. These books imagine children as creative and spontaneous in their approach to journal and diary activities. And though 'My Lockdown Diary' invites children to engage, it invites them to do so on their own terms. Ransom and Manning (2013) argue that children are good at seeing and resisting what they perceive to be 'busy work' (189). The timeliness, openness and simplicity of McCarthy's activities likely made them more meaningful to the children who worked on them. The prompts are, as McCarthy suggests, a mix of pre-formatted illustrative and written prompts, and large blank spaces where McCarthy envisions free drawing and writing.

\* \* \*

As this book project developed, and I have thought more and more about the presence and absence of children's voices in the public sphere, I have felt a more urgent need to include children's voices as readers, critics and writers of biographies. Though generically, 'My Lockdown Diary' was presented as a 'diary' rather than a biography, its timely presence represented an opportunity for me, in this study, to look at this as an example of children's life narrative. This was an entirely unique moment in history to consider how children might tell stories about their lives and the lives of others.

My ethics approval for this project included information sheets for parents and children, and consent and assent forms for parents and children respectively. It was important that both children and parents were aware of the potential benefits and risks inherent in participation, and how I was going to study the diaries. As well as outlining the practicalities of distribution and return, it was important that I let parents know the following:

> I would like to make a copy of your child's 'My Lockdown Diary' diary for analysis in our study. However, we want to urge you to respect your child's privacy during this process. If your child does not want you to look at certain pages of the diary – this might be because they feel self-conscious about what they are writing or drawing. Please be encouraging. We are not judging what they write or draw, or what they don't complete.
>
> I am interested in what seems interesting or important to them at this time. There are no right or wrong answers or approaches. I hope that you will encourage your child to enjoy this creative task.

Part of my information to children included the following statements:

> Your parent/carer told me that you like to draw, colour and write, and you might be keen to do a 'Lockdown Diary' during your long school holidays. That would be awesome work! I am interested to see what you think of the activities in the diary. It's okay if you don't finish it, or even if you don't like it. All of this is interesting to me!
>
> Could I please (with your parent's or carer's help) make a copy of your diary when you are finished with it? I would return it to you very soon after. You can choose to not share some of the pages if you don't want to.
>
> Please let you parent/carer know if you would like to participate.

In letting me research your diary, you get to have your voice be a part of history. What did you do during Lockdown? What was important to you?

\* \* \*

I circulated twenty diaries to local primary school children aged between six to ten years.

I organized for the return of the diaries after six weeks. Ten diaries were returned. This was roughly the return rate I anticipated. Of those that were returned, the children's demographics were as follows: all children attended the same primary school in suburban Adelaide, South Australia. Each lived in a proximate suburb in a middle-class area. All children had two parents living in the same household as them and each had at least one sibling. The majority of children had both parents working at home during lockdown though one child had a parent who was a frontline emergency services worker.

Of those ten diaries that were returned, most had at least one page not completed, some had four or five pages unfinished. Some of the reasons why children might not have completed the diaries are: they might have thought their drawings and writings weren't good enough. They might not have wanted to complete the diary under their parents or my watch. They might have had more interesting leisure pursuits. Or perhaps, for various reasons, this might have been the last thing children wanted to do during lockdown. The limitations of this study are numerous. However, what I did gather was rich and fascinating enough for discussion in the study I present here today.

I scanned, de-identified and saved the diaries, then returned them to their authors. Though I will offer general analyses of what I observe in the diaries, the limits of this chapter context mean that I cannot offer a detailed analysis of each diary page/activity completed by each of the children. I did not want to impose restrictive genre interpretations on the sorts of life narrative that I see here, and I will make comments about themes that emerged. But since this is principally a study of biography, and previous chapters have reported children's tendencies towards producing relational life narratives, my analysis is particularly tuned into these aspects of the diary. The diaries did contain prompts to elicit biographical representation, but there were also many and varied spontaneous representations that the child authors made of other people, places or objects. This turned out to be a fascinating and important way of engaging with these diaries.

Of the twenty-nine activity pages in the 'Lockdown Diary', there are inevitably many diaristic activities, activities that ask children to detail their day's activities, draw their day and so forth. I have defined nine of them as 'biographical activities', whether asking children for their representation of family and friends, places or objects. For example, the first page asks, 'Who are you in lockdown with? What do you appreciate about these people?' Of all of the diaries that I collected, each of the authors completed this particular page (arguably this could be because this was the first page), but perhaps also because it seemed like a fun, easy activity in which they could write about what they know. Further pages ask 'Isolation: What do you appreciate about your family?'; 'Isolation: What do you appreciate about your friends?'. Again, all of the children completed these pages, drawing pictures of family members, friends and pets, and writing about their qualities. These representations of family members were most often positive, perhaps responding to the prompt which explicitly asked for a positive spin ('appreciation'), some of the narratives about siblings were frank assessments about annoyance, how much noise their siblings make, feeling sad when they will not play, cheating in games and taking more than their share of time on the computer or game console. These representations are a great example of how the children hacked the prompts to tell the story that they wanted to tell. They were not always limited by text's suggestions, but able to offer representations that felt meaningful to their own experiences.

Subsequent pages ask questions such as:

Draw the view from your bedroom window. Is there something you didn't notice before?; What's for dinner? Draw what you have on your plate;

Listen to your favourite song. Really listen. What are the words about?;

If you can talk a walk outside, list four things you remember;

Pantry: Draw what's in your cupboards at home.

Write a note to you in the future. How to keep calm and cool. Dear future me.

One of the most popular pages was the writing a note to the future self. All diarists completed this page, and I will discuss this prompt further on in this chapter. In 'My Lockdown Diary', there is also space for biographical representations on activity pages that do not explicitly ask for such a response. For instance, list 'Five awesome things about today' was another popular prompt in which respondents again wrote about things they did with family members and conversations they had (for instance, on FaceTime etc.) with extended family members and school friends. Though the activities often have a focus on the self and reflecting on the self in the present, there is also a strong focus on looking outwards and connecting the self with people and places. As previously argued, this is feature of children's life narrative and life narrative for children: a deep interrogation of the '/' in auto/biography, an acknowledgement of the inevitably of relational representation when it comes to the representation of children's lives.

My tools for analysis were life-narrative theory and narrative analysis: close reading of the texts including close reading of children's drawings. I draw on methods for written and visual analysis, and theoretical work on children's development and its impact on their drawings. In this analysis, I was indebted to interdisciplinary scholars who have analysed children's drawings including Josephine Deguara (2019); Caroline Lenette, Prasheela Karan, Dearna Chrysostomou and Anthea Athanasopoulos (2017); Eva Maagerø's and Tone Sund (2016); Cumming and Visser (2019); Farley and Mishra Tarc (2014); and Mayhew (2015).[3]

However, when I settled on this method for analysis, it seemed inadequate. What I had centrally learnt from my research to the point was the importance of not only engaging with children's voice and creativity through my own interpretations of their work, but also centring children's own interpretations. So, I revised my ethics, and once I had decided on the particular images I wanted to discuss, I went back to the children and sought artists' statements for the particular pages included here. They are quoted below.

## Discussion: Children, relational lives and biography

Though many themes emerged across the lockdown diaries, for feasibility I am going to look at three that emerged robustly and allow for a discussion about the ways children drew on and developed methods for making biographical representation. These three themes are:

1. Children defaulting to biographical representations in prompts that did not directly ask for them;
2. Children writing and drawing biographies of parents and siblings;
3. Children creating a biographical future self.

The overarching theme in these representations, perhaps not surprisingly, was empathy – an ability and tendency to look outwards rather than inwards, to offer representations of others including an imagined future self.

Children's depiction of immediate family emerged strongly in the representations made in the lockdown diaries. Though there were prompts that specifically asked for children to represent their family (for instance, 'Who are you home with?' and 'Appreciation Day'), there was a propensity to do so outside of these prompts. For example, on the prompts that asked the children to represent a walk, what they had for dinner and their favourite song, seven of the ten authors wrote about siblings as participants in these entries and eight of ten authors mentioned parents as the facilitators. For example, two authors mentioned that their parent was a 'great cook'; one author suggested that he listened to his favourite song with his dad, and it made him happy; four authors wrote and drew about enjoying the extra time to have walks and plays with siblings and parents. Three respondents wrote about missing grandparents when prompted to talk about people they appreciated. They wrote about how grandparents would FaceTime or Skype them and make them laugh, read stories to them and ask them about their day.

These represent 'hacks' to what was presented in the prompt: instead of writing about their own experience, they necessarily implicate those around them, those people they admire, love and feel close to. This is what Hall refers to as children positioning themselves in powerful ways. As in her study, instead of simply replicating predictable templates, children made these activities meaningful for themselves through the representations they made. They saw the prompts as ways in. As previously suggested, the children also felt empowered enough to write frankly about the things that were annoying them: siblings, not being able to see their friends, not being able to play sport, feeling bored. Even though the diary's tone was overtly positive (with a focus on appreciation, future optimism, finding beauty in things around you, awesome things about your day, something new you have learned, highlights of the week) the children offered representations that were not positive, but in doing so, likely felt more authentic to them.

In the 'Lockdown Diary' examples where the child authors were explicitly prompted to represent their immediate families, the representations were very detailed and specific. See Figure 8.1, an example of the 'Who are you home with?' page which asks directly for biographical representations of immediate family. In this example, author two, aged five, describes each of his siblings and his parents in seemingly honest ways. We might find humour in the ways that he offers both positive and negative assessments of his family members: his sisters are 'fun', 'kind' and have 'good ideas' but are also 'bossy' and 'mean'. Unlike the overtly complimentary representations of mothers in Chapter 7, it seems that siblings are more likely to be subjects of honest, often amusing, biographical representations! This was certainly a theme across the different children's 'Lockdown Diaries'.

*Artist's statement*

*It was easy to write about my family as they were all there for me to look at and think about what I wanted to say. I have the best family in the world, but three sisters can be a bit annoying sometimes. I think that is okay to say.*

*Artist's statement*

*I miss Molly so much. I am used to seeing her every day at school and we also play at each other's houses a lot too. I definitely appreciate having her and my other friends in my life even more now that we can't see each other.*

As previously suggested, all diarists completed the 'Appreciation Day' page that invited them to write about their friends. Almost all of the representations were effusively positive, in Figure 8.2, author one, aged eight, offers a direct representation of her friend 'Molly'. She draws the two of them standing together under clouds. She writes of how her friends make her laugh and smile, and play with her when she is sad. The prompt is positive, likely mindful of the confusion or difficulties children are facing; it asks children to reflect on what they appreciate about their friends during this time of absence. Author one

**Figure 8.1** 'Who Are You Home With?' (author two, aged five). Courtesy of the author.

**Figure 8.2** 'Appreciation Day (a)' (author one, aged eight). Courtesy of the author.

**Figure 8.3** 'Appreciation Day (b)' (author three, aged eight). Courtesy of the author.

writes generally about her friends before focusing on a particular friendship. Similarly, author three (Figure 8.3) represents the importance of friendship and the value of friends for play at a time when playdates are more limited. Amusingly, after the prompt 'What do you appreciate about your friends?' author three has crossed out 'for being smelly', however it remains visible in the narrative. This constitutes a 'hack' to the diary. While we might expect to read only positive comments here, the author has offered something humorous or silly. In the artist's statement later below, she suggests it is because she felt silly about doing the picture. It might also be a reflection on the genre: the author knew she was not meant to write something like this and crossed it out. The picture seems to focus on the kindness of a friend after the author has hurt herself on some play equipment (as signalled by the 'oh no!' statement). It is clear that this is something children commonly value about each other: their friends' ability to make things better when bad things happen. It is these memories that return at a time when friends are absent and children are in lockdown.

*Artist's statement*

*I was only joking when I wrote smelly. I was feeling a bit silly about drawing the picture, but I feel really lucky to have my friends especially to play sports and games with. I miss them a lot right now.*

The final prompt I want to discuss is 'Dear future me'. In Figure 8.4, author one writes to herself at age twenty-one. She draws a picture of her future self and imagines that she will have two dogs, two cats and a fish, her favourite colour will be yellow and her favourite sport will be soccer. There are no prompts to suggest what the children should write in this section, but the author's responses follow established 'about me' templates that children are often asked to complete at school (much like in Claire Lynch's, 2013 'ante-autobiography' which I discussed in Chapter 7 of this study). She presents her life according to expected templates (job, interests, pets). What is fascinating about what author one does here is readily (and seemingly easily) imagine and represent a future, older, version of herself. She imagines herself as a nurse or paramedic who is able to help people 'because right now the world is not so good'. It's apparent from the narrative that she is inspired by her older sister: she wants to be a

**Figure 8.4** 'Write a Note to You in the Future (a)' (author one, aged eight). Courtesy of the author.

nurse or paramedic 'like' her. She is able to build a biography with confidence and certainty of her future self through self-knowledge and knowledge about how the genre works. Other respondents offered something similar in the way of clear and confident representations of a future self with a nominated job, families, types of houses, cars and pets. These seem to reflect and respond to ideas about how auto/biography works as a genre. The biography offers an idealized version of the self in which life will be as it should. The future self is a role model for the child now. Writing the story of their future is equal to writing the future.

Some respondents framed their responses as questions to a future self. These narrations reflect a more uncertain relationship with life narration, and reveal something of the instability of biography as a genre. These narratives become speculative or futuristic narrations. In these examples, the authors imagine this future self exists as a formed human being and thus do not construct this person themselves (as author one and others cited above do) but rather ask questions that might function as wishful thinking. One asks, 'are you rich do you have a mansion do you have a bod' (I presume the latter means dog). He addresses a future self in aspirational terms, perhaps reflecting what he imagines now is a desirable future for an adult. Another diarist (Figure 8.5) asks 'do we still have Covid in the future? I am curious to know the answer'. And another asks 'what do you look like? Do you like your job and your family?' The latter two comments do not make clear, optimistic assumptions about their futures, rather, they ask questions, reflecting perhaps future wishes, but also uncertainties about what the future looks like. Considered together, these two different types of approaches offer some indication of what children know about what auto/biography should be and a contribution they might make to it.

*Artist's statement*

*My mum is a paramedic and still has to go to work every day during the lockdown. This is what made me think about ways that I can help people when we have something else like this happen in the future. I think I will still have the same favourite sport when I am 21 as I do now. And I love the pets I have now so hope I will have the s ame sorts of ones in the future.*

**Figure 8.5** 'Write a Note to You in the Future (b)' (author two, aged nine). Courtesy of the author.

## Conclusion

Alexander and McMaster (2006) offer this call-to-action on how we might better respect and appreciate child writers:

> In the twenty-first century, the time has come to listen to the authentic literary voice of the child – to the extent that we can identify such a thing – or children's literature properly so called: that is, literature *by* children … there should be a place for what children have to tell us of themselves. (1)

In constructing 'The Lockdown Diary', McCarthy's assumptions about how the diary would work proved to be correct: though the children did embrace his prompts, the children did also 'hack' his prompts and engage in unexpected 'free' writing and drawing. They skipped some pages and put a lot of energy into others. As in my study more widely, the examples in this chapter have shown that children are prolific auto/biographers. Children understand the genres and have experience to respond in both predictable and formulaic ways, as well as unpredictable, fun and creative ways.

The findings of this chapter show that when it comes to children's life narrative, prompts can be okay. Children are used to being disciplined subjects in education, sports, home life and so on. This isn't necessarily something we should be afraid or steer children away from when it comes to constructing life narrative as it can be informative to them and to us. If there are no prompts, perhaps with some children, we would receive nothing. As we can see in these lockdown diaries, understanding and responding to creative prompts doesn't necessarily affect children's creativity and originality. The effect can be quite the opposite.

As I started working on this chapter, I could immediately see the limitations in the possibility of imposing my interpretations of the children's creations. Though the written text does act as a type of annotation to the prompt and drawing, as Hall (2015: 146) argues, 'the ethically aware researcher is always concerned with foregrounding children's personal meanings'.

In seeking and including their artist's statements, I was able to structure my interpretation around theirs and offer an interpretation that was much more child centred, collaborative and meaningful. Having access to these diaries, at this moment in history, made me think about their (and indeed life writing's more generally) interdisciplinary potential as artefacts to better comprehend children's experiences of lockdown, of the psychological effects, its impact on relationships, creativity and so forth. I have no doubt this research is in train across the globe, and I hope that my discussion here has made a small contribution to this inquiry.

## Acknowledgements:

I would like to acknowledge and thank the children who completed and contributed lockdown diaries to this project. I appreciated your generous and creative approach to this task and I hope our collaborative interpretations here do justice to your auto/biographical representations. This chapter was completed with the support of the Flinders University Social and Behavioural Sciences Research Ethics Committee (Project number 2147).

## Notes

1 Arguably there are richer contexts than Adelaide, South Australia, when thinking about children's experiences of Covid-19 and lockdown. South Australia has experienced relatively short periods of lockdown compared with other parts of Australia and indeed the world. Public schools were only closed for a few weeks, though distance learning was possible for children whose families chose to keep them at home. However, it was the case that many children were (indeed are, at the time of writing) unable to see interstate or overseas family and friends for extended periods. The impact of this on children will likely be significant.

I live and work in Adelaide and all of my studies from this project have happened here. It would have been very difficult to complete studies anywhere else during 2020–1. Future studies might consider some of these child biographer and child reader methods in different contexts. For instance, in their study of children's experiences of lockdown in Spain, Nahia Idoiaga Mondragona, Naiara Berasategi Sanchob, Maria Dosil Santamariac and Amaia Eiguren Munitisb (2021) note how restricted children's experiences were in Spain during 2020. On the 14 March 2020, the prime minister of Spain declared a state emergency and national lockdown, the president outlined a very stringent set of rules to be followed during this lockdown, which, at the time, were possibly the harshest in Europe, and even the world. At the time of this speech there was not a single mention of children, although the rules were particularly rigid for them. Children were forbidden to leave their homes, with Spain being the only European country where children were not allowed to go out (Idoiaga et al., 2021: 180).

2   I made a donation to McCarthy of €50. I also wrote to him via his website to let him know about this study.

3   In her paper, 'Young Children's Drawings: A Methodological Tool for Data Analysis' Josephine Deguara (2019) offers a sophisticated social semiotics tool for the analysis of children's drawings in which she considers semiotic (modes) and configuration (themes) and interprets each of them as 'complex' or 'simple' (157). I adapted her methods in this discussion.

# Conclusion: What next for children's biography?

As I was about to finish writing this book, I became aware of the publication of an incredibly powerful book, *Heroes, Rebels and Innovators: Inspiring Aboriginal and Torres Strait Islander People from History*, written by Karen Wyld and illustrated by Jaelyn Biumaiwai. Reading this book reminded me that any current study of biographies for children now is bound to be nothing more than a work in progress. But *Heroes, Rebels and Innovators* seems an important text to conclude this study on, because it reveals how subjects for children's biography are ever expanding and diversity is a central project. *Heroes, Rebels and Innovators: Inspiring Aboriginal and Torres Strait Islander People from History* is a children's picture book, but its themes and representations are complex, so it would likely appeal to both children being read to, early readers, and more competent primary-school-aged children who recognize some of the historical figures represented and want to read more.

The book contains seven stories that are structured as two narratives over four pages (or two double-paged). The first double page represents the biographical narrative over a page and a half with a small picture, representing the colonial encounter between the Indigenous-biographical subject and their white collaborator. The first narrative reads like a poem or song, formatted in verses and stanzas. This approach offers stylistic diversity for the child reader, but also reminds us of the strong oral and songline histories of Indigenous Australian cultures. The second part of the biographical narration is the short biography on the left side, with a full-page illustration of the subject on the right side. In each of these full-page portraits, the subject is appearing serious, distinguished and beautiful. In all instances, the portrait is a close-up, head-and-shoulders representation, much like traditional or classic portraiture which shows the subject as they are, true to life. But representing these subjects in this way elevates them beyond the colonial subjects represented in *Heroes, Rebels and Innovators*. For once, the story is not about the so-called great explorers or pioneers' family from history textbooks of the late twentieth century, or those commemorated so often by monuments.

The stories themselves are filled with intelligence, heroism and adventure. For instance, Patyegerang, a young Darug woman, shared her language with a Lieutenant from the First Fleet, William Dawes. Together they 'make the first books featuring Aboriginal languages' (Wyld and Biumaiwai, 2021: 5). The illustration shows them together looking at the sky, but it is Patyegarang who is pointing and explaining something to Dawes. It is her knowledge that is valued. Patyegarang's role in making these records with Dawes has become highly significant in the preservation of Darug language for future generations.

Bungaree, a leader of his people, boldly inserted himself into colonial activities and histories through his friendship with Matthew Flinders. He travelled with him and taught Flinders and his crew what foods were safe to eat. Again, as in the illustration of Patyegarang, it is Bungaree who is depicted as the leader in the illustration of Bungaree and Matthew Flinders. It is Bungaree who is looking through the telescope and wearing the Royal Navy hat. Flinders looks on, taking notes! (Wyld and Biumaiwai, 2021: 9). Bungaree's leadership and knowledge is foregrounded; this image offers a simple but powerful inversion of dominant Australian colonial history (Wyld and Biumaiwai, 2021: 9). *Heroes, Rebels and Innovators* represents freedom fighter Tarenorerer who escaped from slavery to defend her territory and people; writer and inventor David Unaipon and environmental activist, Fanny Bulbuk Yooreel aimed to educate white people to care for the environment.

In each of these stories, Indigenous knowledge is privileged; it is shown to be superior to white knowledge of the colonial landscape. For example, Yarri and Jacky had warned the settlers not to build on the Murrumbidgee flood plains. But they did. The floods came and resulted in seventy lives being lost. More lives would have been lost were it not for Yarri and Jacky who saved many lives. Mohara Wacando-Lifu showed courage and superior skills in saving lives during tropical cyclone Mahina in 1899.

The core aim of each of these brief biographies is to bring an Indigenous history from the early years of colonization to children's attention. However, a strong theme also emerges relating to the ways in which lives are recorded and memorialized. For example, though history reveals what happened to William Dawes when he returned to England, 'there is no record of what happened to Patyegarang' (Wyld and Biumaiwai, 2021: 6). Similarly, 'recognised as a diplomat and explorer, Bungaree was given the title *King of Broken Bay* by Governor Macquarie. *But no monument was raised in his honour*' (Wyld and Biumaiwai, 2021: 10).

Biographies for children, then, are to play a role beyond the memorial, beyond what has already been recorded in history. In her author's note to *Heroes, Rebels and Innovators*, Karen Wyld writes,

> I encourage readers of all ages to learn more about Aboriginal and Torres Strait Islander peoples, languages and histories … There are Teacher's Notes on the Hachette website that will assist in further discussion, research and learning. (32)

Biographies for children create a space for education, historical revision and an overt respect for diverse lives. They open up conversations between children and adults on some of the biggest issues facing us in the twenty-first century. The book does not represent the end of the dialogue; these books most often conclude with offers of further reading, resources and so on. They are explicitly open-ended texts, inviting further inquiry. In seeing the subjects as rebels, and being invited to be rebels themselves, child readers are encouraged to redefine rebelliousness as an altogether positive subversion. The rebels in these biographies use their powers for good.

*  *  *

Biography has always been an important subgenre of children's literature. In this study I have explored children's relationship to biography. In doing so, I have considered examples of children as readers and as writers of biography. Children have been reading biographical texts for as long as children have been reading and, though my overview of these reading practices is not exhaustive, I have isolated some significant trends. Biography for children has long been associated with and aligned to principles of civic education and moral instruction. As these biographies represent children and childhood, they reflect dominant ideas about children and childhood that circulated at the time of their production. Though this might also be true of much of children's literature more generally, when narratives are presented to children as 'true', their ideological weight and responsibility shifts. Children are invited to read biography differently to how they read fiction. Biographies have traditionally been role-model texts, and a means by which cultural stakeholders have sought to reproduce cultural, religious and moral values through children and towards the future. Biographies for children, through their inclusion and omission of certain subjects and representations, define for child readers what makes a valuable life.

In the late twentieth and early twenty-first centuries we can see a shift in biographies for children, and this shift is a direct response to what was published previously. Though there are many conservative books for children in circulation across the globe, it is not within the scope of this study to review them. If we look to some of the most famous biographies for children published over the past five years, we can see these texts now have a much broader mandate. Books like *Goodnight Stories for Rebel Girls*, *Great Women Who Changed the World* and *Heroes, Rebels and Innovators: Inspiring Aboriginal and Torres Strait Islander People from History* invite their child readers to learn about subjects that are absent or might appear differently in other history books they have read. They ask children to have empathy for those represented, to think more deeply about diversity and to recognize the world we live in as filled with people (and animals) whose experiences of life are very different from each other's and potentially from the reader's. In exploring the collaborative biographies of child asylum-seekers, in considering the experiences of courageous children from across the globe and in following the narratives of rebel dogs, children are reading and recognizing diversity. In accepting these stories into their lives, in witnessing them, children are acknowledging these narratives as genuine and vital to the world we live in. Children are supporting these books' revision of history and coming to understand their own role as drivers of cultural change.

The other notable trend in the production of these biographies is the inclusion of interactive elements within the books. From blank pages in the texts that encourage children to add their own rebel narratives, to companion texts that are exclusively about children creating their own biographical writings and drawings, the relationship between reading and creating is emphasized and celebrated by twenty-first-century biographies for children.

Reading a biography is the first step towards interactivity, whether being inspired by the narratives to make changes in your own world or considering how creating your own biography texts might be productive. We could read these inclusions with scepticism: as a simple consumerist hook designed to ensure children want to buy more of these books. And while this perspective is persuasive, we should not deny children's desire to want to create their own texts and the books' clever recognition of this. Children like to interact with texts, whether through active reading approaches, for instance, the adventure-reading-style approach to the *Great Women* books or through writing in the books themselves. As discussed in Chapter 2, this once taboo idea has become the norm in these biographies and there is definitely scope for future studies to explore the positive payoffs of such interactive approaches to how children read. The blank pages offer space for children to add their knowledge and creative instincts to what biography is and does.

Another layer of interactivity common to twenty-first-century biography for children is the inclusion of 'further reading' lists and links. Such inclusions invite children to think about the limits of the biographical text and its relationship to '*the* truth'. These books let children know that this biography is not exhaustive, and they are encouraged to develop their knowledge further. These are very important transferable skills for children at a time of increasing fake news and where the norm is many versions of the truth in circulation across mainstream media.

* * *

As my study progressed, so did my sense of the parameters of biography. Adopting an increasingly broad definition of biography allowed me to consider new ways that children might be interacting with an old genre and in doing so, reinvigorating it. This interaction goes beyond the published books, towards other ways that children might engage with the genre as creators of biography. Children are prolific life narrators and do so across various private and public spaces in their lives. In doing so, they engage deeply with ideas of truth, power and change, and complete important work with relational lives at the intersection of autobiography and biography. While it might seem a leap to talk about the drawings of child asylum-seekers in detention alongside primary-school children's lockdown diaries and biographical texts about their mothers, these small archives each offer snapshots and contribute to our knowledge of the diverse ways in which children live in the twenty-first century, and how they come to construct aspects of life through auto/biographical texts. What I learned through looking at these texts was that children see their lives relationally and might be inclined to represent the lives of others over their own. Children will, without being prompted, represent the less-than-positive aspects of life. They will respond to prompts but will also readily hack them. Children will anticipate a response to their auto/biography, and they will assume that what they produced will be valued. Each of these findings might be developed in future research as we seek to learn more about children's relationship and engagements with life-narrative knowledge and practice.

Children read and make meaning from what they read. Further research might focus more closely on children's relationship to the various non-fiction genres that they read, particularly how they negotiate the 'truths' within. In my discussion of my kids' book club sessions, I present a rosy picture. The children loved the books they read as part of this study. However, in the session that followed (which did not form part of this study), we read a book which contained short narratives of young environmentalists from across the globe. The children reported finding these stories 'boring' and 'too much the same'. In future research, I aim to embrace and celebrate the difficulties and complexities around children's reading of non-fiction. I will take this chapter's methods and aims to different locations in Australia to investigate how children read biography, with the goal of discovering more about how diverse personal and geographical contexts might impact on children's interpretation of biography.

New studies might consider different spaces in which children create biography and other types of life narrative. The three case studies included here indicate that there are myriad ways in which children make biography. Researchers might look to ways to engage collaboratively with the public sites and discourses in which this is occurring (similar to the asylum-seeker drawings) for example, as a means for supporting activist projects and to consider how researchers might act as champions for child artists and activists in their pursuit of social justice.

In the micro, intimate spaces in which children create life narrative, I again predominantly presented positive example texts. We might look to add more nuance here, though this is ethically tricky, as issues of ownership, permission and the ethics of representation always come into play when exploring relational life narratives. One 'way in' here might be to engage children more overtly and powerfully in the interpretation of their own texts.

*  *  *

Biography in the twenty-first century is a fast-changing genre and children's biography is making a significant contribution to this change. As readers and as creators of biography, children are engaging in and starting conversations with adults about truth and representations; about rebels, heroes and role models; about love and influence; and about power and cultural change. Australia's (then) Commissioner for Children, Megan Mitchell, has stressed the importance of listening to children's voices in ensuring that children are included in decisions affecting their lives. However, children's voices are frequently marginalized and adults more commonly speak on their behalf. A recent survey of Australian youth revealed that 80 per cent of respondents (aged under eighteen) feel that they don't get to participate in decisions that affect them (Australia Human Rights Commission, 2018). When children engage in research about their own lives and well-being, this positively impacts upon their dignity and sense of self (Albers, 2016; Bargiel, Beck, Koblitz, O'Connor; Pierce and Wolf, 1997; Douglas and Poletti, 2016). In tracing the responses of children to biography in *Children and Biography: Reading and Writing Life Stories* in this project, I hope that I have delivered useful knowledge on children's literacy, cultural engagement and perspectives on the future.

# References

Abawi, A. (2019), *A Land of Permanent Goodbyes*, London: Penguin.

Abrahamson, R. F. and B. Carter (1992), 'What We Know About Nonfiction and Young Adult Readers and What We Need to Do About It', *Publishing Research Quarterly*, 8 (1): 41–54.

Albers, P. (2016), 'Why Stories Matter for Children's Learning', *The Conversation*, 5 January.

Alexander, C. and J. McMaster (2006), *The Child Writer from Austen to Woolf*, Baltimore: Johns Hopkins University Press.

Alexander, J. and R. Jarman (2018), 'The Pleasures of Reading Non-Fiction', *Literacy*, 52 (2): 78–85.

Aliagas, C. and A. M. Margallo (2017), 'Children's Responses to the Interactivity of Storybook Apps in Family Shared Reading Events Involving the iPad', *Literacy*, 51 (1): 44–52.

Alter, A. (2017), 'Why Children's Authors Are Taking on the Refugee Crisis', *The Independent*, 15 August.

Anderson, K. J. and D. Cavallaro (2002), 'Parents or Pop Culture? Children's Heroes and Role Models', *Childhood Education*, 78 (3): 161–8.

Anderson, V. (2020), 'Christchurch Artist Makes Lockdown Diary for Children', *Stuff*, 1 April. Available online: https://www.stuff.co.nz/national/120706383/christchurch-artist-makes-lockdown-diary-for-children. (Accessed 12 July 2021).

Arizpe, E. (2015), 'Foreword', in J. Evans (ed.), *Challenging and Controversial Picturebooks: Creative and Critical Responses to Visual Texts*, xvii–xx, London: Routledge.

Aukerman, M. (2015), 'How Should Readers Develop across Time? Mapping Change without a Deficit Perspective', *Language Arts*, 93: 55–62.

Austin, G. (2007), 'Drawing Trauma: Visual Testimony in *Caché* and *J'ai 8 ans*', *Screen*, 48 (4): 529–36.

Australian Human Rights Commission (2014), 'Survey Elevates Voices of Children in Australia'. Available online: https://humanrights.gov.au/about/news/survey-elevates-voices-children-australia. (Accessed 27 December 2021).

Backman, A. (2020), 'Shadow in Children's Picturebooks: Highlighting Children's Perspectives', *International Journal of Early Years Education*, 7 September.

Available online: https://www.tandfonline.com/doi/full/10.1080/09669 760.2020.1814217. (Accessed 20 August 2021).

Bargiel, S., S. Beck, D. Koblitz, A. O'Connor, K. Pierce and S. Wolf (1997), 'Bringing Life's Issues into Classrooms', *Language Arts*, 74 (6): 482–90.

Barone, D. (2011), 'Making Meaning: Individual and Group Response within a Book Club Structure', *Journal of Early Childhood Literacy*, 13 (1): 3–25.

Baroutsis, A., L. Kervin, A. Woods and B. Comber (2019), 'Understanding Children's Perspectives of Classroom Writing Practices through Drawings', *Contemporary Issues in Early Childhood*, 20 (2): 177–93.

Barzillai, M., J. Thomson, S. Schroeder and P. van den Broek (2018), *Learning to Read in a Digital World*, Amsterdam: John Benjamins.

Beauvais, C. (2019), 'Is There a Text in This Child? Childness and the Child-Authored Text', *Children's Literature in Education*, 50: 60–75.

Beckett, S. L. (2015), 'From Traditional Tales, Fairy Stories, Cautionary Tales to Controversial Visual Texts: Do We Need to Be Fearful?', in J. Evans (ed.), *Challenging and Controversial Picturebooks: Creative and Critical Responses to Visual Texts*, 49–70, London: Routledge.

Beckton, D. (2015), 'Bestselling Young Adult Fiction: Trends, Genres and Readership', *TEXT*, 32. Available online: http://www.textjournal.com.au/speciss/issue32/Beckton.pdf.

Bender, L. (2013), 'Children's Nonfiction Publishing Comes of Age', *Publishing Perspectives*, 25 March.

Benton, M. (1999), 'Readers, Texts, Contexts: Reader-Response Criticism', in P. Hunt (ed.), *Understanding Children's Literature*, 81–99, London: Routledge.

Bishop, R. S. (1990), 'Mirrors, Windows, and Sliding Glass Doors', *Perspectives*, 6: ix–xi.

Bland, D. (2012), 'Analysing Children's Drawings: Applied Imagination', *International Journal of Research & Method in Education*, 35 (3): 235–42.

Bode, K. and R. Dixon, eds (2009), *Resourceful Reading: The New Empiricism, eResearch and Australian Literary Culture*, Sydney: Sydney University Press.

Botelho, M. J. and M. K. Rudman (2009), *Critical Multicultural Analysis of Children's Literature: Mirrors, Windows, and Doors*, New York: Routledge.

Brien, D. L. (2015), 'What About Young Adult Non-Fiction?: Profiling the Young Adult Memoir', *TEXT*, 32.

Brooks, B. and Q. Winter (2018a), *Stories for Kids Who Dare to Be Different*, London: Quercus.

Brooks, B. and Q. Winter (2018b), *Stories for Boys Who Dare to Be Different*, London: Quercus.

Brown, M. (2019), 'Latinx Children's Biographies: Inspiring Transformation and Transcendence', *Language Arts*, 96 (3): 202–4.

Cardell, K. and K. Douglas (2020a), 'Circuits of Children's Testimony: Reading Syrian Children's Drawings of *Home*', *Life Writing*, 17 (4): 493–502.

Cardell, K. and K. Douglas (2020b), 'Emma González, Silence and Youth Testimony.' *Women: A Cultural Review*, 31 (1): 1–22.

Cardona, Ruby, and Isobel Lundie, illus. (2020), *Women in Science: Temple Grandin*, Brighton: Salariya.

Carter, D. J. and G. M. Montgomery (2017), 'The Social Justice Reading Group: Helping Youth Explore Culture, Difference, and (In)Equity Through Children's Literature,' *Michigan Reading Journal*, 49 (3): 44–8.

Castiglione, B. ([1528] 2001), *The Book of the Courtier*, London: Penguin.

Chute, H. L. (2016), *Disaster Drawn: Visual Witness, Comics and Documentary Form*, Cambridge, MA: Belknap/Harvard University Press.

Clark, B. (2016), 'Kids' Books Make Great Story', *Herald Sun*, 7 October.

Coats, K. (2018), *The Bloomsbury Introduction to Children's and Young Adult Literature*, London: Bloomsbury.

Coleman, J. (2010), 'Vested Interests: The Con Artist, the Historian, and the Feminist Biographer', *a/b: Auto/Biography Studies*, 25 (1): 18–31.

Cosslett, T. (2002), 'Child's Place in Nature: Talking Animals in Victorian Children's Fiction, *Nineteenth Century Contexts*, 23 (4): 475–95.

Cottrell, A. and A. Woods (2018), 'A Lunchtime Writing Club in Primary School? How Would That Possibly Work?', *Practical Literacy*, 23 (3): 14–17.

Couser, G. T. (2011), *Memoir: An Introduction*, Oxford: Oxford University Press.

Cumming, P. (2017), 'Introduction to "Another Children's Literature": Writing by Children and Youth Taking Writing by Children and Youth Seriously', *Bookbird: A Journal of International Children's Literature*, 55 (2): 4–9.

Cumming, S. and J. Visser (2019), 'Using Art with Vulnerable Children', *Art & Behaviour Support for Learning*, 24 (4): 151–8.

Cunningham, H. (2014), *Children and Childhood in Western Society Since 1500*, London: Routledge.

Darling-McQuistan, K. (2017), 'Beyond Representation: Exploring Drawing as Part of Children's Meaning-Making', *The International Journal of Art and Design Education*, 36 (3): 281–91.

Deguara, J. (2019), 'Young Children's Drawings: A Methodological Tool for Data Analysis', *Journal of Early Childhood Research*, 17 (2): 157–74.

Del Rizzo, S. (2017), *My Beautiful Birds*, Toronto: Pajama Press.

DeMello, M. (2018), 'Online Animal (Auto-)Biographies: What Does It Mean When We "Give Animals a Voice?"', in A. Krebber and M. Roscher (eds), *Animal Biography: Re-framing Animal Lives*, 243–59, Cham: Palgrave/Springer.

Do, A. (2010), *The Happiest Refugee: My Journey from Tragedy to Comedy*, Sydney: Allen & Unwin.

Do, A. and S. Do (2011), *The Little Refugee*, Sydney: Allen & Unwin.

Douglas, K. (2006), 'Lost and Found: The Life Narratives of Child Asylum Seekers', *Life Writing*, 3 (1): 41–59.

Douglas, K. (2010), *Contesting Childhood: Autobiography, Trauma and Memory*, New Brunswick: Rutgers.

Douglas, K. (2017), 'Malala Yousafzai, Life Narrative and the Collaborative Archive', *Life Writing*, 14 (3): 297–311.

Douglas, K. (2019), 'Autobiographical Writing for Children', in Jo Parnell (ed.), *New and Unusual Ways of Writing Lives*, 22–31, Houndsmill: Palgrave.

Douglas, K. (2020) '@Alabedbana: Twitter, the Child, and the War Diary', *Textual Practice*, 34 (6): 1021–39.

Douglas, K. and A. Poletti (2016), *Life Narratives and Youth Culture*, London: Palgrave.

Dollins, C. A. (2016), 'Crafting Creative Nonfiction: From Close Reading to Close Writing', *The Reading Teacher*, 70 (1): 49–58.

'Drawings by Children in Immigration Detention.' (2014). Available online: https://www.flickr.com/photos/23930202@N06/albums/72157645938124048. (Accessed 25 January 2021).

Drogos, K. L. (2021), 'Media Literacy Lessons for American Children in the Kids' Antiracist Bookclub', *Journal of Children and Media*, 15 (1): 117–21.

Eaton, G. (2006), *Well-Dressed Role Models: The Portrayal of Women in Biographies for Children*, Lanham: Scarecrow.

Ebenezer, Miller (1824), *Scripture History, With the Lives of the Most Celebrated Apostles. Designed for the Improvement of Youth*, London: T. Kelly Publishing.

Einarsdottir, J., S. Dockett and B. Perry (2009), 'Making Meaning: Children's Perspectives Expressed Through Drawings', *Early Child Development and Care*, 179 (2): 217–32.

Evans, J. (2015), *Challenging and Controversial Picturebooks: Creative and Critical Responses to Visual Texts*, London: Routledge.

Farley, L. and A. P. Tarc (2014), 'Drawing Trauma: The Therapeutic Potential of Witnessing the Child's Visual Testimony of War', *Journal of the American Psychoanalytic Association*, 62 (5): 835–54.

Farris, P. and C. Furhler (1994), 'Developing Social Studies Concepts Through Picture Books', *The Reading Teacher*, 47 (5): 380–7.
Favilli, E. and F. Cavallo (2017), *Goodnight Stories for Rebel Girls*, London: Penguin.
Favilli, E. and F. Cavallo (2018), *Goodnight Stories for Rebel Girls 2*, London: Penguin.
Favilli, E. and F. Cavallo (2018), *I am a Rebel Girl: A Journal to Start Revolutions*, London: Timbuktu.
Flores, T. (2019), 'The Family Writing Workshop: Latinx Families Cultivando Comunidad Through Stories', *Language Arts*, 97 (2): 59–71.
Favilli, E. and P. Gruber (2020), *Good Night Stories for Rebel Girls: 100 Immigrant Women Who Changed the World*, London: Penguin.
Favilli, E. and F. Cavallo (2021), *Rebel Girls Champions: 25 Tales of Unstoppable Athletes*, New York: Rebel Girls Inc.
Favilli, E. and F. Cavallo (2021), *Rebel Girls Lead: 25 Tales of Powerful Women*, New York: Rebel Girls Inc.
Favilli, E. and F. Cavallo (2021), *One-Hundred Real-Life Tales of Black Girl Magic*, New York: Rebel Girls Inc.
*The Forgotten Children Report: National Inquiry into Children in Immigration Detention* (2014), *Human Rights*. Available online: https://humanrights.gov.au/sites/default/files/document/publication/forgotten_children_2014.pdf. (Accessed 25 January 2021).
Fuchs, M. (2004), *The Text Is Myself: Women's Life Writing and Catastrophe*, Minneapolis: The University of Minnesota Press.
Gardner, S. (1991), 'My First Rhetoric of Domination: The Columbian Encounter in Children's Biographies,' *Children's Literature in Education*, 22 (4): 275–90.
Garner, H. (2006), *Joe Cinque's Consolation*, Brisbane: Pan Macmillian.
Gene, G. (2021), *Living with Mochi*, Kansas City: Andrews: McMeel Publishing.
'Georgiou Library Receives Collection of Picture Book Biographies from Leonard Marcus, Children's Literature Historian', (2015), *NYU Steinhardt News*, 25 October. Available online: https://www.nyu.edu/about/news-publications/news/2015/october/georgiou-library-receives-collection-of-picture-book-biographies-from-childrens-lit-authority-leonard-marcus.html.
Gernhardt, A., H. Keller and H. Rubeling (2016), 'Children's Family Drawings as Expressions of Attachment Representations Across Cultures: Possibilities and Limitations', *Child Development*, 87 (4): 1069–78.
Gibson, F. (2007), 'Conducting Focus Groups with Children and Young People: Strategies for Success', *Journal of Research in Nursing*, 12 (5): 473–83.

Girard, L. W. (1989), 'Series Thinking and the Art of Biography for Children', *Children's Literature Association Quarterly*, 14 (4): 187–92.

Girard, L. W. (1990), 'The Renaissance of Biography', *Five Owls*, 5 (1): 1–3.

Glaveanu, V. P. (2013), 'Creativity Development in Community Contexts: The Case of Folk Art', *Thinking Skills and Creativity*, 9: 152–64.

Gonen, M. and T. Guler (2011), 'The Environment and Its Place in Children's Picture Story Books', *Procedia Social and Behavioral Sciences*, 15: 3633–9.

Graham, P. (2016), 'Re-viewing the Lives of Others: "New Biography" in the Early Twenty-First Century', PhD diss., Flinders University, School of Humanities and Creative Arts, Adelaide.

Grenby, M. O. and A. Immel, eds (2009), *The Cambridge Companion to Children's Literature*, Cambridge: Cambridge University Press.

Grenby, M. O. (2007), 'Chapbooks, Children, and Children's Literature', *The Library*, 8 (3): 277–303.

Grenby, M. O. (2009), 'The Origins of Children's Literature', in M. O. Grenby and Andrea Immel (eds), *The Cambridge Companion to Children's Literature*, 3–18, Cambridge: Cambridge University Press.

Gross, J. and Hayne, H. (1998), 'Drawing Facilitates Children's Verbal Reports of Emotionally Laden Events', *Journal of Experimental Psychology*, 4: 163–79.

Habermas, T. (2010), 'Autobiographical Reasoning: Arguing and Narrating from a Biographical Perspective', *New Directions for Children and Adolescent Development*, 131: 1–17.

*Hachi: A Dog's Tale* (2009), dir. Lasse Hallstrom, Affirm Films.

Hall, E. (2015), 'The Ethics of "Using" Children's Drawings in Research', in D. Yamada-Rice and E. Stirling (eds), *Visual Methods with Children and Young People: Academics and Visual Industries in Dialogue*, 140–63, Basingstoke: Palgrave Macmillan.

Harkin, P. (2005), *The Reception of Reader-Response Theory. College Composition and Communication*, 56 (3): 410–25.

Harper, J. R. (2019), 'Folk Art', *The Canadian Encyclopedia*, Toronto: Historica Canada.

Haertling, T. A. and R. R. Schmidt (2017), 'Challenging, Rewarding Emotion Work: Critical Witnessing in an After-School Book Club', *Language Arts*, 94 (5): 313–25.

Hamilton, K. (2018), *Rebel Cats: Brave Tales of Feisty Felines*, New York: Scholastic.

Hamilton, K. (2019), *Rebel Dogs: Heroic Tales of Trusty Hounds*, New York: Scholastic.

Hamilton, N. (2010), *Biography: A Brief History*, Cambridge: Harvard University Press.
Harvey and Darton (1824), *Juvenile Biography; Being Some Account of the Childhood of Persons Who Were Eminent in Maturer Years for Piety, Genius, and Learning*.
Haynes, R. Elizabeth ([1921] 2019), *Unsung Heroes*, Sydney: Wentworth Press.
Herman, D. (2016), 'Animal Autobiography; or, Narration Beyond the Human,' *Humanities*, 5: 82.
Hewin, Caroline (1882), *Books for the Young*, New York: F. Leypoldt.
Hill, S., A. Glover and M. Colbung (2011), 'My Favourite Book! Young Aboriginal Children's Book Choices', *Australasian Journal of Early Childhood*, 36 (1): 77–84.
Hintz, C. and E. L. Tribunella (2019), *Reading Children's Literature: A Critical Introduction*, Peterborough: Broadview.
Hoberman, R. (2001), 'Biography', *Encyclopedia of Life Writing: Autobiographical and Biographical Forms*, 112, London: Routledge.
Hoffman, A. R. (2010), 'The BFG and the Spaghetti Book Club: A Case Study of Children as Critics', *Children's Literature in Education*, 41: 234–50.
Hopperstad, Marit Holm. 'Studying Meaning in Children's Drawings'. *Journal of Early Childhood Literacy* 10, no. 4 (December 2010): 430–52. https://doi.org/10.1177/1468798410383251.
Hourihan, M. (1997), *Deconstructing the Hero: Literary Theory and Children's Literature*, London: Routledge.
Howes, W. C. (2020), 'Life Writing – Genre, Practice, Environment.' *Oxford Research Encyclopedias*, 27 October. Available online: https://doi.org/10.1093/acref ore/9780190201098.013.1146. (Accessed 12 July 2021).
Huff, C. (2017), 'After Auto, After Bio: Posthumanism and Life Writing', *a/b: Auto/Biography Studies*, 32 (2): 279–82.
Huff, C. and J. Haefner (2012), 'His Master's Voice: Animalographies, Life Writing, and the Posthuman', *Biography*, 35 (1): 153–69.
Huff, C. Ann, ed. (2005), *Women's Life Writing and Imagined Communities*, London: Routledge.
Human Rights Commission (2014), 'Drawings by Children in Immigration Detention.' *Human Rights*, 11 August. Available online: https://www.humanrig hts.gov.au/news/photos/drawings-children-immigration-detention. (Accessed 8 January 2021).
Hunger, C. (2021), *How Stella Learned to Talk*, New York: William Morrow.
Idoiaga Mondragona, N., N. B. Sanchob, M. D. Santamariac and A. E. Munitisb (2021), 'Struggling to Breathe: A Qualitative Study of Children's Wellbeing During Lockdown in Spain,' *Psychology and Health*, 36 (2): 179–94.

Immel, A. (2009), 'Children's Books and Constructions of Childhood', in M. O. Grenby and Andrea Immel (eds), *The Cambridge Companion to Children's Literature*, 19–34, Cambridge: Cambridge University Press.

Interview with Francesca Sanna. Available online: https://vimeo.com/210912683. (Accessed 5 May 2021).

*The Interesting and Affecting History of Prince Lee Boo, a Native of the Pelew Islands, Brought to England by Capt. Wilson. To Which is Prefixed, a Short Account of Those Islands* ([1789] 2018), Farmington Hills: ECCO Gale.

Iordanaki, L. (2020), 'Older Children's Responses to Wordless Picturebooks: Making Connections', *Children's Literature in Education*, 52: 493–510.

Jaques, Z. (2015), *Children's Literature and the Posthuman*, New York: Routledge.

James, A. and A. Prout (1997), *Constructing and Reconstructing Childhood: Contemporary Issues in the Sociological Study of Childhood*, London: Routledge.

Janeway, J. ([1671] 2021), *A Token for Children*, Maroussi: Alpa Edition.

Jolley, R. (2010), *Children and Pictures: Drawing and Understanding*, Chichester: Wiley-Blackwell.

Jolly, M. (2008), *In Love and Struggle: Letters in Contemporary Feminism*, New York: Columbia University Press.

Jones, D. and T. Watkins (2000), *A Necessary Fantasy?: The Heroic Figure in Children's Popular Culture*, London: Routledge.

John, F. ([1890] 2010), *Reading for the Young*, Memphis: General Books.

Johnson, R. ([1790] 2010), *The Adventure of a Silver Penny*, Whitefish: Kessinger Publishing.

*The Journey* (2016), (Website publicity). Available online: https://www.penguinrandomhouse.com/books/585963/the-journey-by-francesca-sanna/9781909263994/. (Accessed 12 August 2021).

Jurich, M. (1972) 'What's Left Out of Biography for Children', *Children's Literature*, 1: 143–51.

Kaemaek, F. and B. Logas Beverly (2000), 'Spider, Kid Curlers, and White Shoes: Telling and Writing Stories Across Generations', *The Reading Teacher*, 53 (3): 446–51.

Kalb, D. (2017), 'Q&A with Suzanne Del Rizzo', 4 May. Available online: http://deborahkalbbooks.blogspot.com/2017/05/q-with-suzanne-del-rizzo.html. (Accessed 5 May 2021).

Kaplun, C. (2019), 'Children's Drawings Speak a Thousand Words in Their Transition to School', *Australasian Journal of Early Childhood*, 44 (4): 392–407.

Katz, C. and L. Hamama (2013), '"Draw Me Everything That Happened to You": Exploring Children's Drawings of Sexual Abuse', *Children and Youth Services Review*, 35: 877–82.

Kellond, J. (2020), 'The Reproduction of Mothering: Second Wave Legacies in Alison Bechdel's *Are You My Mother?*', *Free Associations: Psychoanalysis and Culture, Media, Groups, Politics*, 78. Available online: http://www.freeassociations.org.uk. (Accessed 5 May 2021).

Kelly, R. G. (1973), 'American Biographies for Children, 1870–1900', *American Literary Realism, 1870–1910*, 6 (2): 123–36.

Kilner, D. ([1793] 2002), *The Life and Perambulations of a Mouse*, IndyPublish.com.

Knight, L. (2013), 'Not as It Seems: Using Deleuzian Concepts of the Imaginary to Rethink Children's Drawings', *Global Studies of Childhood*, 3 (3): 254–64.

Koutsoftas, A. D. (2018), 'Writing: Process Products of Fourth and Sixth-Grade Children', *The Elementary School Journal*, 118 (4): 632–53.

Krebber, A. and M. Roscher (2018), *Animal Biography: Re-framing Animal Lives*, Cham: Palgrave/Springer.

Lechner, J. V. (1997), 'Accuracy in Biographies for Children', *The New Advocate*, 10 (3): 229–42.

Ledger, S. and M. K. Merga (2018), 'Reading Aloud: Children's Attitudes Toward Being Read To at Home and at School', *Australian Journal of Teacher Education*, 43 (3): 124–39.

Lee, H. (2009), *Biography: A Very Short Introduction*, Oxford: Oxford University Press.

Lenette, C., P. Karan, D. Chrysostomou and A. Athanasopoulos (2017), 'What Is It Like Living in Detention? Insights from Asylum Seeker Children's Drawings', *Australian Journal of Human Rights*, 23 (1): 42–60.

Leieune, Philippe (1975), *Le Pacte qutobiographique*, Paris: Seuill.

Linder, Lauri. A., Bratton, Heather., Nguyen, Anna., Parker, Kori., and Wawrzynski, Sarah (2018), 'Symptoms and Self-Management Strategies Identified by Children with Cancer Using Draw-and-Tell Interviews', *Oncology nursing forum*, 45 (3): 290–300. https://doi.org/10.1188/18.ONF.290-300

*Little People, Big Dreams* (2021). Available online: https://littlepeoplebigdreams.com/ (Accessed 5 May 2021).

*The Lion King* (1994), dirs. Roger Allers and Rob Minkoff, Walk Disney Pictures.

Locke, Mason ([1800] 1996), *The Life of Washington*, London: Taylor and Francis.

Locke, J. ([1693] 1998), *An Essay Concerning Human Understanding*, London: Penguin.

Locke, J. ([1693] 2000), *Some Thoughts Concerning Education*, Oxford: Oxford University Press.

Looman, W. S. (2006), 'A Developmental Approach to Understanding Drawings and Narratives from Children Displaced by Hurricane Katrina', *Journal of Pediatric Health Care*, 20 (3): 158–66.

Loumeau-May, L. V., E. Seibel-Nicol, M. Pellicci Hamilton and C. A. Malchiodi (2014), 'Art Therapy as an Intervention for Mass Terrorism and Violence', in C. A. Malchiodi (ed.), *Creative Interventions with Traumatized Children*, 2nd edition, New York: Guilford Publications.

Lowther, T. (2018), 'Why No Stories for Rebel Children? Don't Divide Young Readers by Gender', *The Guardian*, 24 April. Available online: https://www.theguardian.com/commentisfree/2018/apr/24/rebel-childrens-books-women-gender-girls-boys. (10 Sept 2021).

Lynch, C. (2013), 'Ante-Autobiography and the Archive of Childhood', *Prose Studies*, 35 (1): 97–112.

Maagerø, E. and T. Tone Sunde (2016), 'What Makes Me Happy, and What Makes Me Scared? An Analysis of Drawings Made by Norwegian and Palestinian Children', *European Early Childhood Education Research Journal*, 24 (2): 287–304.

Maguire, E. (2018), *Girls, Autobiography, Media: Gender and Self-Mediation in Digital Economies*, London: Palgrave.

Maine, F., S. Rojas-Drummond, R. Hoffman and M. J. Barrera (2020), 'Symmetries and Asymmetries in Children's Peer-Group Reading Discussions', *Australian Journal of Language and Literacy*, 43 (1): 17–32.

Mantzicopoulos, P. and H. Patrick (2011), 'Reading Picture Books and Learning Science: Engaging Young Children with Informational Text', *Theory into Practice*, 50 (4): 269–76.

Marcus, L. S. (1980), 'Life Drawings: Some Notes on Children's Picture Book Biographies', *The Lion and the Unicorn*, 4 (1): 15–31.

Marshall, E. (2019), 'Life Writing and the Language Arts', *Language Arts*, 96 (3): 167–78.

Martínez García, A. B. (2018), 'TED Talks as Life Writing: Online and Offline Activism', *Life Writing*, 15 (4): 487–503.

Martínez García, A. B. (2019), 'Construction and Collaboration in Life-Writing Projects: Malala Yousafzai's Activist "I"', *Journal of Writing in Creative Practice*, 12 (1–2): 201–17.

Martínez García, A. B. (2020), 'Constructing an Activist Self: Greta Thunberg's Climate Activism as Life Writing', *Prose Studies*, 41 (3): 349–66.

Mavers, D. (2010), *Children's Drawing and Writing: The Remarkable in the Unremarkable*, London: Routledge.

Maxwell, T. (2015), 'What Can Year-5 Children's Drawings Tell Us about Their Primary School Experiences', *Pastoral Care in Education*, 33 (2): 83–95.

Mayhew, M. (2015), 'What Can We Draw from Pictures by Detained Child Asylum Seekers?', *The Conversation*, 23 February. Available online: https://theconversation.com/what-can-we-draw-from-pictures-by-detained-child-asylum-seekers-37647. (Accessed 5 May 2021).

McCance, D. (2013), *Critical Animal Studies: An Introduction*, Albany, NY: SUNY Press.

McCreary, J. J. and G. L. Marchant (2017), 'Reading and Empathy', *Reading Psychology*, 38 (2): 182–202.

McCulloch, F. (2011), *Children's Literature in Context*, London: Continuum.

McGowan, J. ([1793] 2017), *Life of Joseph, the Son of Israel: In Eight Books, Chiefly Designed for the Use of Youth*, Norderstedt: Hansebooks.

McHugh, S. (2009), 'Animal Farm's Lesson for Literary (and) Animal Studies', *Humanimalia*, 1 (1): 24–39.

McMaster, J. (2001), '"Adults' Literature", by Children', *The Lion & The Unicorn*, 25 (2): 277–99.

Merga, M. K. (2017), 'Interactive Reading Opportunities Beyond the Early Years: What Educators Need to Consider', *Australian Journal of Education*, 61 (3): 328–43.

Merga, M. and S. M. Roni (2018), 'Children Prefer to Read Books on Paper Rather Than Screens', *The Journal for the School Information Professional*, 22 (3): 17–26.

Meyer, R. J. (2010), *Official Portraits and Unofficial Counterportraits of At Risk Students Writing Spaces in Hard Times*, New York: Routledge.

Mickenberg, J. (2002), 'Civil Rights, History, and the Left: Inventing the Juvenile Black Biography', *MELUS*, 27 (2): 65–94.

Middelhoff, F. (2018), 'Recovering and Reconstructing Animal Selves in Literary Autozoographies', in A. Krebber and M. Roscher (eds), *Animal Biography: Re-framing Animal Lives*, 57–79, Cham: Palgrave/Springer.

Morgan, H. (2009), 'Picture Book Biographies for Children: A Way to Teach Multiple Perspectives', *Early Childhood Education Journal*, 37: 219–27.

Murray, K. (1999), *Tough Stuff: True Stories of About Kids and Courage*, Sherborne: Ragged Bears.

Murray, K. (2019), *Kids Who Did: Real Kids Who Ruled, Rebelled, Survived and Thrived*, Sydney: Allen and Unwin.

Nash, J. C. and S. Pinto (2020), 'Strange Intimacies: Reading Black Maternal Memoirs', *Public Culture*, 32 (3): 491–512.

Natov, R. (2018), *The Courage to Imagine: The Child Hero in Children's Literature*, London: Bloomsbury.

Newberry, J. ([1944] 2009), *A Little Pretty Pocket Books*, Gloucester: Dodo Press.

Newbery, Elizabeth, Cummyng, Mrs. Susannah, Josse, Augustin Louis (2019), *Juvenile Biography; or, Lives of Celebrated Children. Inculcating virtue by eminent examples from real life. To which are added moral reflections, addressed to the youth of both sexes. By Mr. Josse, professor of Spanish and French languages. Translated by Mrs. Cummyng, translatress of Estelle. The Women's Print History Project*, 12703. Available online https://www.womensprinthistoryproject.com/title/12703 (accessed 2 April 2022).

Ní Dhúill, C. (2020), *Metabiography, Palgrave Studies in Life Writing*, London: Palgrave.

Nocella II, A. J., J. Sorenson, K. Socha and A. Matsuoka, eds (2014), *Defining Critical Animal Studies: An Intersectional Social Justice Approach for Liberation*, New York: Peter Lang.

Nodelman, P. (2015), 'The Scandal of the Commonplace: The Strangeness of Best-Selling Picturebooks', in J. Evans (ed.), *Challenging and Controversial Picturebooks: Creative and Critical Responses to Visual Texts*, 33–48, London: Routledge.

Norton, D. (1985), 'Moral Stages of Children's Biographical Literature, 1800s–1900', *Vita Scholasticae*, 4 (1): 77–89.

Norwich, B. and G. Koutsouris (2020), 'An Inclusive Model of Targeted Literacy Teaching for 7–8-Year-Old Children Who Are Struggling to Learn to Read: The Integrated Group Reading (IGR) Approach', *e Education: Global Issues and Controversies*, 216–33, Leiden: Brill.

Nuttman-Shwartz, O., E. Huss and A. Altman (2010), 'The Experience of Forced Relocation as Expressed in Children's Drawings', *Clinical Social Work Journal*, 38 (4): 397–407.

'NYU's Georgiou Library Receives Collection of Picture Book Biographies from Children's Literature Authority Leonard Marcus' (2015), NYU Press Release, 26 October. Available online: https://www.nyu.edu/about/news-publications/news/2015/october/georgiou-library-receives-collection-of-picture-book-biographies-from-childrens-lit-authority-leonard-marcus.html. (Accessed 15 May 2021).

O'Dell, L. (2008), 'Representations of the "Damaged" Child: "Child Saving" in a British Children's Charity Ad Campaign', *Children & Society*, 22: 383–92.

Olmstead, K. and Bobbie Kabuto (2018), 'Writing Artefacts as Narratives of Emotion', *Language and Literacy*, 20 (2): 102–24.

Onwuemezi, N. (2018), 'Non-Fiction and Middle Grade: The Growth Areas for Children's Publishing', *The Bookseller*, 20 August.

Oztabak, M. U. (2020), 'Refugee Children's Drawings: Reflections of Migration and War', *International Journal of Educational Methodology*, 6 (2): 481–95.

Pankhurst, K. (2016), *Fantastically Great Women Who Changed the World*, London: Bloomsbury.

Pankhurst, K. (2018), *Fantastically Great Women Who Made History*, London: Bloomsbury.

Pankhurst, K. (2017), *Fantastically Great Women Who Made History Activity Book*, London: Bloomsbury.

Pankhurst, K. (2018), *Fantastically Great Women Who Made History Activity Book*, London: Bloomsbury.

Peterson-Sweeney, K. (2005), 'The Use of Focus Groups in Pediatric and Adolescent Research', *Journal of Pediatric Health Care*, 19 (2): 104–10.

Pickering Jr. S. F. (1977), 'The Evolution of a Genre: Fictional Biographies for Children in the Eighteenth Century', *The Journal of Narrative Technique*, 7 (1): 1–23.

Pierce, P. (1999), *The Country of Lost Children: An Australian Anxiety*, Cambridge: Cambridge University Press.

Pierce, N. (2020), *Women in Science: Ada Lovelace*, Brighton: Salariya.

Pooley, S. (2015), 'Children's Writing and the Popular Press in England 1876–1914', *History Workshop Journal*, 80: 75–98.

Q&A with Kimberlie Hamilton (2018), *Scholastic*, 8 November. Available online: https://www.scholastic.co.uk/blog/Q-and-A-with-Kimberlie-Hamilton-37243. (Accessed 13 February 2021).

Q&A with Maria Isabel Sánchez Vegara (2018), *World Book Day*. Available online: https://www.worldbookday.com/2018/09/qa-isabel-sanchez-vergara-creator-little-people-big-dreams-series/. (Accessed 13 February 2021).

Quilty, B. (2018), *Home: Drawings by Syrian Children*, Melbourne: Penguin.

Rabakukk, G. (2017), 'New Voice: Author–Illustrator Suzanne Del Rizzo', *Cynsations*, 5 April. Available online: http://cynthialeitchsmith.blogspot.com/2017/04/new-voice-author-illustrator-Suzanne.html. (Accessed 30 November 2021).

Ransom, M. and M. Manning (2013), 'Teaching Strategies: Worksheets, Worksheets, Worksheets', *Childhood Education*, 89 (3): 188–90.

Rahn, S. (1991), 'An Evolving Past: The Story of Historical Fiction and Nonfiction for Children', *The Lion and the Unicorn*, 15 (1): 1–26.

Rak, J. (2013), *Boom!: Manufacturing Memoir for the Popular Market*, Waterloo: Wilfred Laurier.

'Rebel Dogs: An Interview with Kimberlie Hamilton', by Sarah Farrell (2019), *The Reading Realm*, 10 August. Available online: https://thereadingrealm.co.uk/2019/08/10/rebel-dogs-an-interview-with-kimberlie-hamilton/. (Accessed 21 February 2021).

Reynolds, K. (2011), *Children's Literature: A Very Short Introduction*, Oxford: Oxford University Press.

Rooney, A. and I. Lundie (2020), *Women in Science: Rachel Carson*, Brighton: Salariya.

Rosen, H. (2015), 'Is Children's Nonfiction Having Its Moment?', *Publisher's Weekly*, 17 July. Available online: https://www.publishersweekly.com/pw/by-topic/childrens/childrens-industry-news/article/67549-is-nonfiction-having-its-moment.html (Accessed 15 July 2021).

Sánchez Vegara, M. I. and A. Weckman (2020), *Little People, Big Dreams: Greta Thunberg*, London: Frances Lincoln.

Sánchez Vegara, M. I. and P. Morgan (2021), *Little People, Big Dreams: Megan Rapinoe*, London: Frances Lincoln.

Sanna, F. (2016), *The Journey*, London: Flying Eye Books.

Schaub, M. (2017), 'Does Aung San Suu Kyi Belong in a Children's Book of Heroic Women, "Rebel Girls"?', *Los Angeles Times*, 27 December. Available online: https://www.latimes.com/books/jacketcopy/la-et-jc-rebel-girls-20171227-story.html. (Accessed 30 March 2021).

*Shout Out to the Girls: A Celebration of Awesome Australian Women* (2018), Sydney: Random House.

Short, K. G. (2018), 'What's Trending in Children's Literature and Why It Matters', *Language Arts*, 95 (5): 287–98.

*A Street Cat Named Bob* (2016), dir. Roger Spottiswoode, Stage 6 Films.

Skabelund, A. (2018), 'A Dog's Life: The Challenges and Possibilities of Animal Biography', in A. Krebber and M. Roscher (eds), *Animal Biography: Re-framing Animal Lives*, 83–102, Cham: Palgrave/Springer.

Skloot, R. (2011), *The Immortal Life of Henrietta Lacks*, New York: Crown.

Skrlac Lo, R. and S. Dahlstrom (2020), 'Comic Moments in the School Library: Reflections on an After-School Book Club', *Bookbird: A Journal of International Children's Literature*, 58 (1): 61–7.

Smith, K. (2013), *Wreck My Journal*, London: Penguin.

Smith, S. and J. Watson (1996), *Getting a Life: Everyday Uses of Autobiography*, Minneapolis: University of Minnesota Press.

Smith, S. and J. Watson (1998), *Women, Autobiography, Theory: A Reader*, Minneapolis: The University of Minnesota Press.

Smith, S. and J. Watson (2010), *Reading Autobiography*, Minneapolis: University of Minnesota Press.

Soundy, C. S. (2012), 'Searching for Deeper Meaning in Children's Drawings', *Childhood Education*, 88 (1): 45–51.

Stabell, I. L. (2013), 'Model Patriots: The First Children's Biographies of George Washington and Benjamin Franklin', *Children's Literature*, 41: 91.

Strachey, L. ([1918] 2009), *Eminent Victorians*, Oxford: Oxford World Classics.

Strehle, E. (1999), 'Connecting Children to Their World', *Children's Literature in Education*, 30 (3): 212–20.

Sutcliff Sanders, J. (2017), *A Literature of Questions Nonfiction for the Critical Child*, Minneapolis: The University of Minnesota Press.

Tang, J. (2017), 'The Children's Hour', *THINK Australian*, Books and Publishing. Available online: https://www.booksandpublishing.com.au/ThinkAustralian/ThinkAustralian2017.pdf.

Tompkins, G. E. and P. D. Jones (2018), *Teaching Writing: Balancing Process and Product*, New York: Pearson.

Tomsic, M. (2019), 'Children's Art: Histories and Cultural Meanings of Creative Expression by Displaced Children', in K. Moruzi, N. Musgrove and C. Pascoe Leahy (eds), *Children's Voices from the Past: New Historical and Interdisciplinary Perspectives*, 137–58, London: Palgrave.

'Turkey says Rebel Girls Children's Book Should Be Treated Like Porn' (2019), *The Guardian*, 4 October. Available online: https://www.theguardian.com/world/2019/oct/04/good-night-stories-for-rebel-girls-turkey-says-porn. (Accessed 2 June 2021).

Twine, R. (2015), *Animals as Biotechnology. Ethics, Sustainability and Critical Animal Studies*, London: Routledge.

Van Bergen, E., M. Snowling, E. L. de Zeeuw, C. E. M. van Beiksterveldt, C. V. Dolan and D. I. Boomsma (2018), 'Why Do Children Read More? The Influence of Reading Ability on Voluntary Reading Practices', *The Journal of Child Psychology and Psychiatry*, 59 (11): 1205–14.

VanderHaagen, S. (2012), 'Practical Truths: Black Feminist Agency and Public Memory Biographies for Children,' *Women's Studies in Communication*, 35 (1): 18–41.

VanderHaagen, S. C. (2018), 'A World of Inspiration: Biographical Sketches in Early African American Children's Literature', *Children's Biographies of*

*African American Women: Rhetoric, Public Memory, and Agency*, Columbia, SC: University of South Carolina Press.

Van Horn, S. E. (2015), '"How Do You Have Two Moms?" Challenging Heteronormativity While Sharing LGBTQ-Inclusive Children's Literature', *Talking Points*, 27 (1): 1–12.

Vreeland, P. (1998), 'The Family Tree: Nurturing Language Growth Through "All the Parts of Me"', *Voices from the Middle*, 6 (1): 17–22.

Wahlström Henriksson, H. (2021), 'Moms, Memories, Materialities: Sons Write Their Mothers' Bodies', *a/b: Auto/Biography Studies*, 36 (1): 139–60.

Watts, R. (2010), 'Responding to Children's Drawings', *Education*, 38 (2): 137–53.

Wollman-Bonilla, J. (2000), *Family Message Journals: Teaching Writing Through Family Involvement*, Urbana, IL: National Council of Teachers of English.

Woolf, A. and I. Lundie (2020), *Women in Science: Jane Goodall*, Brighton: Salariya.

Woolf, V. (1979), *Diaries*, London: Mariner Books.

Woolf, V. (1981), *The Diary of Virginia Woolf*, 3: 1925–30, Boston: Mainer Books.

Wyld, K. and J. Biumaiwai (2021), *Heroes, Rebels and Innovators: Inspiring Aboriginal and Torres Strait Islander People from History*, Sydney: Lothian.

Yousafzai, M. (2017), *Malala's Magic Pencil*, London: Penguin.

Yousafzai, M. with C. Lamb (2013), *I am Malala: The Girl Who Stood Up for Education and Was Shot by the Taliban*, New York: Little Brown.

# Index

Alexander, Christine and Juliet McMaster 142, 169, 188
animal biography 8, 14–15, 24, 82, 83–99
ante-autobiography 16, 148, 162, 184
Arizpe, Evelyn 103, 104, 108, 112
artist's statements 156, 180, 184, 186, 188
asylum seeker narratives (*see* 'refugee narratives') 15, 16, 99, 101–21, 123–39, 195–6
auto/biography 3, 10, 60, 61, 89, 90, 120, 124, 137, 162, 166, 170, 178, 186, 196

Barone, Diane 66, 72
Beauvais Clémentine 142, 143, 144, 145
biographical collage (*see also* 'collaborative biography') 15, 101–21, 135, 172, 188, 194
biography (definitions, history of) 3, 4–8
　biobits 7
　metabiography 6, 7, 87
　new biography 5, 6, 7
　pre twenty-first century biography, theory 4–8, 19–37
　twenty-first century biography, theory 3, 4–8, 39–63
biography for children 8–10
　African-American (*see also* 'Black lives') 30–5, 42, 43, 50, 52, 58
　as activism 2, 9, 15, 29, 34, 35, 39, 43, 45, 46, 48, 69, 73, 74, 83, 84, 88, 95, 98, 125–6, 144, 192, 196
　Black lives (*see also* 'African-American') 30–5, 42, 43, 50, 52, 58
　citizenship, relationship to 4, 8–10, 20, 27, 34, 71, 163
　diversity in representation 3, 9, 17, 20, 25, 30, 41, 43, 48, 49, 66, 81, 85, 87, 103, 107, 111, 115, 147, 150, 191, 194
　environment, representation of 9, 14, 22, 43, 45, 46, 53, 58, 63, 71, 74, 75, 76, 77, 79, 103, 146, 192, 196

　feminism 1, 31, 35, 39–63
　girlhood, representation of 39–63
　historical figures, representation of 2, 3, 8, 19–37
　history of 4–8, 19–37
　Indigenous peoples, representation of 47, 70, 191–3
　LGBTIQA+, representation of 43, 47–9
　marginal subjects, representation of 3, 4–8, 33, 36, 40, 41, 42, 49, 79, 88, 98, 102, 147, 169, 172, 173, 197
　moral education 2, 3, 13, 20–6, 32, 33, 36, 48, 69, 98, 193, 194
　of spaces, places and sites 8, 123–39
　posthuman 8, 66, 83–99
　revisionist histories, as 4–8, 41, 193, 194
　role models, representation of 8, 9, 20, 25, 28, 29, 30, 32, 48, 78, 186, 194, 197
　social justice, relationship to 31, 48, 75, 98, 136, 138, 162, 163, 196
　sports, representation of 39, 47–9
　truth, relationship to 4, 8, 10, 11, 14, 24, 28, 33, 41, 108, 114, 119, 138, 195–7
Bland, Derek 171–2
book clubs, for children (*see also* 'Kids' Book Club') 17, 19, 46, 67–82, 94–9, 196

Cardell, Kylie and Kate Douglas 126, 129, 130, 171
Carter, Dorinda, J. and Georgina M. Montgomery 67, 71, 75, 79
Cavallo, Francesca 13, 57, 59
child readers (*see also* 'children's responses to biography') 12, 65–82, 94–9
children as biographers 142–67, 169–90
　biographical activities 57–62, 142–67, 169–90
children's drawings 16, 106, 117, 123–39, 141, 148, 149, 151, 169–90, 195–6
children's literature 82, 84, 86, 98, 103–4, 110, 114, 124, 142, 145, 188, 193

stakeholders 3, 8, 11, 13, 20, 25, 26, 67, 103, 194
children's responses to biography (*see also* 'child readers') 12, 65–82, 94–9
collaborative biography (*see also* 'biographical collage') 15, 101–21, 135, 172, 188, 194
Covid-19 narratives 60, 78, 79, 166, 169–90

Darling-McQuistan, Kirstin 171, 174
Del Rizzo, Suzanne 15, 101, 105, 113–20
'Dear future me' 61, 177, 184–5, 187
Diaries 169–90
didacticism and children's biography (*see also* 'childhood education') 3, 4, 5, 9, 13, 19, 20, 22, 23, 24, 25, 28, 30, 32, 36, 39, 43, 47, 48, 51, 67, 103, 104, 119, 193
Douglas, Kate 2, 9, 17, 42, 125, 126
Douglas, Kate and Anna Poletti 40, 126, 128, 197

ethics of witnessing 105, 114–15, 136–8
Evans, Janet 103, 104, 110

*Fantastically Great Women Who Made History* 13, 40
*Fantastically Great Women Who Changed the World* 13, 40
Favilli, Elena 13, 57, 59
*The Forgotten Children: National Inquiry into Children in Immigration Detention* 16, 123–39

Girard, Linda Walvoord 29, 41, 105
*Goodnight Stories for Rebel Girls* 9, 13, 40, 57–62
Grenby, Matthew O. 11, 22, 23

Hall, Emese 170, 179, 188
Hamilton, Kimberlie 14, 58, 83, 88–93, 97
hero 57–8, 62, 65–9, 71, 73, 75, 77, 81, 82, 83, 84–5, 92, 93, 96, 112, 113, 131, 134, 153, 164, 166, 191–4, 197
*Heroes, Rebels and Innovators: Inspiring Aboriginal and Torres Strait Islander People from History* 58, 191–4
Huff, Cynthia 40, 90
Huff, Cynthia and Joel Haefner 85–6

'Isolation Appreciation Day' 177, 182, 184
*I am a Rebel Girl: A Journal to Start Revolutions* 60–1

Jaques, Zoe 11, 95
*(The) Journey* 15, 101, 102–13, 114, 119–20, 131
Jurich, Marilyn 36, 107

Kids' Book Club (*see also* 'book club') 17, 19, 46, 67–82, 94–9, 196
*Kids Who Did: Real Kids Who Ruled, Rebelled, Survived and Thrived* 14, 63, 65–82, 94
Krebber, Andre and Mieke Roscher 86–9, 97

Lenette, Caroline, Karan Prasheela, Dearna Chrysostomou and Anthea Athanasopoulos 129, 133, 136, 178
*Little People, Big Dreams* 13, 39, 42–9, 53, 62
Lovelace, Ada 13, 39, 42, 53–7
Lynch, Claire 148, 162–4

McCarthy, Stephen 16, 169, 173–4, 188
Marcus, Leonard S. 9, 26
Marshall, Elizabeth 31, 41, 44, 48, 51
Mavers, Diane 145, 163, 169
methods, working with children's biography 12, 68, 70–3, 82, 135, 149–51, 173–8
Mickenberg, Julia 31, 33, 34
Murray, Kristy 14, 63, 65, 68, 69, 73
*My Beautiful Birds* 15, 101, 102, 105, 106, 113–17, 119, 120
*My Lockdown Diary* 16, 169–89

Ní Dhúill, Caitríona 6, 7, 66, 81, 87
Nodelman, Perry 28, 103

Pankhurst, Kate 13, 40, 42, 49
pedagogy (*see also* 'didacticism and children's biography') 3, 4, 5, 9, 13, 19, 20, 22, 23, 24, 25, 28, 30, 32, 36, 39, 43, 47, 48, 51, 67, 103, 104, 119, 193
picture books 2, 8, 9, 13, 15, 29, 39, 40, 42, 43, 49, 99, 101–19

Quilty, Ben, *Home: Drawings By Syrian Children* 106, 119, 127, 130

Rahn, Suzanne 27–30, 32, 33
Rapinoe, Megan 44, 47, 49
rebel 8, 40, 52, 58, 62, 91, 94, 95, 96, 193, 194, 197
*Rebel Dogs: Heroic Tales of Trusty Hounds* 14, 58, 83–99
refugee narratives (*see* 'asylum seeker narratives') 15, 16, 99, 101–21, 123–39, 195–6

Sanchez Vegara, Maria Isabel 39, 43, 44
Sanna, Francesca 15, 101, 102, 105, 107–14, 119, 120, 131
Skrlac Lo, Rachel and Sue Dahlstrom 67, 68
Smith, Sidonie and Julia Watson 10, 16, 40, 166
Stabell, Ivy Linton 26, 27

testimony 15, 16, 101, 102, 105, 106, 120, 123–39, 170
Thunberg, Greta 44–6, 75
Tomsic, Mary 130, 131, 136
trauma narratives 99, 102, 104–6, 110, 112, 114–15, 119, 123–38

*Value Tales* 1–3
VanderHaagen, Sara 30–5, 71

'Who are you Home With?' 179–81
*Women in Science* 13, 39, 43, 49, 53–6
Woolf, Virginia 4, 83, 142
writers' statements 151–9
Wyld, Karen and by Jaelyn Biumaiwai 58, 191–3

Yousafzai, Malala 9, 42, 126, 144

www.ingramcontent.com/pod-product-compliance
Lightning Source LLC
Chambersburg PA
CBHW062223300426
44115CB00012BA/2197